# Prisoner of the Japanese

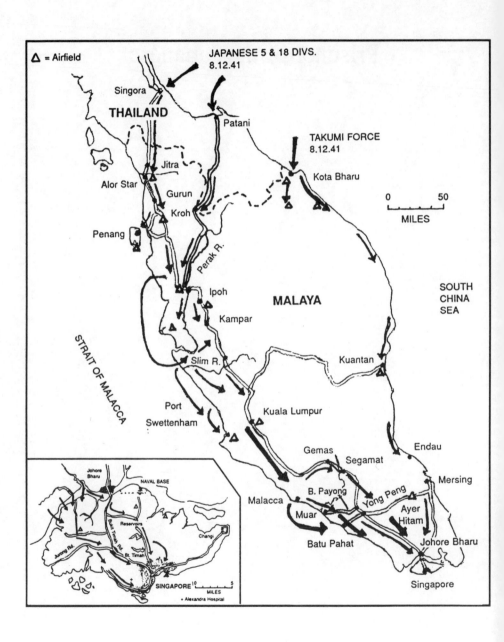

△ = Airfield

JAPANESE 5 & 18 DIVS.
8.12.41

Singora

THAILAND

Patani

TAKUMI FORCE
8.12.41

Jitra

Kota Bharu

Alor Star

Gurun

Kroh

0        50

MILES

Penang

Perak R.

Ipoh

MALAYA

Kampar

SOUTH
CHINA
SEA

STRAIT OF MALACCA

Slim R.

Kuantan

Port
Swettenham

Kuala Lumpur

Gemas

Segamat

Endau

Johore
Bharu

NAVAL BASE

Reservoirs

Bukit Timah Rd.

Jurong Rd.

Bt. Timah

Changi

SINGAPORE    10        5

MILES

• Alexandra Hospital

B. Payong

Yong Peng

Mersing

Malacca

Muar

Ayer
Hitam

Batu Pahat

Johore Bharu

Singapore

# PRISONER

## OF THE

# JAPANESE

*From Changi to Tokyo*

Tom Henling Wade

Kangaroo Press

**Acknowledgments**

I would like to thank Chappell Music Publishers for the use of the words from 'As Time Goes By'. Thanks also to my daughter, Catherine Christie, for her help with the wordprocessing.

Cover design by Darian Causby.
Inset: The author.
Main picture: An illustration of No. 6 Barrack, quarters for 120 men, commanded by the author from October 1943 to January 1945. All wood construction with earth floor. The author's calligraphy reads:
*Tokyo Furyo-Shuyoshu Dai Ichi Bunsho*
Tokyo Prisoner-of-War Detention Place, No. 1 Camp

*First published in 1994 by Kangaroo Press Pty Ltd*
*3 Whitehall Road Kenthurst NSW 2156 Australia*
*PO Box 6125 Dural Delivery Centre NSW 2158*
*Printed by McPherson's Printing Group, Maryborough, Vic. 3465*

ISBN 0 86417 602 3

To my family
above all,
four generations of them,
to those prisoners of war
who did not return
from the Far East
and to those survivors,
scarred but sturdy,
who returned to an
uncomprehending
country

# Contents

# 1

# Introducing the Japanese

The Japanese generals, bemedalled and be-starred, white-gloved hands pushing forward the pommels of their samurai swords, chatted quietly with each other or smiled confidently in small talk with Chinese politicians. The latter, in black or deep blue silk gowns, beamed and nodded; they had forfeited the respect of most of their countrymen, but they had well-paid posts in the city government of Greater Shanghai, they enjoyed full Japanese support and the ceremony they were attending was the inauguration of the approved new mayor.

The great hall, under a traditional Chinese green-tiled roof, was brightly decorated with large baskets of flowers beside the red pillars. The open doors of the hall faced a broad flight of 50 steps, beside which a uniformed Chinese band was playing martial music. Was it deliberate or was it accidental when they slipped into 'Hail, Hail, the Gang's All Here'?

English and American pressmen, including the writer, mentally polished phrases about puppet politicians while white-gowned servants distributed portable lunches— Japanese *bento*, chopsticks and beer.

'Not even Shanghai beer—it's Asahi,' a correspondent observed.

In the distance the towers of the International Settlement raised their heads, rich but out of reach to the Japanese unless they were prepared to go to war with the West, and that, in 1940, they were not prepared to do.

Just then twelve Japanese Army coaches drew up below and 400 Japanese geisha in beautiful, flowered kimonos swarmed up the steps in their clipping *geta*, sounding like an army of locusts. With their black lacquered hairstyles and white powdered skin, these seductive entertainers were the Chinese politicians' reward for their collaboration with the invader.

The time was early 1940, the place, Kiangwan Civic Centre, Shanghai, in Japanese-occupied China, and I was a teenaged reporter for the *Shanghai Times*.

Born in China, raised partly in China, I have been a student of Chinese politics and Far Eastern affairs since I edited a single-copy newspaper at the age of ten with a younger American cousin as fashion editress and my sister as cub reporter. The newspaper, which we called *Echo*, was published in our home in Tientsin; its readers were our parents and friends, who each had to pay 10 cents to read it. All profits went to buying sweets.

The front page carried the China news: the marching and counter-marching of the warlords, mobilisation of the local Volunteers, the background manoeuvring of Japan. I gleaned my news from the two North China English-language newspapers, adding personal observation of the Volunteers on duty at the perimeter of the British Concession. Pages two and three were a double-spread on fashion by the two girls, while page four might be anything.

I continued to produce that newspaper each time there was an outbreak of hostilities: the Japanese annexation of Manchuria in 1931, the Sino–Japanese War of 1932–3. Earlier than this, instead of calling our game 'bobbies and thieves' or 'cops and robbers', we often called it 'Chang Tso-lin's men against Wu Peifu's men,' using the names of the two leading warlords then ravaging North China with civil war. I always supported Chang Tso-lin, the Manchu general from the north, I think, because he was more successful.

Suddenly Chang Tso-lin was killed. The Japanese Army blew up his train with him in it on a line they were guarding. Japan, already in occupation of most of Manchuria, was stepping into the open and taking a direct part in North China affairs. Her plan was the annexation of Manchuria and later the conquest of China, carried out by her own troops in her own name, because of a special 'divine mission' of the Japanese to rule China on account of her 'geographical propinquity'.

From this moment forward Far Eastern affairs were dominated by Japan; you could not consider Chinese politics without discussing the policy, puppets or presence of the Japanese. Of course, Chinese leaders had been suspicious of Japanese ambition ever since the war between the two nations in 1895, by which Japan acquired Taiwan; the presentation of the Twenty-One Demands in 1915, which would have given Japan virtual economic and political control of China; and Japan's obvious interest in Manchuria ever since the Russo–Japanese War of 1904–5. Ever since these events, the Japanese had revealed a tendency to despatch troops into China on the smallest pretext. Japan was feared, but the liberal elements in Tokyo were still powerful enough to restrain expansionist plans, and it was only after the proved success in Manchuria that the militarists gained a greater hold on power and succeeding steps of the program of imperialist expansion could be taken ever more quickly and ever more openly.

I developed considerable enthusiasm and sympathy for the Japanese in 1931–2. For years I had heard hundreds of Europeans living in China and making their living there, say that what China needed was a strong and stable government and no one could do that better for her than the leading Asian nation, the energetic and enterprising Japanese. These foreigners were tired of civil wars, weak government and 'squeeze' or corruption. They admired the Westernisation of Japan with its technical efficiency and commercial prosperity; they even admired the Japanese Army, whose soldiers, they sincerely believed, did not loot, and they believed a Japanese conquest of North

China would bring order. The history of the 1930s is the history of the surrender of power to totalitarianism in the name of order.

I accepted the opinions of my elders. I expected to see the efficient modern army of Japan defeat the ill-equipped, cloth-shod mobs of Chinese soldiers, who carried umbrellas in case it rained, ceased fighting on feast days and whose generals frequently bargained with each other beforehand about who should advance or keep the town and then, having a result, dispensed with the battle.

Difficult now to understand these eleven-year-old feelings. Now I realise that those battles were highly civilised. If only all nations would fight wars in this slipshod, civilised way the whole matter of warfare would become a joke, ambitious militarists and aggressive dictators would be treated with the amusement and contempt they deserve and peace would be bolstered by a widespread outbreak of sanity.

But then came Nippon's aggressive war against China in 1932. A huge area of North China was occupied, Japanese regiments stood at the gates of Peking and a local war developed in Shanghai. Here the invader met an unexpectedly stout resistance and a hard battle was fought in the industrial districts of northern Shanghai. Losses on both sides were heavy, but despite superiority in equipment and training, Japanese progress was slow, thanks to the stubborn defence of the 19th Route Army, and some 'big-sword' soldiers in silent shoes and with old-fashioned scimitars.

This stubborn defence made me realise that there was a new spirit awakening in China and that these ill-equipped soldiers were fighting for something they valued as highly as peace and civilised living—their country. So the main ideological lesson that Western civilisation has to teach had been learnt by the Chinese: they were becoming nationalistic. I wonder if Europe is ready to face all the consequences of the nationalism she has taught the rest of the world. If not, why doesn't she change the fashion?

From 1933 I was in school in England, but I followed Far Eastern affairs carefully in the not over-curious British press. Letters from my parents showed me how war clouds were slowly gathering in those middle '30s until in 1937 the Chinese were beginning to feel confident that they were sufficiently united and sufficiently strong to defy the Japanese and Tokyo was watching for a pretext to crush China before she became any stronger.

I was in Officers Training Corps camp at Tidworth Pennings during the sunny days of early August 1937, when one day a newspaper boy came running between the lines of tents shouting 'War!' I looked up quickly and read on his placard, 'Tientsin Bombed'.

This was the first time I had ever read the name of my 'home town' on a newspaper placard, the first time I had ever heard it mentioned in England and the first time I had ever read that the town where my family lived had been bombed.

With Oriental fatalism I walked into the shade inside the tent without buying a paper to sit and think. I was there for several minutes, squatting with my knees under my chin, wondering in silence while the paperboy's cries faded into the distance. Then one of my tent-mates burst in.

'Gosh, you look miserable. Have you seen the paper?'

'No.'

'Have you heard the news?'

'Yes.'

'Aren't your people in Tientsin?'

'Yes.'

'You're a queer chap. Why don't you buy a paper? I'll go and get one!'

He came back a minute later with a copy and I read that Japanese bombers had bombed the Chinese city, causing much damage, but that it was not believed that any bombs had fallen on the foreign section of the city.

I was comforted. I asked myself why I had not bought a paper to get this news immediately. It was because seeing the newspaper instantly or after some minutes could make no difference to the facts: at that moment my family were either alive or dead; time alone would show.

When I returned from camp, I found letters from my parents and sister waiting for me. They told of the Lukouchiao (Marco Polo bridge) incident near Peking, which was the spark that began the whole long China War of 1937–45. The family had driven to Peking soon after and found the Marco Polo bridge held by Japanese troops, who had put up fortifications and were curt and quick on the trigger because they were being fired on regularly by the Chinese. Japanese reinforcements were being poured into North China. 'I think this will become a full-scale war,' my father wrote, 'but the Japanese will easily take northern China.'

I forgot Spain for months even though I had had some sympathy for the Republicans, but here was war in 'my own country'. I knew the Marco Polo bridge, white and broad, just outside Peking; I knew Tientsin and the Chinese city which had been bombed; how many times had I watched football matches or shot snipe near Nankai University which had been burned to the ground? I knew Hungjao aerodrome outside Shanghai where the incident occurred which precipitated the 1937 Shanghai war front, and I knew Woosung, Hongkew, Chapei and the Soochow Creek. Strange names these to the newspaper readers of the world, but to me they were more familiar than Tilbury, Whitechapel and Mayfair.

My heart ached for China, for the desperate and costly fighting that lay before her, for the sufferings her people would undergo and the ravages the country would suffer. My war against Japan had begun: I could not dream what Japan had still to do to me.

# 2
# Occupied China

I finished school and decided to become a journalist—in Shanghai. My family was in Tientsin in the north, but I believed Shanghai was the critical point of the Far East in 1939, so I became a reporter on the *Shanghai Times*.

There were three English-language morning newspapers in Shanghai at that time: the *North China Daily News*, old, famous and conservative; the *China Press*, a bold, pro-Chinese American-organised daily, and the newspaper which I had just joined. It had once been a close rival of the NCDN, but its rather pro-Japanese editorial policy and its part ownership by the Yokohama Specie Bank had lost it popularity. This leader policy did not affect our reporting of local news, except that courtesy was shown to the Japanese and we could not describe Chinese sycophants and collaborators as puppets, which the *China Press* could.

Publishing newspapers was a hazardous enterprise in neutral Shanghai in the centre of Japanese-occupied China. The Japanese did not dare to offend the United States, Britain and France by occupying the International Settlement and French Concession of Shanghai. Nevertheless they hated the criticism levelled against them by the foreign press published in the city. They knew that there was wealth, support and intelligence for Chiang Kaishek inside those few square miles of inviolable territory. It was a city of refuge for Nationalists escaping from their grasp and they coveted it.

Either they must ignore it, or attempt to crush it through terrorism. Being increasingly totalitarian and in the hands of the army, the Japanese opted for the latter. Bombs were thrown into the offices of the *China Press*, the *Shanghai Evening Post and Mercury* and three or more of the Chinese newspapers.

Avenue Edward VII, 'the Fleet Street of Shanghai', became a fortified highway with three pillboxes and three permanently parked armoured cars all standing in the last 250 yards of the Avenue. For here were all the newspapers and news agencies of the city (except one). At night, one foreign sergeant and two or three Chinese constables came into each newspaper editorial office and printing room. These men were all strongly armed; Shanghai police didn't play about with truncheons and pistols, they carried heavy Browning sub-machine guns.

The sound of a bomb bursting on the floor above somehow did not frighten us as much as it should have; all my press friends were exhilarated rather than cowed by this terrorist attack. The newspaper on the floor above us had strong wire netting stretching from the public counter to the ceiling in its office so that any bombs thrown would rebound on the thrower. For this work, the Japanese did not use their own subjects; the capture of a Japanese terrorist would have proved to the world their complicity. So they hired penniless Chinese for these tasks. Several Chinese compositors were killed in these attacks.

The western outskirts of the Settlement were an area of dangerous lawlessness. Hundreds of gambling dens and scores of opium dens were established here on Chinese territory beyond the reach of the Settlement Police, who were restricted to the roads. Armed robbery and murder thrived in this western district, which became known as 'the Badlands'. In this area too, the Japanese were suspected of hiring the gunmen who terrorised the district and fought armed battles with the police. Armoured cars were constantly on patrol and in three years a score of policemen and many more terrorists were killed.

The Japanese would then deplore this disorder to the Shanghai Municipal Council and demand a larger role in the government of the city.

At the same time the Japanese Navy exercised full control of river trade on the Yangtze and the army exercised control of movement and trade on the railways and in many ports and cities, yet the Japanese government said that they were not at war with China, but merely dealing with an 'incident' and that they were in China for her own good. No one who lived there in those days could believe that, for, besides recognising the aggressive and imperialist character of the war, the world also knew that Japan was smuggling thousands of tons of opium, heroin and cocaine into China in order to encourage drug-taking and thus undermine the national character and will to resist. Also, beating, torture and murder were practised by the Japanese *kempeitai* or military police against outspoken and patriotic Chinese.

British and American newsmen in Shanghai were all united in opposing the Japanese war in China, all shocked by events like the rape of Nanking and the sinking of the USS *Panay* in the Yangtze. Most attended the Japanese biweekly news conferences, but paid scant attention to Japanese claims of skirmishes won on the Yangtze front. They were always the same: 'A small party of Japanese soldiers was attacked by a large number of Chinese troops. The Chinese were annihilated and left behind four machine-guns, 67 rifles and 532 rounds of ammunition.'

Yet in spite of four or five alleged successes like this each week, China could not be defeated.

I remember once a missionary lady called Miss Wilkinson had disappeared while making a long journey across exceedingly rough hill country on a donkey in remote Japanese-occupied China. Weeks passed without news of her, then the Japanese Army spokesman announced with delight that the lady had been found after three weeks in the saddle, was unhurt and taken to a garrison. An American correspondent stubbed out his cigar and asked, 'And how's Miss Wilkinson's ass?'

The Japanese members of the press conference were pleasant, amiable men. One of them later became consul-general in Singapore, but I did not renew our acquaintanceship. And the foreign correspondents attending included some quite famous names.

In June 1940 came Dunkirk and the fall of France. I gave notice to my paper and went north to Tientsin. British civilians there had been subjected to great indignities at the hands of the Japanese. The British Concession was surrounded by the Japanese Army and barriers erected to keep Britons inside as far as possible. Passports had to be shown at the perimeter and, in 1938, Japanese sentries started slapping many who showed British passports. Next, men and women were made to strip their clothing so that the Japanese could search them for 'arms or contraband'. This 'strip-teasing' went on till the end of 1939 and the British government could do nothing about it but lodge protests in Tokyo, which the Japanese government ignored. The critical situation in Europe and later the war prevented any stronger action by a Britain too busy in Europe to take risks in Asia.

My father was stripped only twice in spite of crossing the line a dozen times a week; a few times he crossed in Volunteer uniform with war medals and shouted '*Shikan*'—officer—and was saluted by puzzled sentries. My mother and friends once rushed the barrier in a car and got away with one bullet in the back of the shiny Buick, and my sister and other teenagers showed driving licences and said they were Irish and never had any trouble.

I met early school friends again. The men had been almost continually on duty with the Volunteers since 1937. Frequently they lived in posts, wore uniform and carried arms for weeks on end, and, during a great flood in 1939 when most business ceased, they did months of service. The Emergency Corps was as efficient a unit as the Shanghai and Hong Kong Volunteer Forces, and in 1938–9 had far longer active service.

I revisited the scenes of my boyhood in Tientsin and Peitaiho, the delightful seaside resort not far from the end of the Great Wall, and revisited imperial Peking, the most majestic capital in the world. Then I returned to Shanghai, by rail through 900 miles of Japanese-occupied China, and tried to work a passage to Canada or England to join the army.

# 3
# Five Dollar Private

August in Shanghai was intensely hot as I toiled round the shipping offices trying to work a one-way passage to Canada or Britain; but it was in vain. I was not a member of the union. This would not have been a handicap fifteen years earlier, but it was now.

How galling too, when Nazi Germany had occupied nine countries in Europe[1], when Britain, alone, was fighting a desperate air battle and expecting invasion. The Germans in Shanghai smiled with self-confidence.

An Italian businessman, a family friend, called one evening and ardently urged me not to enlist. 'Don't go,' he said with a piercing stare. 'Germany and Italy are going to win.'

'We don't think so,' I replied.

At that moment the British government amended its instruction that all British subjects in the Far East should continue their jobs to promote British trade and gain foreign exchange. The clamour of young men in the Far East to be allowed to join the services was now heard. A local body was set up to interview and medically examine volunteers and a recruiting officer soon came up from Singapore to enlist them.

Within several weeks the first party of 56 young men was ready and sailed from Shanghai in September, I among them; sixteen bound for Singapore and the rest for India. Watching the crowd waving on the Bund, I reflected that my father had sailed from this same Customs Jetty in October 1914 with the first contingent of volunteers from Shanghai bound for France and the Western Front.

The *Viceroy of India*, blacked out at night, carried us down to Hong Kong, where we spent three delightful days swimming at Repulse Bay, drinking with friends, driving round this jewel of an island and dancing in honky tonks in Wanchai—later, much later, to be known as 'Suzy Wong country'.

After dusty Shanghai, this British colony looked so steadfast with its Sikh policemen and well-kept British roads. It had defences too; we saw pillboxes among the bathing bungalows at Repulse Bay and in the hills, all supported with tactical wire. It was

---

1. Austria, Czechoslovakia, Poland, Denmark, Norway, Holland, Belgium, Luxembourg and France.

certain the Japanese knew the situation of all these gunposts, but at least they were prepared positions.

As we sailed out of Hong Kong, I wondered if Japan would join in Germany's war and scatter British defences in the Far East as she had constantly scuttled British prestige over the past few years. If she did attack, could Hong Kong last more than two weeks?

It was the end of September when our ship docked in Singapore. The city was white, sunbright and smelt of sandalwood, coconut and ripe fruit as I remembered from three previous visits. A staff major came aboard and told us for which units we were destined; sergeants with trucks then drove us out to Changi. About seven of us were deposited on the grass among the tents of the East Surrey Regiment's camp—and no one knew anything about us. Apart from the urgent order to collect us, the battalion had not been warned to expect us or what to do with us. A tent and camp beds were supplied, but no mess tins, cutlery or uniforms of any sort. So there we were for weeks in civilian tropical suits and so on getting spottier and dirtier every day.

After thirteen days we were formally enlisted, but did not receive uniforms or equipment for three weeks. The men of the regiment found this almost as strange as we did and they dropped in regularly at our tent to chat and hear our opinions or simply to escape the orderly sergeant. Our tent became a clubhouse and we made many friends in the battalion. Our friends in the artillery were having the same experience and even after a month no real training had begun. Consequently one man left the army, joined the navy and received a commission and two brothers got themselves to New Zealand and joined the forces there.

The army in Malaya was not very quick off the mark in October 1940.

Quite soon the East Surreys moved camp to the Chinese High School on Bukit Timah Road, which had the advantage of being much closer to town. We were proceeding with our drill and weapon training at last and learning to be 'old-soldiers' very quickly. The troops never ceased telling us of the dodges round the little problems that beset a private's life, and as we hardly ever saw the officers and never spoke to them, we were rapidly acquiring the troops' point of view. It was odd that the officers should be so distant. We had met many of them in clubs in China and one had joined the regiment in Tientsin. He had been a member of the Tientsin Volunteers which my father commanded, yet one embarrassed grin was the sum total of his intercourse with me in Malaya. Strange how officer status affects some people.

Intensive training had begun and so had the rainy season. We marched and crept in banana and rubber plantations and thick bush and returned to barracks soaking wet with both rain and perspiration each night. The army paid us between $6 and $7 a week for these services, holding back over a dollar for benefits, leaving us $5 a week for entertainment, extra drinks and food, Blanco and polishes. That was just enough to buy one soft drink in the middle of a long morning, one bottle of beer each night and steak-egg-and-chips once a week at a cafe in town to be followed by free dancing with Chinese and Malay partners at the New World or Happy World dance hall.

To the East Surreys the purchasing power of the Singapore dollar was a bitter blow after the very favourable exchange rate they had enjoyed in Shanghai and Tientsin. There their pay amounted to hundreds of dollars and the extraordinary thing was that one could buy almost the same goods and services with the Chinese dollar in Shanghai as one could with the Straits Settlements dollar in Singapore. British other ranks, therefore, disliked Malaya. Their favourite song, to the tune of 'Trees', went:

*I pray that I shall never see*
*Another bloody rubber tree!*

For the British civilians in the country did almost nothing to entertain the NCOs and privates of all the infantry, artillery and corps units of the British Army or to make them feel wanted or respected. The same was true of the RAF other ranks and later of the Australians.

Of course, there were too many troops; Malayan European society is short of women at any time and in 1941 most British girls in Malaya went out only with officers. There was even a surplus of young officers, giving the girls a very wide choice. But all other ranks were left to get on as best they could with Asian women. When a party of us were invited to an American lady's house for tea, I heard two British ladies expressing surprise that these soldiers, whom they had expected to be uncouth, should be well-behaved.

As a factor in the development of the morale with which the British troops later faced the Japanese invasion, I believe it is worth stating that the British troops had no sympathy whatsoever with the Malayan colonial government or the British civilians in Malaya. They hated them and hated the country which they were told was so wealthy, but which could not give them any value in return for their money or even respect in return for their presence.

I said goodbye to a hundred solid friends in the battalion when I left to go to the Officers Cadet Training Unit for Malaya. As I said goodbye to all those familiar types— rugged sergeants, 'old-soldier' corporals, Cockneys, East Enders, 'Paddy' the Irishman, intellectual company clerks, ex-public schoolmen in the ranks and 'barrack room lawyers'—I knew the army would do its best to raise a barrier between us once I was commissioned and I hoped I would not lose their friendship and that they would never think so unflatteringly of me as I had heard them speak of almost all officers.

Where there is a gulf between officers and men, the British Army deepens it, and where there is no gulf, the army creates it.

# 4

# Malayan Paradise

I enjoyed the OCTU, which I attended from January to April 1941. One received useful information on the work, scope, theory and dogma of a large organisation like the army and the British way of war. They did not tell us much about the Germans or the Japanese, nor did they tell us anything about the topography and peoples of Malaya, the country we were likely to have to defend. In one lecture hall, we had a vivid sand-table model, some 20 feet by 9, showing every farmhouse, hedge, hill and copse in a Cotswold area near Stow-on-the-Wold. I could still guide you to every wood and hamlet in the area. Why, why were we not shown as clearly the topography of Malaya or a part of Malaya?

In April I was commissioned and posted to the Loyal Regiment (North Lancs), a regular unit. 'Nol' Gouda, also from Shanghai, came with me.

We found that we had the privilege of joining a well-trained, disciplined and smart unit, which had served in Shanghai in the protection of the International Settlement in 1937, when the Sino–Japanese War raged close beside them. The men, 75 per cent regular soldiers, were mostly from Lancashire; some were hard to get to know, but the majority were straightforward, reliable and a little wry, not as talkative as the Cockneys, but still able to size up a situation with that terseness and shattering wit which is a characteristic of the British Tommy.

The officers made up one of the most friendly and fraternal messes in Singapore, and it was inspiring to feel the *esprit de corps* of all officers and men in the battalion. All officers of the rank of captain and above were also regulars and one felt that in such company, even if we were not fully trained, the power and discipline of the whole fighting unit would carry one through.

Proud as I was of the unit, I was privately rather critical of the way officers spent their time in Singapore. Units worked from eight till twelve each morning and were free the rest of the day except for guards, pickets, etc. These involved few officers so that their afternoons were free for siestas till four (very common) followed by sport, then drinks and dinner in the mess or out to dinner at one of the clubs, hotels or parties which were so popular in Malaya and Singapore then. I noticed too that there was no pressure on anyone to learn Malay.

The social life of the European civilians and service officers in Singapore was a roundabout of parties. The famous Singapore hotels—Raffles, Seaview and Adelphi— held dances attended by large parties of officers in uniform every night. The Tanglin Club, Singapore Swimming Club and Cathay restaurant were thronged with all the pageantry of British uniforms: tropical khaki, flashing brass, leather belts, kilts, RAF wings and naval gold braid surrounded one on all sides in every nightspot in the city. And after the dancing and drinking, some would drive to a cool hilltop overlooking the calm sea, with the hush of palm trees in their ears and the golden tropical moon above.

Romantic, but unwarlike; Britain was neck-deep in war. She was being heavily bombed; in the Middle East our forces were hanging on to Egypt by a whisker after the loss of Greece and Crete. Nazi power seemed unlimited as the Germans opened a thousand-mile front against the Russians and pressed relentlessly towards Moscow, and in the Orient, an empire of 80 million loyal, brave and devoted subjects of the Emperor watched and waited their opportunity to attempt their long-cherished ambition, the conquest of a South Pacific empire and the capture of Singapore.

Officers fresh out from England were shocked at the complacency of the services in Malaya, the spit and polish, 'regimental' attitude of mind, the insistence on exact colours and measurements in tailoring and impeccable turnout. But there was nothing they could do; it required a complete change of thinking at the top to achieve this, and that was not forthcoming.

*Tid'apa* is the Malay expression for 'it doesn't matter' and in that sleepy climate is heard as often as '*mañana*' is elsewhere. One of the troops in Changi summed up the whole Malayan attitude of mind when he said the whole country was rotten with '*tidapathy*'.

Acid but realistic rhymes and jokes were invented by troops to describe the army, government and civilians of Malaya. One especially well-written rhyme gained such currency that all copies were ordered to be destroyed.

Militarily too, Malaya was appallingly complacent. The main defences of Singapore Island were big naval guns facing the sea, as in the '20s seaborne invasion was what the British envisaged. But by 1940 there were RAF airfields right up to the Thai border and so the entire peninsula had to be defended. There were not nearly enough troops, planes or ships to ensure this as, compared with the active warfronts, Malaya suffered a low priority for supplies. Yet little anxiety or urgency was visible. Invasion overland from the north was not discounted; blockhouses and other defences were constructed at Kota Bharu, near Thailand, in the north-east and in Kedah in the north-west, also at Mersing on the east coast of Johore. But no defences were constructed on the northern shores of Singapore Island. Most damning of all, once the invasion had started and it was clear that the main Japanese thrust would be down the peninsula from the north— and with all the native labour available—still no defences were constructed on the northern and western shores of Singapore Island.

There was a divergence of policy between the services on the one hand and the civil governments of the Straits Settlements and the Federated and Unfederated Malay States on the other. The colonial administration had orders from London to maintain peacetime conditions in Malaya, to carry on as usual, to produce the maximum amount of rubber and tin and to keep the native population content and free from alarm or the thought of war.

Clashes there were between the army and colonial government, but the civilian interest usually won. Thus fields of fire could not be cleared, blockhouses could not be built because they had been sited in private gardens or 'blocking someone's view of the sea', and troops on exercise could be fined for the destruction of rubber trees in the plantations.

Noel Coward, while visiting Malaya years before, described the British there as 'lower class people living upper class lives'. This was scarcely true, but not entirely untrue. The generally middle-class Britons in Malaya with their many servants, large houses and gardens and sometimes cars where they had had none in Britain, lived at a much higher standard than they had left behind and they resented this kind of observation as strongly as they resented many of Somerset Maugham's comments in his Malayan stories. They lived a highly privileged life, which they had come to feel was their due. They had no wish for the services or anyone else to limit it or spoil it—not even in wartime, not even when there was a risk of invasion.

But the civilians alone should not bear full responsibility for this attitude of mind; top and final responsibility rested with the Governor, the Colonial Office in London and the General Officer Commanding, Malaya. Had the Governor and the Colonial Office been prepared to revolutionise their ideas and whole-heartedly cooperate in making Malaya fully prepared and strong, the scene might have been different. And had the GOC, Lieutenant General A. E. Percival, been strong enough and determined enough to insist on all necessary military measures being implemented, Malaya could have been ready for the Japanese invasion in December 1941.

Malaya was living in a fool's paradise until 8 December that year. The government, civilians and services alike hoped that war would never strike this prosperous peninsula, apparently so far from all warfronts. The high-living civilians and many officers played and danced as the sands ran out of the hourglass as the aristocrats of the kingdom of France had once done till the very hour of revolution. *'Après moi le déluge'*; *Tid'apa*— it is the same story.

# 5
# Tropical Blitzkrieg

At the Staff College, Quetta, western India (now Pakistan), selected officers from the Royal Navy, the British and Indian Armies and the RAF studied problems in the defence of the British Empire. In 1935 they were set the problem of the defence of Singapore against a Japanese attack, one syndicate of officers representing the Japanese and another the British, each having to decide on its best strategy to win such a war. They were free to decide on grand strategy, troop numbers, naval and air requirements and ground tactics.

After many hours of study, the team representing the Japanese presented their plan to capture Singapore by invading Malaya at Mersing and Endau on the east coast and driving south, mostly by road through jungle and rubber plantations, to take Singapore from the north, from the land side.

Colonel (later Field Marshal) Bernard Montgomery, the senior instructor, who set the problem and controlled the exercise, suggested to them that to speed up their advance in that steamy tropical climate they use bicycles as the roads in Malaya were good. This was accepted and the invasion plan was voted effective.

The conclusions of this study would have been available to senior British officers stationed in Malaya and faced with this same problem in 1941.

Two years later, Colonel A. E. Percival, as senior staff officer Malaya, forecast for the War Office that if the Japanese planned to capture Singapore, they would land at Kota Bharu in north-east Malaya and Singora and Patani, two ports in Thailand, and drive south down the western side of the peninsula to Singapore.

Now that he was a lieutenant general and in command in Malaya, surely he would know how best to fight a Japanese invasion whose route, time would soon show, he had so accurately foreseen.

The most that any junior officer or NCO could read on the defence problems of Malaya and the type of warfare likely to be fought there was a small green booklet four inches by three and a half and one-twelfth of an inch thick, entitled *Tactical Notes on Malaya*.

Everything in it was sound, but there was so little of it. Once a soldier had read that, knew his weapons and had done some manoeuvres in open country, he was regarded as trained for the defence of Malaya. There was one thing in which troops received little information and little practical experience, and that was—the jungle.

About 75 per cent of Malaya is covered with thick, equatorial jungle: a choking green world, infested with animals and insects warring on each other. Blind, difficult country, but man can penetrate it. This fact was disregarded in the training of troops in Malaya and in the siting of lines of defence. Where the jungle was marked on the map as thick and swampy, high-ranking officers would airily announce: 'The jungle there is impenetrable, so our defensive lines need not stretch beyond here and here'.

Then when Japan struck, all the way down the 600-mile of withdrawal each British position stretched as far as the edge of the jungle and every time the Japanese would outflank the resistance by working round through the jungle and arriving behind our troops.

The pamphlet also taught that Malaya was not tank country. Because of the narrow roads and heavily treed borders, leaving little space to manoeuvre, tanks were discounted. Consequently, when the Japanese used light but powerful tanks they ruled the roads and gained an invaluable moral advantage.

So Malaya basked in the sunshine of optimism and wishful thinking even after the Japanese occupied French Indo-China and General Tojo became prime minister and the negotiations with the United States in Washington slowed almost to a stop. In fact, in November the tensing Pacific situation was electric. We were informed in late November that Japanese troops in Indo-China had been issued with maps of Malaya and had completed their jungle training.

On 6 December 1941, two large fleets of Japanese transports were sighted heading from southern Indo-China towards Thailand, north of the Malayan border. Next day contact was lost.

Late on the night of 7/8 December as I lay asleep in bed, a low roar wakened me. I sat up, recognising the sound of bombs. I jumped out of bed and looked out of my glassless window at the starlit sky. There was no sign of bombers, but I could see the glow of street lights and city lights and realised that every light in the city was blazing like a carnival night, lighting up this great inviting target. The bombers dropped their loads on the city centre and in a native residential district and left—and the lights were *still on*.

Companies of my battalion had left barracks earlier that night to round up Japanese civilians living in the city and not long after the men were divided into two shiploads and I, with my platoon, escorted over 200 Japanese fishermen and merchants by sea to Port Swettenham in central Malaya. Most of the fishing around Malaya was done by Japanese, so the Imperial Navy knew every rock, shallow and beach defence around the peninsula.

Before we left port, we heard of the attack on Pearl Harbor, the destruction of half the American battle fleet, the attack on Hong Kong, the occupation of Shanghai and a landing in the Philippines; also that the Japanese had landed at Kota Bharu where they had broken through the Indian regiments deployed in defence, captured the airfield and were about to move south. Worst blow of all two days later, the newly arrived battleship, *Prince of Wales*, and battlecruiser, *Repulse*, were caught off the east coast of Malaya by Japanese torpedo-bomber squadrons and sunk. They had arrived only eight days ago and they were already both sunk. They had had no air cover. How would air cover be for the army when it came to battle the Japanese—we had only 154 or so largely obsolescent aircraft in Malaya?

The Yangtze riverboat steamed through calm and silent seas up the coast of Malaya and deposited the Japanese civilians in Port Swettenham, then returned to Singapore. Within a few days those Japanese internees were evacuated from Malaya to India because the Japanese advance was sweeping down the peninsula.

There had been a plan to anticipate the Japanese by occupying the corner of Thailand just north of the FMS border and thus deny the enemy an unopposed landing and use of the ports of Singora and Patani. But Malaya Command hesitated when sight of the troopships was lost and after the Japanese landing it was too late.

My battalion, the Loyals, was mobile reserve for Singapore Island. We spent December 1941 chasing imagined fifth columnists, paratroops and mystery lights in and around Singapore.

Two Indian Divisions faced the Japanese in the north: one around Kota Bharu in the east and the other in a prepared position at Jitra in the state of Kedah on the west coast. With three-quarters of Malaya under jungle and most of that mountainous as well, these positions simply guarded the road and rail gateways to the country and the most advanced airfields, leaving the interlying areas and a thousand miles of coastline undefended. However, owing to the physical nature of the country and to the comparatively small numbers of troops employed by both sides, it was obvious that the main arteries of communication would dictate the path of invasion. The British were prepared for this, but they were not prepared for the fanatical pressure with which the Japanese attacks were pressed home, the appearance of tanks, infiltration of enemy dressed as Malay and Chinese labourers, and the spreading of alarmist rumours by a small fifth column.

After landing unopposed in Thailand, the Japanese raced across the Malayan frontier led by tanks, overwhelmed two outpost battalions in steaming monsoon rain and hit the Jitra line repeatedly at a single point until it weakened. Twenty-two hours later they burst through and poured south. The Indian division in defence was split asunder and forced into retreat with most of its guns and vehicles left behind. With Kota Bharu also lost the withdrawal had begun. To the rear the best natural defensive positions in Malaya were known but had not been prepared, and throughout the campaign the retreating troops, after days and later weeks of fighting and marching, had to dig their own hasty weapon pits and improvise their own tank obstacles.

With Jitra lost and also an interim position at Gurun, Malaya Command decided that Penang could not be defended, and so, within eight days, Penang, the second largest port in Malaya, was abandoned to the enemy. The white British residents were evacuated to Singapore, but hundreds of thousands of British Asians and British Eurasians were left in the port along with warehouses full of rubber and tin and hundreds of small boats and launches. What did this tell the Indians? Half our army was Indian.

The Resident Councillor of Penang, from the moment of arrival in Singapore, in the press and the council chamber, urged the local authorities to prepare for air attack and invasion and not to be caught napping like Penang. But his warning was not heeded, or if heeded, not acted upon. Singaporeans went on dancing and drinking at the clubs and hotels and hoped that *somebody* would stop the Japanese.

The news the forces heard of the Japanese was little short of frightening. They were almost invincible. Every man was said to be armed with an automatic weapon. They had tanks. They had command of the air. They had Stuka dive-bombers. They penetrated impossible jungle and swamp. Their snipers were wonderfully accurate.

Oh, how surprised everyone was! In spite of warnings from military attachés who had studied the Japanese Army at first hand and maintained that it was efficient, daring and strong, everyone thought that because it could not conquer China it was a musical comedy army and all Japanese were short-sighted, bandy-legged, comic little men who hissed through their teeth and could not shoot straight or fly straight or bomb straight.

I know who was short-sighted.

The Japanese stormed on, reaching each new British position earlier than expected, attacking immediately with great ferocity and breaking through. Rivers, which they were expected to take three days to bridge, were crossed in about 30 hours. Already six good airfields were in Japanese hands and over a quarter of our air force destroyed. The East Surreys and Leicesters, who had fought since Jitra, were so much reduced in strength that they were amalgamated into a single unit, the 'British Battalion'. The 6th and 15th Indian Brigades were amalgamated into one. Ipoh, a major town, was abandoned and our forces dug in at Kampar. However, the Argyll and Sutherland Highlanders, our only jungle-trained battalion, were putting up a bonnie fight and had probably frustrated a Japanese pincer move to encircle our troops in the north-west.

On New Year's Day, the Japanese attacked not only at Kampar but also at Kuantan on the east coast, which they captured. The hard battle at Kampar lasted three days, the British Battalion holding the Japanese and their tanks to a standstill on three ridges in spite of repeated *Banzai* charges. But retreat became inevitable when a Japanese force, using boats captured at Penang, landed by sea south of this position and threatened its communication. Our forces withdrew to the Slim River. By now nearly half the length of Malaya (420 miles by road) had been lost to the enemy in 26 days. In effect we were fighting a rearguard action with lengthening withdrawals rearward between battles. People in Singapore could *not* grasp the seriousness of it.

But the news got only worse: Japanese tanks burst right through the Hyderabads, Punjabis and Argylls in succession, caught one Punjabi and two Gurkha battalions on the march, crossed the Slim River bridge and were finally halted seventeen miles to the rear by a howitzer firing at 30 yards range. The Slim River disaster was so serious that nothing could now save Kuala Lumpur, the federal capital. We heard that Seremban and Malacca would not be defended and that the next line of resistance might be in Johore, the last Malay state before Singapore Island. Here two Australian brigades were in position, one on the east coast at Mersing and the other in the centre around Segamat, reinforced by roughly four Indian brigades, three of them very weary.

On 10 January, three days after the Slim River disaster, my battalion received sudden orders to reinforce the Aussies at Segamat (SeGAHmat). At an hour's notice, the colonel, adjutant and I, as intelligence officer, drove from Singapore through the night towards northern Johore. A breezy Indian Army general (Major General A. Barstow), red-ringed cap on the back of his head, met us at the bridge at Segamat.

'You are to defend Segamat to the last man and the last round,' he said. 'No one is to cross this river.'

We quickly reconnoitred company defence and billeting areas, and I found a plan of the town. Segamat was a ghost town; not a soul was to be seen in any street or at any window. Next afternoon our 800-strong battalion and transport arrived by rail and road and immediately commenced to dig.

Some days later the Japanese cycled into a trap laid by the Aussies at Gemas; nine of their tanks and some hundreds of infantry were destroyed in one ambush. It was a welcome success. But instead of continuing their pressure down this main north–south road, the Japanese switched attack to the west coast. They thrust across the Muar River, scattered the 45th Indian Brigade and an Aussie battery and threatened to surround them. Two Australian battalions were rushed across Johore to prevent this and now this whole force was battling with great courage to avoid encirclement and annihilation. Orders reached us to leave Segamat and join a newly-arrived East Anglian brigade which had been rushed forward virtually from the docks at Singapore to relieve the surrounded Aussies and Indians.

As we waited to cross the only bridge out of Segamat that night, I watched an Indian Frontier Force battalion withdrawing. The long-striding sepoys carried souvenirs: bundles, shawls and one man a large pink lampshade. It did not augur well.

Our trucks drove south-west. Approaching the 53rd East Anglian Brigade, we found the countryside a vast level swamp with jungle and patches of banana. The road was almost a causeway above the morass. Ahead it crossed an unexpected and prominent ridge: Bukit Payong, we called it (more correctly, Bukit Pelandok). It completely dominated the plain. Beyond this range, some nine miles, lay Parit Sulong, where the Aussies and Indians were struggling to break the Japanese stranglehold. Two East Anglian battalions had failed to capture the pass; one of our companies was sent up to attempt the same by stealth; our battalion then arrived and was ordered to take the ridge. Why had we allowed the Japanese to reach this the most important high ground within 50 miles' radius while we had so many troops on the far side? Our colonel requested a delay of twelve hours so that our first company could rejoin. The brigadier agreed; help for us, no help for the Aussies.

As we waited at the foot of the sheer ridge for a short artillery barrage which never came, thus delaying our attack, suddenly shining silver Mitsubishi bombers circled overhead, dropped height and bombed our regiment as it lay in neat lines awaiting the whistle to attack.

The bombing killed nine men and wounded over 30. The attack was cancelled and we withdrew to better cover. In a small banana plantation with a farmhouse, there was a single shot. Two privates dragged the Chinese houseowner dressed in a white singlet, shorts and slippers to me. He fired the rifleshot, they said. Had he a rifle? No. Ammunition? No, but it must have been him. Can we shoot him? No, I replied, but they took the unfortunate man to a higher ranking officer, got permission and a minute later shot him dead behind his house.

Reports came that the Aussies had broken the ring and were withdrawing. Towards midday we received orders to withdraw. I led off with two support platoons. A patch of jungle only 300 yards wide took us an hour to cut though, so we returned to the road. Minutes earlier the Japanese Imperial Guards Division swarmed down the hilltop road with tanks in the lead. Our two forward companies fought a grim battle without the aid of any anti-tank guns. I had a glimpse of khaki tanks, their guns swivelling, followed by running soldiers, unencumbered by equipment. With one company overrun, two embroiled, but the tanks halted and the causeway blown, our (half) battalion received orders to hasten to Yong Peng to face the Japanese already well south of Segamat.

The battle of the Muar River was irretrievably lost; the British did not 'get there fastest with the mostest'. A much reduced remnant of the Australians and Indians surrounded beyond the ridge cut their way through jungle and swamp and regained our lines days later, badly in need of rest and reorganisation.

As we retreated through Yong Peng and beyond, we saw hardly a single Malay or Chinese; village after village was empty, shops were closed. The Asians were not involved. There was a game of war on in Malaya and only members of the club were allowed to play.

I slept late that night in a Malay hut above rooting pigs. Earlier I had patrolled the road by motorbike on the lookout for Japanese infiltration. I rode into Ayer Hitam on the old imaginary Mersing–Batu Pahat defence line and was shocked but not greatly surprised to see no troops and no roadblocks at this important crossroad. We'll be in Singapore in a week, I decided.

We took up a position near the 63rd mile post amid swamp and low hills. At midday, one of my intelligence section lookouts cycled into headquarters from his forward position and reported Japanese approaching. I was sent forward to report more fully.

On my motorbike I accompanied my lookout on his cycle and he led me round a bend smack into a Japanese ambush. Fire came at us from two sides; he turned his bike and was gone. I turned my heavy motorbike and stalled the engine. As I was kicking it to restart with bullets slapping the road beyond me, a rifleshot hit me in the left shoulder; my arm sprang up like a snapped wire and I fell flat on the ground. My helmet was off and blood jolting out of the exit wound in my shoulder. I slapped my pistol into my armpit and held it there to stem the blood loss. It slowed the flow and I staggered off. Behind me the Japanese infantrymen and our forward company were exchanging fire.

As I staggered along the road, a Bren-gun carrier came screaming by, its crew shouting 'Tanks!' I lurched off the road into thigh-deep swamp and put 30 yards between me and the road. Weaker now, I threw off my belt and equipment, mapcase and water-bottle, keeping only my pistol. But wading through swamp water was too slow and no tanks had appeared, so I returned to the road. A gunner officer, seeing my faintness, left his anti-tank gun to give me a pick-a-back for 60 yards then ran back to his gun. I staggered on another 200 yards and reeled into battalion headquarters and dropped onto a groundsheet at the doctor's aid post. He offered me a lighted cigarette.

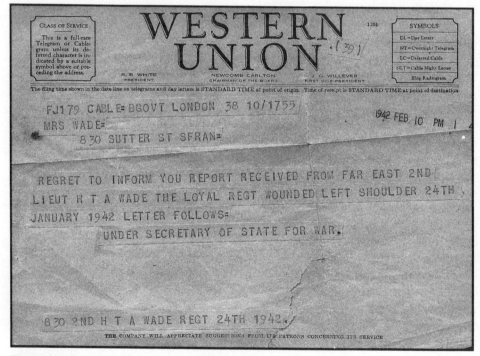

The cable received by the author's mother in San Francisco on 10 February 1942—seventeen days after the event, but accurate in all details.

'No thanks, I don't smoke,' I murmured automatically. He gave me a mug of sweet tea and a morphine pellet and sketched an M on my forehead. Joking cheerfully, he fixed a shell dressing on my shoulder and put my arm in a sling. Mortar shells exploded among the banana trees and huts of battalion headquarters. The battalion was holding the Japanese nicely. Other wounded came in. Once he had seven wounded ready, the doctor had us loaded into an ambulance he had commandeered. The battle receded behind us as the vehicle bounced along the road southwards towards the casualty clearing station. A Japanese Zero dived and fired a burst at our ambulance. At the CCS I went straight onto the operating table. The bullet had entered near the spine, passed an inch from the heart and out the left shoulder near the main artery. Next day I was delivered to the Alexandra Military Hospital, outside Singapore, weak and very, very hungry.

In the hospital ward, I heard that the battle in Johore had continued badly. Withdrawing two miles from the 63 mp our colonel met the 2/30 Australians in position. He offered to place his shrunken regiment under the command of Lieutenant Colonel Galleghan. This was instantly accepted and the Loyals' remaining 70 riflemen, mortars, signals, two carriers, drivers and headquarters team fought their next battle shoulder to shoulder and sharing ditches with the 2/30 Battalion AIF. Next day near Ayer Hitam, my decimated battalion was withdrawn and the Gordon Highlanders took over. I also learnt that the Australian wounded left at Parit Sulong—at least 130 of them—had been massacred by the exultant Japanese. The British Battalion and others, fighting south of Batu Pahat, had finally to be taken off by sea.

From my bed I watched two of the 70 Hurricane fighters which had arrived by crate or from the deck of an aircraft carrier. We hadn't seen a British plane since the first day at Segamat, nor had most of the troops on the mainland. One aerodrome, we knew, had been abandoned in panic while the enemy was miles away and bombs, petrol and runways left intact for the Japanese to use.

By the end of January, a gap in the causeway had been blown and the Japanese were in Johore Bahru, just across the causeway connecting Singapore Island with the mainland, while for hundreds of miles north, small parties of British troops, cut off by the swift advance, were wandering through jungle and rubber trying to make their way south. Many died in the jungle or fell into Japanese hands and were shot, but some reached the island.

During the whole 500-mile retreat, the British generals seemed to have little control of the battle. The Japanese had the initiative all the way and no counter-attacks on anything but the smallest scale were ever attempted. The decision to withdraw was often made by the commander on the spot when he saw that his line of retreat was about to be cut.

Back on the island, the weary troops who had fought all the way down the peninsula were disgusted to find that they had to defend the north of the island and therefore face the main Japanese attack, while the 'fortress' troops, who had still not fired a shot, and were fresh, were left on their beach defences facing the sea. Neither was it encouraging to hear that the navy had all cleared out and also most of the air force.

On about 23 January our transport officer had found a marked map in a shop in Yong Peng, accurately showing the main routes of the Japanese invasion from Thailand to Singapore. They indicated that the attack on the island would come from the north and west. One hoped therefore that this area would be allotted the most troops and defensive equipment. The map had, of course, been sent immediately to headquarters.

It was the Australians who were given the west and north-west of the island to defend, but no digging or wiring had been done in or near the mangrove swamps that covered most of their front. Nor had any work been done on the rest of the northern shore. All this had to be attempted now. And even with the navy and Naval Base to draw upon, no attempt was made to mine the narrow strait dividing the island from the mainland.

There was an uncanny silence for a few days as the Japanese piled up men and material for the final assault. On the island, troops were digging those positions that should have been dug in December or even in peacetime, some officers were at last arming 2000 Chinese volunteers and the last ships were evacuating most of the British (white) women and children and a few Asians; some men forced themselves aboard these ships. And some officers were still managing to drink at the Raffles Hotel.

Soon after I came to Malaya, I had wondered why the British did not recruit a few Chinese regiments. If anybody knew how to fight the Japanese, if anybody hated them at this time, it was the Chinese. The two countries had been fighting since 1932 and, especially, since 1937, yet the British colonial administration did not trust the Chinese sufficiently to let them join in the defence of Malaya or even let them defend themselves.

As I say, there was a game of war on in Malaya and only 'members of the club' were allowed to play.

The British in Malaya were very ready to explain why they adopted this policy towards the Chinese. There were two and a half million Chinese in Malaya, slightly fewer Malays and 700 000 Indians. Besides being the largest racial group, the Chinese were the wealthiest. By nature industrious and independent, they owned every village shop and most of the thriving industries of the towns; their millionaires' homes in Singapore were famous. But in the '30s, there had been some Chinese Communist agitators who had caused riots and incited the people. Because of these incidents the Chinese were feared. It was thought that they might attempt to throw the British out of Malaya. That the Communists were a minority of young extremists and that most of the middle class Chinese had no sympathy for them made no difference; neither did the obvious change in the political situation after 1937. Chinese help was not wanted in the defence of Malaya. They were permitted to join the Singapore Volunteers, but for the rest, as at the clubs, the rule was 'Asiatics keep out'.

Shortly before the Pacific war started, an officer of my regiment had given a 'hate' lecture to the troops of the battalion. Knowing the man, I am certain the lecture was not of his own composition but a piece of prepared propaganda issued by Malaya Command.

It was a 'hate' tirade against the Chinese. It made much of the belief that the Chinese dislike the smell of Europeans. 'They say we smell of meat. They say we stink like corpses,' he sneered. 'They would welcome the Japanese.' The Eurasians, he added, were untrustworthy and sided with the Asiatics.

So *over half* the population of Malaya, for whom Malaya was home, were written off as unreliable and even as our enemies.

As I lay in hospital in Singapore waiting for the Japanese invasion of the island, I thought of all the stories I had heard of the fighting up-country, which showed that the Chinese were almost 100 per cent reliable and pro-British, while the Malays had maintained strict neutrality and scores of them had denounced parties of British soldiers to the Japanese, given our men wrong directions, refused food and water to the dying and, above all, acted as guides to the enemy.

How badly Britain misjudged some of her colonial peoples!

The Chinese guerilla volunteers were given a blue armband and a rifle and posted in the mangrove swamp and rubber. Most were killed, some by our own men. The Chinese members of the Straits Settlements Volunteer Force who were detected as having belonged to this corps were led on to the beach near Singapore after the surrender and shot in their hundreds by the Japanese. At least 5000 were executed. Yet the Chinese would willingly have raised a brigade if they had been trusted.

In truth, Malaya was the most heterogeneous and disunited colony in the British Commonwealth. The races rarely mixed; friendship and trust between them was minimal. How could such a divided federation hope to resist the united, patriotic, homogeneous Japanese? The British administration in Malaya had no roots in the people, it did not represent the people. There was little sympathy or understanding between British and Asians and even less friendship. No effort was ever made to unite all the races or to make them understand that they were all 'Malayans'. Class and above all racial distinctions reigned supreme and inviolable.

# 6

# Last Days of the Fortress

A thunderous barrage from 500 guns was the signal for the Japanese assault on the island, the 'fortress' of Singapore.

Need it be said after all that has gone before that Singapore was not a fortress in any sense of the word. Millions of pounds had been spent with the idea of making it one, but millions more would still be needed. The money spent had bought it a well-equipped naval base, a giant floating dock, five 15-inch guns set in the hills facing the sea and a number of 9.2- and 6-inch batteries guarding the sea approaches. It had also bought many fine, large barrack buildings, three airfields and a well-defended small island, Blakang Mati, beside the harbour. But it provided no defences of any kind on the northern, western and even portions of the southern shore of the island.

Any infantry officer or sergeant-major or sergeant could have told the British government that this was the case in 1940 and 1941. Other officers too. But this was not the way to success in the army. The army does not look kindly on juniors who criticise the strategic decisions of their seniors. I thought one afternoon that I should write to Churchill about this lack, but I immediately abandoned this thought. It would only get me into appalling trouble.

There was even a scandal about the pillboxes on the beaches of Singapore. Too much sand had been used in their construction. The officer in charge of the work had been gaoled. But the sandy pillboxes remained.

But there were no pillboxes, crumbly or strong, on the north-western coast of Singapore Island where the Japanese landed in hundreds of small landing craft in pitch darkness. Shaken by the barrage, their lights knocked out, communication poor and the mangrove thick, the Australians could not stop the Japanese landing and fanning out. A beachhead was firmly established. It was 8 February.

Air attack on the whole of Singapore Island was continuous. Squadrons of 27 Japanese bombers, flying in perfect V formation, dropped their pattern of bombs in one shower, then returned to reload. Fighter planes machine-gunned exposed troops. Oil tanks and petrol dumps were ablaze and volcanic columns of black smoke darkened the island. Most of the 70 Hurricanes had already been destroyed or had been withdrawn to Sumatra. Few British planes took the sky.

Heavily outnumbered, the Aussies were pushed back and bypassed; the Japanese advanced from the north too. Soon they were pressing towards Bukit Timah, the hill dominating the island and the three reservoirs. The 'line' between the Jurong and Kranji rivers was pierced. I was scarcely surprised; it had had neither weapon pits, trenches nor wire. On Friday the 13th they overran the seaward-facing 15-inch guns at Buena Vista. That night, the Japanese burst into Alexandra Hospital, four miles outside of Singapore, whose corridors and verandahs were lined with wounded soldiers, and bayonetted or shot nearly 100 wounded, officers and orderlies. The surgeon, anaesthetist, patient on the operating table and theatre staff were all bayonetted; only the surgeon survived, feigning death. Some 200 other wounded and orderlies were wired together and packed into 9 by 9 foot coolie quarters and the doors nailed. Next day they were led out in batches and bayonetted. Altogether some 320 are believed to have perished in this obscene atrocity.

On 'Black Friday', the doctor in charge gave all patients who could leave to discharge themselves from hospital as the Japanese were a mile away. Some left but many stayed. I believed the enemy would reach the hospital within hours so I begged a lift in an Indian Army ambulance bound for the city. As we left, Punjabi troops were retreating past the gates. The ambulance dropped me in a temporary hospital for the Indian wounded in an ordinary house in a suburb of Singapore. In the blacked-out house with nearly 40 beds covering the floorspace, there was only one orderly. Men groaned in pain and others cried 'Pani, pani!' ('Water, water!') but there was only one man to aid them. I lay on a camp bed in my clothes, sweating.

Next morning I left that sad house, having halted a passing army three-ton lorry. I hitched a ride towards the city. As we drove down Orchard Road, a sniper put a bullet smack through the windscreen and through the shoulder of the driver. He may have been in a tree. The lorry lurched across the road into the three-foot monsoon drain and I smashed my left shoulder against the windscreen. With my arm in a sling, I could barely help the wounded driver out of the cab. He was pale and faint, but I got a rough dressing on his wound. We left the truck in the drain and walked towards the Cathay Cinema. My wound was bleeding. I met an officer from headquarters who told me where my regiment was believed to be. I then got my wound dressing changed in a first aid post in the cinema.

Singapore was littered with burnt cars and trucks. Lost soldiers roamed the streets looking for their units and for food and drink. All shops and cafes were boarded up. There were several fires, and overhead black smoke rolled across the sky from the abandoned Naval Base and from Pulau Bukum island offshore, where our largest oil installation was going up in flames. There was nothing to eat or drink anywhere.

I came to St Andrew's Cathedral, almost white in the sun under its tall spire, and saw about a thousand British and Australian soldiers outside it on the lawn. Most of them were wearing Red Cross armbands, yet I could hardly believe that they were all RAMC and AAMC. Many were sitting on the cathedral chairs and pews, set out in rows on the grass. They seemed to be waiting like men in a cinema. Some were wounded and the cathedral was being used as a hospital. Across the green *padang* a battery of howitzers was aligned in its final position with the trails of the guns only yards from the harbour. I rested for some minutes on the steps of the government buildings taking in this strange, dreamlike scene.

In the next 200 yards I encountered five lost men from my battalion. We crossed the bridge and on Collyer Quay saw cars and several bodies burning. Private cars were being pushed off the quay into the waters of the harbour. Across the street on a small verandah at the General Post Office, they were burning money. A single man was emptying boxes of notes on to a fire; notes floated away on the breeze and drifted down to the street. No one seemed to be picking them up.

I wasn't sure exactly what I expected to see in a besieged city, but it was not this calm, mild behaviour. There were no staff officers or military police rounding up men and building defensive lines or erecting barricades. I had expected to see Chinese, Malay and Indian civilians weeping in anguish or running in and out of buildings trying to save their businesses or their families. But there were none in sight; only some soldiers sitting in doorways. In spite of the clamour of close and distant shelling and bombing, there was a hollowness and deadness about the city; no civilians, just a litter of fallen electric cables, brick, glass, wood and asphalt rubble, yet the streets mainly clear and passable. Among the Red Cross orderlies and even the gunteams in the streets, there was a lack of ardour, as if they suspected that their jobs might not last much longer. A fire-fighting vehicle hurried by, but otherwise there was no excited movement, no shouts; soldiers seemed quiet and fatalistic. Enthusiasm was quite absent, and so, I guessed, was hope.

We shared out some bully beef and water and began the long stretch past the docks. There were no ships and some of the docks were burning. We didn't look at them with any interest as we had no thought of escaping from the island. But we heard that some groups of soldiers had forced their way at gunpoint aboard passenger ships busy evacuating civilians and fled the island in that way. We also heard the Japanese had reached the reservoirs. After this there began to be some talk of boats, but everyone said there were no boats left. We reached the railway station and informally attached ourselves to a large unit there. By now I had seven men with me, but had lost two. That evening we scrounged a light meal and a soldier gave me a small bottle of Foster's Melbourne Bitter—pure nectar. We slept on some sacks.

Next morning, Sunday 15 February, we continued west along Keppel Road towards Pasir Panjang, hoping to find our battalion. Squadrons of 27 Japanese bombers poured their bombs on this main west coast highway and the docks and shells smashed and battered the small shops and godowns across the road. The nearby Normanton oil dump was also burning. A couple of soldiers from our unit appeared. They told us the battalion's transport had been badly shelled and set ablaze somewhere behind Gillman Barracks and that what was left of the battalion had dispersed into the hills.

Rumours were now rife that we were about to surrender. The three reservoirs for the city had been captured and that morning we turned on taps and got no water. Men were still seeking boats to escape towards Sumatra. We heard that special groups of men had been given permission by our high command to escape in motor launches held ready for this purpose. We knew that such a course was forbidden to us.

A captain from Fort Canning, Command Headquarters, appeared, who was organising additional lines of defence. He enlisted us and a truck took us to a point north of Tanglin Club where a reserve line was being established. We were left there without food or ammunition. There was no line of command; and I was still unarmed. Shelling and machine-gun attacks from the air continued. Black smoke rolled endlessly over the city. The hot, long, hungry day dragged on. A rumour came that we had surrendered at four o'clock. I denied this to the men, but the rumour persisted. An eye-witness described an armoured car with a white flag flying driving up the Bukit Timah Road. We waited and wondered. It was clear we were about to capitulate; there was no water, no air power, no organisation of any counter-attack, no rescue from the sea. Sometime after 8 p.m. we heard that the surrender had indeed occurred and first the shelling, then the rifle fire ceased. In the darkened city there was a weird unaccustomed silence. We left our weapon pits and slept on the verandahs of deserted bungalows.

A few miles away, I heard later, the remnants of the Loyal Regiment—129 out of the 800—were spread on the hills around Mount Washington, having had the unique experience of fighting a battle through their own barracks, Gillman, over the past two days. The Lancashiremen had battled through the officers' married quarters, house by house, past the canteen, transport and dhobi lines; battalion headquarters had been in the sergeants' mess and the doctor and his crew were back in their peacetime medical inspection room.

Shortly before nine o'clock, a line of Japanese soldiers stood up on a skyline. Officers and men of the Loyals fired Bren-gun bursts. The Japanese dropped out of sight. Then a car drove up the hill with headlights blazing and the word was shouted, 'Cease firing. We've packed in.' To the weary men with Bren guns and fingers permanently on the trigger, the order had to be repeated several times. Then they lowered their gun butts. 'God help us,' one of them murmured.

The last shot had been fired. In the valleys beyond, the Japanese soldiers were cheering the news. The taste of bitter defeat and exhaustion settled on the defenders.

Singapore, the 'city of lions' had fallen. The greatest military name in all Asia and Australasia had been humbled after a 70-day campaign and with it had fallen the richest country of the world, taking into account its population—the rubber-, tin- and copra-bearing Malay States. The defenders and the world were awestruck: a giant had proved to have feet of clay. Singapore had surrendered.

# 7

# Surrender

The fighting troops slept where they lay on the night of 15 February 1942. Many men, who had refused to leave before the resistance ended, now searched among the creeks for boats, junks or any sea-going vessel. A few were found and put off into the night towards Sumatra or Java. Some disorganised troops in the city looked for drink and loot. Over 100 000 soldiers and a million Asians slept uneasily in Singapore that night.

The order to all troops had been to stay where they were and lay down their arms. All over the island next morning an army was to be seen throwing its rifles, machine guns, pistols and ammunition on to great glittering heaps. Goodbye to all that! What next?

About eight o'clock Japanese scouts entered the city. Down the main highways into the city came two dusty figures on foot with bayonetted rifles at the hip. Thousands of the defenders looked at their first Jap. A rifle and three leather pouches of ammunition on his belt was all his equipment; his baggy breeches were bound with puttees from the knee down to his dusty boots, a faded shirt, perhaps even a white one, and a battered little cap. Behold the conqueror!

Without a trace of emotion on their faces, they took up their positions at the main crossroads of the city while a few motor-cycles with officers in sidecars dashed around the city seeing that all was quiet and war correspondents with cameras snapped the piles of surrendered weapons and the swarms of dejected prisoners. I had set out at dawn to try and find my unit and saw these first Japanese arrivals in the city. Less than an hour later, long silent columns of Japanese cyclists came down the empty roads past the watching army to the docks and elsewhere. It seemed that one or two ships in harbour were put in order and that these same troops would be embarking soon for fresh conquests. Other regiments arrived in trucks.

I searched for some time among the hills before finding the remnants of my battalion in a cup in the hills near Mount Washington. Earlier, I heard, a Japanese colonel had walked across the battle-scarred grounds on the western outskirts of Singapore to the little band whose resistance had been so stubborn. He introduced himself to the colonel of the Loyal Regiment.

'I wish to congratulate you and your men on your defence. How many men have you ?'
'A hundred and twenty-nine.'
'Is that all?'
'Yes.'
'What other troops are there here?'
'No more here. Beyond that further hill there are a few.'
'So! You are to be congratulated; you have opposite you a division.'

The Japanese officer added that a big, full-divisional attack had been ordered for the previous night at eight o'clock to sweep right through the city to the sea 'if arrangements were not completed'. Everyone laughed with relief. Then the two colonels saluted each other and the Japanese left.

Besides 129 Loyals about 600 Malays had held the extreme left of the British line. Although officers of the Malay Regiment had confidence in their troops, many outside officers doubted how the Malays would react under modern battlefield conditions. But in the event, the two battalions of the Malay Regiment had fought with courage and tenacity, even though the second battalion was less than eight months old. The behaviour of the Malay Regiment was completely honourable and loyal. It is strange to contrast it with the behaviour of many other Malays in the country.

A messenger brought orders that on the following morning all troops were to march out to Changi, where we would be interned. No transport was allowed beyond the minimum to carry the wounded. Steel helmets were no longer to be worn. We threw our tin hats on to a pile and looked for other headwear.

I was fortunate to sit among 'sitting wounded' in a staff car ahead of our ambulance-trucks for the ride to Changi. Shortly afterwards the surviving Loyals began their nineteen-mile march through heat and dust, carrying most of their kit. Our doctor told me that throughout the campaign he had had to improvise our own ambulances, using trucks, cars and commandeered ambulances; the RAMC, so confident in peacetime that they would evacuate the wounded, rarely approached the regimental aid posts of the fighting units.

As we drove through Singapore, we saw thousands of weary troops beginning their great trek out to Changi. There were crashed cars in every street. Scores of trucks and cars had bullet-shattered front windscreens and some Japanese soldiers in commandeered cars drove wildly round the city, sightseeing and grinning at weary prisoners of war. Others regulated the traffic on the roads to Changi. Many of them, with gestures, demanded watches from passing soldiers. If the man refused, they threatened his stomach with a bayonet point. Thousands of watches were stolen that day. Other Japanese confiscated the motor-cycles which many of our men were attempting to take to Changi.

Looking at the interminable, sad columns of British prisoners making their forced march out to Changi, I suddenly thought: My God, this is the end of the British Empire in the Far East!

Changi, being at the eastern point of the island and commanding the entrance to the Naval Base, had been a military area with several 15-inch and 9.2-inch guns and about 25 large barrack blocks of the standard Singapore pattern. These barracks, mostly built in the '30s, were the finest in the British Empire. Only 30 soldiers slept on each floor measuring about 100 feet by 50. Later the Japanese housed 400 Korean prostitutes, who had come to comfort their troops, in the same room where my 30 men once slept.

But now there were some 68 000 British and Australian troops to dispose amongst these barrack buildings and the rows of semi-detached houses for married families. No more three-yard gaps between beds. Where 30 men slept there were now 200, and where a family of four had occupied a little house there were now 30 men. Every building including laundries, bath-houses and even gas-test chambers became inhabited.

The Australians were separated from us and quartered in Selarang Barracks, a mile nearer Singapore. And further on was Changi gaol, patterned on Sing-Sing, in which British civilians were interned. That was the worst luck of all; theirs was a real prison with blank grey walls and iron gates and bars. We, for the moment, had green fields, palms and trees all around us and a square mile in which to move.

The many Indian prisoners were invited by the Japanese to volunteer for the Indian National Army, soon to be formed. Hundreds joined immediately, thousands resisted pressure to do so and some were tortured, even to death, for their loyalty. Within a few days, some Sikh soldiers, still in British uniforms with a small Japanese flag sewn on their chests, took over patrolling the perimeter of the camp and its main road. They had given up British drill, we noticed, and now slewed their rifles horizontally against the backs of their necks in Japanese fashion.

My much reduced battalion was allotted one barrack block for the NCOs and men and a terrace of Malay married quarters for the officers. The men slept on stone floors with few blankets and few fixtures except bedbugs. The officers were not crowded, but the high walls standing between backyards for religious reasons plus hills on two sides, cut out all breeze.

For the first fortnight, we talked endlessly about the war. Then, having heard everyone else's story in detail, there was no more to be said about it. We also talked about the men who got away. Prisoners were bitter about those men. Unlike Dunkirk, there had been no orders to troops to try to escape. The Royal Navy decided early on that any large evacuation was impossible, therefore men that did escape did so against orders.

It is true that by escaping many of these men were able to serve the Allied cause far better than if they had become prisoners, but that did not lessen the bitterness of the captured, and the names of officers who had fled before the cease-fire were anathema to those that stayed behind.

We made numerous enquiries about lost friends from our own and other units. Some might even be in gaol in Kuala Lumpur; some might still be free in the jungle. We soon learnt that the Argylls, Leicesters, East Surreys and Loyals had probably had the heaviest casualties among British troops; the Australians had suffered as badly, some battalions even worse, and so had the Indians. My battalion had, as I remember, 456 killed or wounded. This was about 70 per cent of those who had fought in the campaign. It was a terrible proportion, yet one regular unit was left in pillboxes facing the sea experiencing few losses, while another was held back far too long. It seemed criminal that well-trained units like these were scarcely used, while Indian troops of six months service and last-minute arrivals such as the 18th Division and 1000 untrained Australians were thrust in to halt the Japanese.

The Army, too, should have made use of the thousands of British planters and other civilians, who were volunteers and had specialised knowledge of Malaya and its languages. Most, except for armoured car and machine-gun units, were held back in reserve. They should have been used as intelligence officers and guides with every platoon, company and battery in action. Never was an army defending a country more foreign to that country than was the British Army in Malaya in 1941–2.

Many British in Changi, in the bitterness of defeat blamed the Indians or the Australians for the collapse. But once one knew that some Indian units were created out of two regular officers and two or three NCOs and all the rest wartime volunteers, sometimes with only six months training, that blame seemed grossly unfair. The Australian 8th Division burned with the desire to perform outstandingly, but had to fight without all the air support, tanks and artillery it would have liked. It wasn't even a full division and at times it was split. Yet all the battalions fought well and suffered heavily. The 2/20th, 2/19th and 2/18th Battalions took the full force of the Japanese landing on Singapore Island and the 2/19th and 2/29th endured the terrible battle and encirclement at Parit Sulong, where a Victoria Cross was awarded to its commander for its heroic resistance.

Why then did Singapore fall?

Because the Japanese had command of the air and command of the sea and proved themselves superior on land. Command of the air and sea could scarcely have been avoided in the Far East at that time, and around a peninsula like Malaya those superiorities were decisive. But superiority on land was due to more thorough training and to greater experience.

The Japanese, who are no more used to jungles than the British, made themselves masters of jungle warfare and all their troops in Malaya fought with an efficiency, determination and speed which only perfect training brings. They used their three main weapons—mortars, infantry guns and tanks—to the best possible effect, and to this they added unflagging determination and breathtaking speed. A great many of their soldiers had had over three years of war experience in China, whereas most of ours had none. The generalship of General Yamashita was brilliant; our generalship was almost always bad and wrong. It was weak and uninspiring; its existence was rarely felt. And, of course, we had dreadfully underestimated the Japanese. Short-sighted, poor marksmen, poor pilots they were said to be. But they did all these things well and their formation bombing was highly effective.

Victorious Japanese troops march into Singapore the day after the fall. Note the relaxed uniforms and white T-shirt at right. Drawing from a photo.

A piece of propaganda fed to our troops which failed them badly was the story that the Japanese did not take prisoners, so a man might as well die fighting as be captured and killed. In fact, this made many men look constantly over their shoulder to see that they were not surrounded, that a way of retreat remained open. They did not plan, at any cost, to be captured.

Before the Japanese had reached halfway down the peninsula, many of us were asking, 'What's wrong with our troops, equipment, tactics and generals?' We seemed to be slow, deliberate, overburdened and roadbound, while the Japanese were fast, light, energetic and daring. We had the wrong concept of war in thickly vegetated Malaya. Thick vegetation could be overcome, but only by an army that was fast, light and daring. We were once again the Redcoats in thick forest while the Japanese were the Red Indians, light, fast and better adapted to the terrain. We had the 'line' mentality, hating to be infiltrated or outflanked; but in thick country such penetration was to be expected. We never thought of the bicycle, but, following our withdrawals, the Japanese moved rapidly down Malaya's excellent roads on 10 000 bicycles.

Could Singapore have been held? I thought at first that had we met the enemy fresh at the Mersing–Batu Pahat line in Johore, it might have worked. But within a year in prison camp and seeing how far their aggression reached, I believed that Singapore could not have been held. Even if the Japanese had had to abandon their drive to Australia and India, they would have made sure of the capture of Singapore in those early months. It was the keystone of southern expansion—also of southern defence.

A few tried to offer excuses for the defeat. They said we ran out of aircraft or ammunition or water. The answer to this was best given by a Lancashire private of the Loyal Regiment, who silenced all opposition with the immortal words: 'The only thing we run out of was land!'

Since their return, the members of the services to Malaya have not been blamed for the collapse of Singapore. But in captivity, they felt unhappy and ashamed, and rightly so. The defence of Malaya was shameful. The British military should learn all the lessons, social, military and psychological of that collapse and take full cognisance of them. Above all, every attempt to gloss over the magnitude of that disaster, now or in the future, should be resisted.

# 8

# Changi

The beauty of Changi contrasted remarkably with the trauma of captivity. Palm trees, scarlet flamboyants, red hibiscus, even a few travellers' palms, like perfect fans, adorned the rolling green hills, dotted with creamy white barrack blocks and red-roofed army family houses. A barbed-wire fence marked the western limit of the prison camp and the seashore the other three sides. The area measured nearly two miles by one. But we were all too conscious of our groaning stomachs to give much thought to bougainvillea or tulip trees. Here we were, a disarmed army stranded beyond the current of world events with men still dying of wounds, others recovering with difficulty, our rations at a lower level than we had ever known and uncertainty everywhere.

Rice was already our staple food and it was of poor quality, brown, broken or too strongly limed. Dirty too, but it was inadvisable to wash it too thoroughly as washing rids rice of part of the nutritive husk and vitamin B content. Our diet consisted of two bowls of rice and a rice flour bun per day; minced into the rice was a little pilchard or the vegetables we grew in our newly tilled vegetable patches. One or two of the following would be used each time: five pounds of meat between 40 men, sugar and fat measured out like condiments and, whenever they ripened in our area, bananas, papayas or sweet potatoes and squash pumpkins. Young hibiscus leaves served as a sort of spinach.

Some of our Lancashire lads started football matches within days of arrival in Changi, not full time, but half an hour each way. After six days the games ended; the players lacked the energy for them. They realised and we all recognised that too much effort had to be spent on raising food, chopping firewood, building ovens and larger kitchens, manufacturing beds and stools, repairing clothes and a thousand other humdrum tasks to waste valuable energy on soccer. Tailoring and cobbling, manufacturing simple oil lamps and candles, carving drinking mugs out of a joint of bamboo and grinding rice for flour—all these filled our days and when darkness fell, only the moon or a few guttering rush lights illumined conversational groups or foursomes at cards.

We felt a burden of emotions as we simply existed through those first days in camp. Despondency, disappointment, also shame at our own performance and our surrender.

We all questioned ourselves: had we done more, dared more, made better decisions, might it not have gone better? The generals too must be asking that, but nothing could help their reputations now. There was bitterness, not only at our defeat, but at the speed of the Japanese conquest—and no one ever used that word. For me there was another emotion: reluctant admiration for the Japanese successes. I had always known that they were capable, patriotic and bold. I should not have allowed the complacency and contempt of those who had never lived amongst the Japanese to overcome my respect learnt from experience. My father, who had closely watched their progress since 1904, had often said: 'They're a great people, clever, united, hard working, highly skilled with their hands; they've got a great future ahead'. Now they had conquered Malaya in 70 days. One had no idea how far they were aiming and how far they would be successful. I had not a second's doubt that the United States and Britain would defeat them in the end, but I felt a reluctant admiration for their military efficiency and undoubted daring.

But each one of us had to come to terms with our despondency and gloom. Prison camp was going to be about survival; one could not afford to mope about a failure; one had to be forward-looking, optimistic, a cheerful comrade to one's fellows in order to survive this ordeal. I noticed how most of the old soldiers in our barrack were cheerful, practical and almost 'at home' in their new surroundings. To them it was just a rather bad army posting; you simply had to make the best of it, did the most you could with what was available, had a laugh, made a joke and 'carried on regardless.' They were right, the old sweats. Learn from them. Smile, be brave, be optimistic. Be ready to take anything the Japs might throw at you—and *survive*.

The Japanese, who had a war to rage, used the British command to pass their orders to the prisoners of war and to maintain discipline within the camp. This was a wise decision as it never fails to give rank and file the impression that unpleasant orders come, not from the enemy, but from their own officers. Men constantly grumbled about our command and paid little attention to explanations.

On the other hand, some men were harshly punished in prison camp. Military law was perpetuated and hard labour tasks were a common sentence. Certainly, the law-abiding majority has to be protected from the offending minority, but the detention barracks, with its zealous military policemen, was the scene of some punishments that must have seriously weakened the culprits and may have contributed to their deaths in prison camp.

With food so short, it was inevitable that some men would scrape through the wire fence and try to buy or barter food from the Chinese outside. A few people did quite well when daring escapades like this and brought back tinned food, soya sauce and other preferably vitamin-rich morsels. Other men were caught by the Indians or Japanese and held in an enclosed tennis court near the Japanese guardhouse and left there in rain and dews for a week or more before punishment. Three gunners were executed at one time and their colonel was obliged by the Japanese to witness the shooting. Later several Aussies were executed for the same offence.

Some men came into camp wounded, badly, lightly or convalescent.Two and later three large barrack blocks were furnished a far as possible as hospitals and from day one men were dying there. Soon after, new patients were entering the hospital; at first it was dysentery that swept them in in hundreds, filling the wards with gaunt, wide-eyed living skeletons; later the effect of a poor diet ruinously short of vitamins caused the first beri-beri deaths.

Beri-beri is caused by the lack of the B range of vitamins, particularly B1. We all experienced constipation and then diarrhoea and then the swelling of ankles, a proneness to fatigue quickly, numbness in toes and fingertips and a tendency to dizziness or even complete black-outs. Another early symptom was particularly uncomfortable; we found ourselves walking awkwardly while trying to keep our legs as far apart as possible. The reason was that the scrotal skin had become raw and inflamed. We called this 'strawberries'.

The well-known vegetable extract, Marmite, often eaten in sandwiches, was collected in Changi from the beginning as it is rich in the B group of vitamins. It went to the doctors who prescribed it in serious beri-beri cases. Our unit doctor gave a spoonful on a piece of paper to a private one day and told him it would cure his 'strawberries'. When the man returned a few days later and the doctor asked if there had been any improvement, the private said: 'No sir. I keep it smeared on all the time, but I'm having a lot of trouble with ants.'

Questioning the doctors, I found that they knew very little about beri-beri and deficiency diseases. Here was a wonderful opportunity for them to study the problem for we were some 60 000 Europeans unused to an Asian diet, swept into an Asian prison situation for perhaps years to come. Surely they would learn a great deal from our sufferings and bring out fascinating studies and statistics after the war. That's what I thought, but nothing of the sort happened. No statistics were collected.

The next stage of beri-beri plus pellagra and general malnutrition is further swelling of the legs and ankles. Now, if one pressed a finger into the skin, it left an impression like a small pit. This would take many minutes to fill out and disappear. This swelling may appear and disappear several times, depending on the value of the food one is eating, and the disease may go no further. Most of us who returned from Japanese prison camps reached this stage at least once but never passed beyond.

But the unlucky ones found their faces swelling up as badly as their ankles. One day a man looked perfectly normal, but the next he would be unrecognisable with a huge, broad, puffy face and closed eyes. Whether treatment were available or not, the swelling would disappear after three or four days almost as quickly as it had come.

If the disease is not halted by this stage, it progressively swells the stomach, face, genitals, and finally the heart, where paralysis, not beri-beri, actually kills. In the last stages the patient suffers terribly from neuritis and spreading paralysis before death ends the torture. And this was the death of some thousands of prisoners of war in the Far East.

Yet, it seems strange that men could die of malnutrition and deficiency diseases in those early months in Changi. Tens of thousands of us lived on much the same level of diet for three and a half more years and never succumbed.

There were six, eight, perhaps more funerals a day in Changi during the early months. I myself attended six burials of men from my former company or armoured car section. One followed the body, wrapped in a sheet on a cart, down to the small cemetery created beside the hospital to see the soldier laid to rest. A small cross was erected above each grave. What was sad was to read the ages of the deceased; on cross after cross one read ages in the early twenties—and there they were, interred, far from home, in the red laterite earth of a derelict colony.

From the very earliest days in Changi there was a subtle return to religion. With so much uncertainty about their present and future and with death ever present, men turned to religion for comfort and for faith. Church services were held under the trees and men flocked to them. To those searching for some truth, some faith, religion became a consolation and a strength for the long years ahead in captivity. Many units built outdoor chapels of coconut logs and palm leaf thatch which attained a simple beauty and services there were always well attended.

On the other hand, there was a considerable minority of men who were apparently completely unaffected by the fearful uncertainty of our life. They might find intellectual stimulus in study at 'Changi University', staffed by lecturers from Raffles College and elsewhere in Singapore. They might concentrate on improving their game of bridge or become news addicts, always gathering and retailing the latest rumours ('boreholes' we called them, after the 40-foot drilled boreholes used as latrines on the hillsides where men of many units often crossed paths). Some tried to distil alcohol, some wrote magazines.

Two young subalterns in my regiment decided to start a magazine for the mess. They asked me to join them and I gladly did. For the next year and a half at irregular intervals, we produced a magazine of some wit and entertainment. We were wrangling about a name.

'What about *Stone Walls*...from "do not a prison make, nor iron bars a cage"?' I asked.

They both grimaced.

'Wait a minute!' I had seen the light. 'What about *Nor Iron Bars*—that's the key part of the quotation?'

So for want of a better title, we used that and never changed it in the next eighteen months. As time passed the quality of the writing and humour improved and each issue was most warmly welcomed in prison camp.

The greatest boon in Changi was the concert party or theatre founded in the early days. The Australians in their camp and the 18th Division also had their own concert groups and the rest of us (Southern Area) had an excellent one. We contributed Jack MacNaughton, a lieutenant from my battalion who was a West End actor with much comedy experience and a mobile and highly expressive face. No. 122 Field Regiment, Royal Artillery, contributed Bombardier Arthur Butler, who was already well-known on the concert stages of Malaya as Miss Gloria d'Earie. Butler was slim and gracious, with small features and ardent brown eyes. He was always known as Gloria and the jokes about him were almost as numerous as they once used to be about Mae West. It was said that when he gave an order to the gunners in his battery, they would always reply, 'Yes, darling'.

The revues, held in a small open-air theatre, were an enchanting escape, full of gaiety and good humour. They conjured up memories of music-hall and musical comedy and seemed to promise a future of lightheartedness and lack of care—exactly what we needed.

Each night the theatre was filled to capacity with an audience from a different group of units and, as soon as all had seen the show, the cast was ready with the next production. It was admirable the way tailors and carpenters provided such colourful and attractive costumes and props. We all contributed what we could in the way of brightly coloured clothing or civilian hats, but most of these things and others like dresses were brought in from working parties in Singapore, always on the look-out for such valuables.

Both MacNaughton and Butler left Changi in the same draft as myself, so their talents remained with us but were lost to Changi. Then the second couple stepped up into the star roles and the new leading lady was one Bobby Spong, who could roll his big eyes wickedly and time his silences most skilfully.

These two young men, slinkily dressed and well made-up, caused immeasurable happiness to thousands of prisoners. They were frankly adored. In POW camp we had no heroes: no war heroes, political heroes, sport heroes. The only people about whom there was any glamour were the actors and most idolised of these were the female impersonators. Crowds escorted them from stage door to their barracks each evening. I often heard troops say, 'If Gloria were a woman I could really go for her', and others, 'I had a wonderful dream about Bobby Spong last night'.

# 9

# Work Camp

The Japanese call Singapore 'Shonan'—Southern Light—and their newspaper, the *Shonan Times* (from the presses of the *Straits Times*) printed a short Japanese lesson each day, but it taught so little and so slowly that we did not waste time with it. Lieutenant George Baker, the signals officer of my battalion, a linguist and midway through university, decided with me very early to learn Japanese. We discovered an officer giving lessons and we joined his classes.

Within a few weeks we had enough words to ask questions of the Japanese sentries accompanying working parties and soon were carrying on lengthy but simple conversations about food, cigarettes, longer rests for the labouring troops and news. We did not read a single character; we spoke only and wrote our notes in romanised (phonetic) Japanese.

Every prisoner in time learnt a fair number of Japanese words, but at this time there was no interest in the subject. Everyone, however, was fascinated to see the authority delegated in the Japanese Army to first-class privates. Working parties of twenty to 100 men were commanded by a single first-class private; a party of 800 men might be commanded by a Japanese corporal with four assisting privates, and the guard for 50 000 British and 17 000 Australian POWs in Changi was a lieutenant with 25 men plus companies of renegade Indians.

I kept wondering how the Japanese would behave towards us; we had had little contact yet. I knew the Japanese as polite, bowing shopkeepers, hotel staff and photographers, also as formal officials, as stiff correct officers and generals and rank after rank of stocky, serviceable soldiers. Then, after 1932 in China, as brusque, surly, aggressive soldiery backed by petulant, secretive officials. Would they now bear any resemblance to the polite shopkeepers of Tientsin, Kobe and Nagasaki? Or would they be arrogant, confident conquerors? To their minds they were extending an empire and had finally, after decades of waiting, subjugated and humiliated the British and Americans.

I accompanied several working parties into Singapore and saw many deserted and looted houses, Japanese flags flying from all the finest buildings while Kallang Airport and some of the docks were crammed with the wreckage of crashed aeroplanes. The Chinese citizens looked at us sadly and occasionally slipped us gifts of food. The Malays and Indians and neutral Europeans ignored us. We picked up food, books, seeds, tools wherever we could and bits of leather, cloth, wire and string to use for repairs in the future.

Several Japanese introduced themselves to our men at various work parties. They had been intelligence agents, they said. Two were naval officers and both had worked as coolies and had helped construct the very beach defences of Singapore. Others were photographers who had photographed hundreds of military installations, bridges etc. One was a brothel keeper and another, a major, who knew our colonel's name. He revealed that he had been the offical interpreter at a court martial held in Gillman Barracks of a gunner charged with the sale of military information to the Japanese. It seemed to me that Japanese intelligence had been as good as their military planning and strategy.

In May, the Japanese began building a war memorial to their dead on top of Bukit Timah hill. It was to be approached by a long driveway. Prisoners, Australian and British, were moved from Changi and housed in new camps north of Singapore near MacRitchie reservoir. A hundred men and ten officers from the Loyals were included in the British party. We were, frankly, delighted when we walked into clean, new suburban houses in Caldecott Estate off Lornie Road. In this four-bedroom house was a modern kitchen and a sparkling white-tiled bathroom. The contrast from cement walls and the 'borehole' privies of Changi could not have been greater. There were even books in a library and colanders, roasting pans, basins and bottles of vanilla essence in the kitchen. Lightly looted though the house had been, there were marvellous deep armchairs in which we could rest, looking out on green hills, and imagine we were in a civilian home in peacetime. Furthermore, as we were a working party, the Japanese *trebled* the Changi rice ration for each of us.

The work was the construction of the highway leading to the war memorial. It meant clearing jungle in the catchment area around the reservoir, digging out the roots, making a flat road bed, breaking stones and laying them, stamping down the stone-bed, then adding gravel on top. It was hard work, but the men were happy as the food was better, our bedding comfortable and the surroundings pleasant.

Baker and I would spend hours talking with Japanese guards and trying to wring out a little news of the war. The Japanese in their turn would ask as many questions as we did.

'Wife-u *arimasu-ka*?'—'No, no wife,' we would reply.

'*Kodomo arimasu-ka*?—'No, no children.'

'*Hei-ya!*' they'd shake their heads. '*Ni-ju-ichi shikashi kodomo ga arimasen*' ('Twenty-one and no children').

But try as we might, we got no good war news. Sumatra, Java and the whole Dutch East Indies had fallen, Burma, the Philippines and Borneo too; in the Battle of the Java

Sea British, American, Dutch and Australian cruisers had gone down before overwhelming Japanese force; this had happened also to the Royal Navy south of Ceylon, giving the Japanese extensive control of the Indian Ocean. The Japanese also claimed a great naval victory in the Coral Sea. Even Sydney Harbour had been attacked by two or three midget submarines.

In Changi a brigadier had forecast three years of captivity for us. Few of us dared to imagine more than two years. I tried not to think about it; most of us, I believe, never thought far beyond the next six, four or even three months ahead.

One day in June, we noticed that there were fewer Japanese around our camp at Caldecott, and we heard that night that a few British troops had slipped through the wire surrounding the camp and gone into town. When they returned, the camp heard that they had been wonderfully treated by the Chinese residents of Singapore and that there were few Japanese soldiers about. They had been welcomed by the Chinese and taken into shops and cafes, treated to cups of tea or coffee and biscuits and given cans of food to take back to camp. That night Caldecott was humming with excited conversation in the troops' quarters where hundreds of men were now considering such escapades.

From dawn the next morning the figures of prisoners with haversacks slung over their shoulders were to be seen darting through the fences and across the fields of tall grass into the rubber plantations, head down for Singapore. Eighty must have gone that day and probably a similar number from the adjoining Australian camp.

When the truants returned that night they had the most amazing stories to tell of the situation in Singapore. There were hundreds of POWs in town, they said, walking through all the streets, sitting in all the Chinese cafes and being feted by the population. Some of them had bumped into Japanese officers when no escape was possible, but instead of having them arrested, the officer had merely returned their nervous salutes and passed on.

No one could understand it. The officers did not dare encourage the men to leave camp like this for fear that the very next day the Japanese might arrest everyone enjoying self-granted leave in town. The penalty of escape, as the Japanese had often said, was death, yet these men had been in town all day and returned safely, laden with gifts of food and cigarettes from the Chinese. Men who went the first day with a haversack, now took the road with an empty kitbag or both! There was limitless canned food, biscuits and sweets being given away by the Chinese, they said, and a thousand men from work camps all round Singapore were pouring in to get their share while the saturnalia lasted.

The Chinese, after the spontaneous welcome of the first days, dipped into the wealthy resources of their residents' association and organised the feeding of prisoners in an efficient manner. They set up a meal kitchen close to Japanese headquarters and fed over a thousand troops each day. Shopkeepers opened crates of canned foods; free meals, free drinks and free rickshaw rides were given to POWs and everywhere they were met with smiles of friendship. Few people on earth have ever been kinder or more generous than the Chinese citizens of Singapore to a few thousand British and Australian prisoners during that unexpected freedom in 1942.

Most British troops in Malaya, as I have explained, had Chinese or occasionally Malay girlfriends in Malaya. Many of them now revisited their paramours during this period and enjoyed blissful reunions. Many men visited the red-light district situated around the picturesquely named Lavender Street, where the girls rushed downstairs to meet them, handed them money earned from Japanese privates and chatted about old times. A few men even stayed in town and lived like kings for a few days, waited on by Chinese friends. They had to go out into the street and find a friend in order to learn news of prison camp.

Perhaps the strangest sight of all was that of an Aussie soldier returning to Caldecott in a rickshaw drawn by a Chinese coolie one evening, sitting back, smoking luxuriously, with a kitbag full of tins at his feet. Reaching the camp gate, the rickshaw puller stopped, helped the Digger out of the rickshaw and hoisted the kitbag on his back. When the Digger motioned that his pockets were empty and he had no money, the rickshaw puller darted his hand into his purse and *he* paid the prisoner.

Those of us who witnessed this incident cheered the rickshawman and he shyly acknowledged our cheers, then mopped his shining face with a dirty cloth and began to walk his vehicle back the five miles to Singapore.

This extraordinary situation lasted for five days and is probably unique in prisoner of war experience. On the fifth day the earlier arrivals from town reported that a number of men had been arrested by the Japanese and taken to gaol. By nightfall we found that we had 30 men missing. At midnight we were suddenly ordered to parade. The roll was called. The Japanese were furious. Next day the 30 were brought back to our camp and locked up on the upper floor of the Japanese sentries' house. They were told they were to be shot.

A gloom settled on the camp. It lasted for days. Then one morning they were released and the camp sighed with relief. The new Japanese garrison had arrived to replace the old, which for five days had left Singapore in the hands of a mere handful of occupying troops.

Not long afterwards, our work ended on this superficially built road and we were returned to Changi.

# 10

# Leaving Changi

Back in Changi once more we quickly picked up the threads of our former life there. I returned to university lectures and Japanese lessons. I revisited my friends—friends from China, from the OCTU, friends from school in England. I met Alan Capstick, who had been at school with me in Tientsin and who had fought with a Gurkha unit from Jitra, up north, right down the peninsula to a place called Serendah near Kuala Lumpur. 'I know,' I said. 'I saw it on the map. I really hoped we'd never have to fight a major battle at a place with that name.' I saw Fee Cooke, who had been the best NCO in the Tientsin Volunteers and whom I had left in the East Surrey Regiment in Singapore. He was now acting intelligence sergeant, but had lost an eye up country.

I met my friend Harold Fabian from Shanghai, who had been commissioned in the navy. His flat-bottomed Yangtze River gunboat had been sunk by Japanese air action somewhere south of Singapore and his crew of about fourteen had clambered on to a raft. They had no water and as day followed day in the blazing sun on the equator, without a drop of rain, men began to go crazy. One drank salt water and went completely mad, another swimming close to the raft was taken by a shark and a third suddenly dropped off the raft and swam off into the blue. They called twice, but he never came back. The rest were picked up by a Japanese cruiser soon after and brought back to Singapore and Changi.

A wing commander of the RAF told us of his attempted escape in an RAF speed launch, together with Rear Admiral E. Spooner and Air Vice-Marshal C. W. Pulford, the senior naval and air force officers in Malaya. The party was stranded on an island in the Banka Straits, south of Singapore, for some weeks. Most of the group caught malaria and blackwater fever. After days of suffering without medicines or relief, several of them died, including both the admiral and the air vice-marshal. The Japanese, mopping up these islands later, brought the sick and emaciated prisoners back to Changi.

And in Changi, I heard the terrible story of the 45 Australian nurses escaping towards Java in a small boat. The ship was sunk and the nurses took refuge on a little island. Japanese ships arrived and sent a party ashore. When they found the Australian nurses, they ordered them to walk towards the water. Then they machine-gunned them. Twenty-one young Australian girls were massacred on that beach.

There were so many stories to hear in Changi and, being interested in hearing first-hand accounts, I walked to all corners of the camp to get the true story. I met men, who after being captured by the Japanese, during their drive south, had been ordered to dig their own graves. After they had dug a couple of feet deep, one man was set aside, the others were shot directly into their graves and the survivor ordered to cover them over. 'I hadn't a glimmer of hope left after that,' one said to me, 'but they just shooed me away towards the rear and continued their advance.'

A corporal in the Loyals was captured with two others after an action in Johore. He was brought before a Japanese officer with sword drawn, who gave orders that our man interpreted as orders to execute the prisoners. While the others were being pushed into a line, my corporal made a dash for it, passing close to the officer. The angry lieutenant swiftly smashed down the samurai sword at him and cut him from the second large vertebra below his neck right down to the bottom of the small of his back in an amazing wound, some sixteen inches long, looking like the split in an over-fried sausage. But the Preston lad survived.

Besides the officers in the Loyals, I had in Changi one of my best friends from Shanghai. Bob Woodhead, the son of H. G. W. Woodhead, a leading Shanghai journalist and authority on Far Eastern affairs, had been an editor in Reuter's when I became a newsman. Later he was promoted to be their Peking correspondent. He had always been a Sinophile and the beauties of the imperial city of Peking and the gentle, civilised life there sent him into ecstasies. He wrote to me of them in Shanghai and in prison camp still talked of them. We both left Shanghai with the first group of volunteers and celebrated our last civilian days together in Hong Kong—and very nosily too. In Malaya, he was posted to the Royal Artillery and I to the East Surreys. Later we both attended the same OCTU, although his course was slightly different from my infantry one.

In prison camp, Bob and I met regularly, comparing our attitudes to his father's in China affairs (his father was inclined to excuse the Japanese) and to discuss his first draft of a book about a young newspaperman on the China coast. I could see a future for him as distinctive as his father's. Dear, hearty, boisterous, voluble Bob. A few weeks after one meeting, my unit was selected to be part of 'A' force, bound for Japan. I pleaded with Bob to volunteer for the same party, but he refused. He said he would leave his fate in the lap of the gods and not make the choice himself. We said goodbye and I never saw him again.

Six months later, he was taken in one of the small Japanese transports to Rabaul in New Britain. Exactly why they sailed there or what work they did may never be known. On 5 March 1943 they sailed from Rabaul for an unknown destination and a few days later the ship was lost with all hands. There are a few graves at Ballale Island, west of the Solomons, and it is suspected that they are those of men who survived the torpedoing only to die on a jungle island. No single survivor has ever appeared.

One day in August 1942, our colonel addressed the officers at lunchtime. 'The general has given me an opportunity to decide if we want to be part of "A" force, which is to sail for Japan this week. I have to give him my answer in two hours.'

This was a shock and also a dangerous decision to make. Most prisoners of war felt that it was foolhardy to tempt fate by volunteering for anything, for if you volunteered and it turned out badly, you would always blame yourself. We sat and pondered and talked. The colonel had already pointed out the main advantage and the main disadvantage: the climate would be temperate and healthier—on the other hand we would undoubtedly be prisoners for the rest of the war.

At the end of our rice and spinach, the colonel took a vote. There was a clear majority in favour of volunteering to sail north and keeping together as a unit. I abstained from voting. Most of those officers knew nothing about the Japanese except as seen at the other end of a rifle. I wondered if they realised how brutal they could be, what contempt they felt for prisoners of war and what Gestapo-like power the *kempeitai* had. I thought of Melville Cox, Reuter correspondent in Tokyo, who after days of grilling by the *kempei* had leapt to his death from his hotel window. I wondered if the Japanese would discover that I had been a journalist in Shanghai and try to use me for their propaganda. One Australian officer, Major Bill Cousens, a well-known broadcaster, had already been sought out by the Japanese and tempted with glowing promises. He had refused and had himself transferred to a working party to escape their attention, but in the end they had got him in their grip and sent him to Tokyo—to broadcast.

I decided to go with the Loyals and not to seek exemption, but I also wondered if I would survive the war in Japan.

We had been six months in prison camp and had not yet received any letters from the outside world. We had been allowed to write one postcard. I knew my mother and sister were in Miami with relatives, having been evacuated from North China by the BAT Co. in the spring of 1941, when the company foresaw war in the Far East. My father was still in Tientsin and, as commander of the local volunteer Emergency Corps, would probably have been arrested by the Japanese early on 8 December '41. (This I later found to be true.) I wondered what sort of fate and conditions he was experiencing with the Imperial Japanese Army in North China and, of course, I missed them all.

Word came that the first Red Cross parcels were on the point of arriving and that we would soon be receiving them. But we continued with our packing and repairing and swopping, trying to prepare ourselves for Japan. I swopped my mosquito net for a sweater and *To Beg I Am Ashamed* for a *Golden Treasury*. Then we paraded on a square outside the Changi wire for a medical inspection as Tokyo had given orders that no dysentery cases or carriers should be sent to the divine islands. Privates, sergeant majors, brigadiers and generals, even the governor of the Straits Settlements had to drop their shorts in the open square, bow to Japanese medical regulations with the rest of us and receive the sleek glass rod. (What did Gloria d'Earie, the female impersonator, say when he received the glass rod? *Ah! Ecstasy!*)

We paraded with packs and bedding rolls, small tin trunks and cardboard suitcases; trucks arrived and we drove that familiar road from Changi to Singapore. No more flames of the forest, tulip trees, coconut palms where we were going... maybe cherry blossom, snow, fog, ice. Ugh! Past Katong, past Raffles Hotel, past the Cricket Club *padang* and suddenly we were looking at an old freighter, scabby with rust, and a tall old-fashioned funnel.

'Is that our ship?' our commanders asked, horrified.

'No, no, that not your ship. Your ship down there.'

We looked and saw an even rustier freighter so deep in the water that only the bridge and funnel were visible above the dockside. Sixteen hundred of us were to squirm into her; she was loaded with bauxite, 'but space for prisoners above.' Groans could be heard on all sides. 'You could sink that ship with a .303 bullet,' said one man.

The generals protested vehemently for three hours and at the end of it their party of 500 was transferred to another vessel. Our 1100 then entered the tall freighter, which was a fumigation ship, were disinfected and powdered for lice, redressed and embarked in our freighter.

We stayed there in port, tied up, overcrowded and sweating for four days before the convoy sailed. As we steamed slowly out of Singapore Harbour, the Red Cross ship arrived with the parcels we had been waiting for. And as we passed Changi, bound for the South China Sea, I looked towards the 15-inch gun site and said: 'And there's our bloody virginal big guns, still looking out to sea!'

# 11

# Korea

Life on a Japanese troopship! The upper part of each hold had been divided by a shelf, leaving a metre of space above and below and in these two tiers, 550 of us would have to live and sleep during the long voyage to Japan. The numbers and conditions were the same in the forward hold. We could not stand or kneel in those shelves; one had to sit, lie or crawl. We stripped off our clothes and sweated on the shelves on straw matting covering the wood or else crowded onto the deck. But the small deck was filled with winches, the cookhouse, cooking vats, an icebox, water tank, life rafts and stores of onions so we were standing, squatting and walking over each other all day. We were given only two meals a day, at 10 a.m. and 4 p.m. The food was rice, well-steamed in the vats, using boiler steam, and a thin soup made of flour and water, a few onions and eighteen tins of Irish stew. Eighteen 14-ounce tins of Irish stew between 1100 men!

Our ship was the *Fukkai Maru*, about 4000 tons, built in England in 1898. *Fukai* means 'deep' in Japanese. Was this the Deep ship? Ominous. But the Japanese had once named a ship *Hsinking Maru*...only the sailors objected too strongly.

I was glad to see Aussies in our company. To a cosmopolitan, representatives of other nationalities are always welcome. We had about 80 of them, and I knew they would add a few oaths and caustic comments to the party. They also added some song. On warm, tropical evenings, a few musical instruments appeared and we enjoyed the Aussies singing 'Waltzing Matilda' and a new Maori song of farewell, 'Now is the Hour'. It was a sad song, but with hunger gnawing at our stomachs, and the Southern Cross dipping slowly below the horizon, such songs suited our mood as we all dreamed of freedom.

The convoy crept into Takao (Kaohsiung) Harbour in Taiwan. The generals disembarked here and we saw them no more. Our men loaded and unloaded ships of bauxite, coal and rice for fourteen days before our voyage continued. Twenty-four serious dysentery cases were left in hospital. At sea again, accompanied by a destroyer, the weather turned chilly, rainy and stormy. The Irish stew ran out and the Japanese fed us a little pork from the 'icebox' which had no ice; consequently the carcases pulled out of it were bright emerald in large patches. The cooks sliced off the worst green edges and threw them overboard where even the seagulls disdained them; the rest went into our soups. All 1100 of us developed diarrhoea. Now the queues for the six wooden latrines suspended over the side of the ship took on new proportions. Many men, after one visit, only felt safe if they returned immediately to the end of the queue once more. And dysentery had reappeared.

Forty-one days after leaving Singapore, we arrived in Fusan (Pusan), Korea. It was 22 September 1942, a grey, windy day. Once more we went through our trouserless bow to the Emperor to provide smears for the Japanese medical service. No dysentery cases would be allowed into Japan. Never mind, these twenty bad cases can be taken to hospital. Ten of them died of dysentery within two weeks. Now at last, we disembarked to be carefully searched, us and all our belongings, by a whole company of *kempei* in their red pigskin boots, and the two characters *ken* (thought) and *hei* (soldier or police) on their brassards.

A week or two later we heard of the torpedoing of the *Lisbon Maru* when travelling from Hong Kong filled with British prisoners of war. Over 900 prisoners were drowned.

Later in Tokyo, I heard from several American officers of a ship of about the same tonnage as the *Fukkai Maru* being crammed with 1500 Americans and nearly 1000 Japanese soldiers. There were nearly 30 deaths on board, including several suicides. Of the suicides, one was an American POW and the rest were Japanese soldiers returning home on leave. Low as the Americans admitted their morale was on that journey, this teaches something about Japanese morale.

But we, and even they, were more fortunate than those comrades of ours in a dozen ships, packed tight with prisoners, which were sunk with the total loss of all the POWs. There were cases where the prisoners were left battened down in the holds and were drowned in their hundreds without being given the chance to save themselves, while in yet other cases, the Japanese guards machine-gunned the few who did break out and reach the deck.

In one notorious case, a Japanese ship was carrying several hundred of their own wounded together with doctors and nurses besides several hundred prisoners of war. When the vessel was torpedoed and about to be abandoned, the Japanese doctors and guards went through the wards and shot dead every wounded Japanese soldier. Then they took to the boats, leaving the Japanese nurses and the POWs aboard. Once the Japanese were clear of the ship, the prisoners escaped, using rafts, and it was the POWs who saved the lives of the Japanese nurses abandoned by their men.

Submarine warfare was beginning to close in on the extended and vulnerable Japanese lines of communication.

After the medical inspection and the search by the *kempei* on the wharf at Fusan, we repacked our belongings and began a march. We were ordered to leave our heaviest baggage behind and, as I did so, I wondered if I had seen the last of my books and a spare pair of boots. For once it was not wiser to carry one's possessions, the heavy baggage did rejoin us later; meanwhile, we marched past the docks, shopping and business districts of the port with the entire population lining the pavements to see us. They stared at us with great curiosity and press photographers snapped every wilting or fainting soldier. The extraordinary thing was that the whole population was in brightly coloured national dress—the Japanese women and children in kimonos and all the Korean women in pink, sky blue, lemon or magenta dresses, while the Korean men were immaculate in white or black and white. The dignified old Korean men wore their miniature top hats of black horsehair held in place with a ribbon tied under the chin and their long jackets and voluminous trousers all of white.

Later we learnt the reason for this festive dress. It was 24 September, the Autumn Equinox and a major holiday in Japan. The inhabitants of Fusan were dressed in their best and brightest attire for this day and the Japanese had skilfully used our arrival to provide an instructive free show for the citizens. I had never before seen a whole city so spectacularly dressed. It must have paralleled the sights witnessed by the first European travellers to visit Korea and Japan in the 1860s after centuries of isolation.

Reaching the far end of the city, we turned twice and found ourselves returning in the direction of the docks once more. We realised that we were merely being shown off to the inhabitants as war booty and were carrying our baggage in a circle. In time we arrived back outside the railway station beside the docks, worn out and exhausted. Many men had fainted on the march. As we sat and lay in exhausted postures in the public square before the station, feeling the blazing sun on our heads, the emptiness of our stomachs and the dryness of our throats, guarded by scores of *kempei* and watched by several thousand citizens of Fusan, the medical officer of my regiment made the best timed remark of the captivity: 'With one bound, Roger Strangeways was free'.

We now heard that we were going to Keijo (Seoul) the capital of Chosen (Korea), 280 miles north. Very few Europeans knew anything about Korea at that time. Even living in North China, only hundreds of miles from it, I had only heard of it as a holiday place for a few honeymooners and businessmen from China and as the source of many of the unpleasant camp followers of the Japanese Army in China. Of course, it had been annexed by Japan in 1910, after occupation during and after the Russo–Japanese War of 1904–5. That war had been fought for the control of the Korean peninsula and suzerainty over Manchuria and Japan had won. Ever since 1910 Japan had hardly encouraged foreigners to visit and study her Korean dominion.

After a train journey through hilly countryside, rich with ricefields, maize, barley and *gaoliang*, also thatched-roofed farmhouses, tiled-roofed villages and glimpses of Korean farmers, nearly all in white national dress (also mourning), we arrived in Keijo. We were suffering badly from dysentery and the worst cases were taken by truck to hospital. Again, press photographers were everywhere. We marched through drab suburbs of Korean huts, houses, small industries and shops, noting how oppressed and miserable the Koreans looked. All the women wore their hair parted in the middle and all the men had a good head of hair, while nearly every Japanese we had seen since Malaya had his hair almost shaved 'to save time owing to war situation'.

We turned into a lane leading to a four-storey warehouse and crunched over gravel to a small parade ground enclosed by a tall wooden fence topped with barbed wire. The place looked small and constricted, but 550 of us were to settle there, while a similar group went on to Jinsen (Inchon), the port, 30 miles away.

# 12

# You Must Endure

The prison yard under the looming warehouse was small and grim. On two sides were wooden buildings which we soon learnt were the cookhouse, bath-house and sickroom. We formed up in ranks to hear an address by the camp commandant, a small, brown-faced lieutenant colonel with a toothbrush moustache, sword and gloves. He stood on a box with his ex-schoolmaster interpreter beside him. After each sentence the aged, hesitant pedagogue interpreted. What we heard was an astonishing and at times almost incomprehensible torrent of verbiage in tortured English. Copies of the speech were given to us later and I carefully preserved mine. It reads:

> I am Colonel Y. Noguchi, Superintendant of the Chosen War Prisoners' Camp. Receiving you here, I should like to give necessary instruction to you all.
>
> I hope you will consider how this Greater East Asia War happened. Nippon's desire for peaceful settlement arising from the conciliatory spirit, rejected by America and Britain in order to attain their ambitious demand to East Asia. Finally they overwhelmed Nippon, the important defenser of Asia, to the extend that they dared to resort to violence of economic disruption.
>
> Promoting Chinese internal confusion and increasing military preparations on all sides of Nippon Empire to challenge us, thus the very existence of our nation being in danger, we stood up resolutely with unity of will, strong as iron, under the name of *Tenno* (Emperor) for the emancipation of the nations and elimination of evil sources in East Asia.
>
> The rise or fall of our Empire that has the glorious history and the progress or decline depend upon the present war. Firm and unshakable is our national resolve, that we should crush the enemy, the USA and Britain.
>
> Heaven is always on the side of Justice. Within ten days after the War Declaration our Navy and Naval Air Forces annihilated both the American Pacific fleet and the British Far Eastern fleet; within a few months American and British long-established Army, Navy and Air Bases were crushed by our Army and Army Air Forces; and now, tide turning in our favour, all parts of regions linked with Burma, Java and Wake Island have already been occupied by us, and the inhabitants there are rejoicing

in co-operation with us for the construction of New Asia. And now these factors have induced the Indian rebellion and Australia come to a crisis of capture. Afterward our belligerents sent their aircrafts and fleets for the rescue, but every time they were to the bottom or destroyed or repulsed, thus the total damages come up to 2,801 vessels and 4,100 aircrafts.

I think these war results do not signify the inferior power of our enemy but rather owe to our absolute indomitable power protected by *Kami* (Heaven). Wherever Nippon Army and Navy advance, *Tenyu Shinjo* (Special Providential Help) always follows; you should recognise the fact and consider the reasons.

Nippon Army and Navy are under the Imperial Command of *Tenno* (Emperor), who is the personification of *Kami* (God), so that the Imperial troops are to be called the Troops of God. Now you have become prisoners because of struggling against *Kami no Gun* (God's Army) and now you are convinced of fearfulness to the marrow and become aware of unsavoury results. What do you think of this?

However you have lost fighting strength now, you once fought fiercely against us. Judging from this fact some of you will hold hostile feeling against us in your hearts; that can never be permission. Accordingly we will punish you if you act against our regulations, for instance disobedience, resistance and escape (even attempt to do so) are understood as manifestation of hostility.

I kindly request you that you must be cautious, not spoiling yourselves by punishment.

But on the other hand, with Nippon's warrior's forgiveness, I express respect to your faithfulness to your country and fulfilment of duty, and feel pitiful for your capitulation after exhaustion.

You should reflect on yourselves. According to the extent of your malice feeling, we also put certain limit to your freedom or severity or lenity on your treatment.

Paroles is of use as proof of wiping away your hostility. I am regretful to say those refuse to swear will be treated as persons of enemy character, will be placed under restraint regarding maintenance of honour, protection of your persons and must endure pain in compensation of hostility.

The details of outline of style of daily life are defined in 'The regulation regarding to daily life'; you should put them into practice strictly after reading them.

Prejudice against labour and grumbling over food, clothing and housing are strictly prohibited because the change in your daily life and custom are inevitable under present war situation.

Closing my instruction, I advise you all to find interest and anxiety in your forthcoming daily life by acting according to the Imperial military discipline.

Colonel Noguchi climbed down from his pedestal and a murmur of conversation followed. There was a mixture of anger, puzzlement and humour in our reactions, but amusement predominated.

'Special Providential Aid,' said the padre. 'It sounds like an insurance company.'

Now, said the Japanese, we had to sign a document swearing never to attempt to escape from 'Japan' on pain of death. Our senior officers tried to explain that we could not sign such a document, but the Japanese were adamant and said we would stay there without food until we did. Finally our seniors decided that we were signing under duress and so one by one we scribbled our names under the promise.

Many were weak and faint after the long parade. They hurried to the drop-pit latrines; dysentery was rampant and pitiless.

Our warehouse was a four-storey brick one, dusty, gloomy and with very small windows. Each floor had been divided into four squadrooms, designed to hold about 30 men each. We decided at once not to use the ground floor with its bare earth underfoot and crowded all 550 of us into the three upper floors. Sixty officers occupied two squadrooms.

Bedspace was staked out on the raised sleeping platform on either side of the central aisle. Boots had to be taken off in the gangway and stowed under the edge of the platform. As it was already chilly, we needed something more on our feet, so we tailored cloth boots out of private blankets to keep them warm. The Japanese had issued us with British winter battledress from stores captured in Hong Kong, so we were no longer in khaki drill, but we had no army overcoats. A month later, a pile was thrown into each squadroom and we found ourselves trying on Japanese Army greatcoats from the 1904 war with Russia. They were threadbare, extremely short and thoroughly inadequate. Being the most junior officer I had the last choice and found that I could actually make out figures and tell dark from light through the weave of my hessian overcoat. In that I faced the Siberian-type winter one is blessed with in Korea.

Morale in the camp was at its lowest at this time. Almost everyone was suffering from amoebic dysentery and there was only enough medicine for the critical cases. The long journey, the disappointment at the conditions in the new camp, the gloom of the hollow warehouse and the depressing view of Korean huts and tin roofs on all sides left us listless and dispirited. The war news was bad too—the Germans were at Stalingrad and near Alexandria at a place called Alamein.

The Regulations Regarding Daily Life were all about death or extremely long terms of imprisonment. Whenever our colonels or doctors made requests or demands, the old Japanese interpreter would answer, 'You must endure'. At first we smiled at his choice of words, but soon we realised that here, in three words, was the creed for a prisoner of war: *'You must endure'*.

Work was soon found for these prisoners living on the Japanese government. There was lifting, loading and sweeping work to do at a large army depot—we called it the Warehouse—where our men began endless months of hefting rice in rice-straw bags and similar tasks. The officers, who accompanied the work parties, had nothing to do beyond relay orders, try to overcome misunderstandings and request better conditions or more rests for the men. It was very boring for all concerned.

But then work was found with civilian contractors and here both the work and the conditions were sometimes better. The contractors made the not very remarkable discovery that the men worked harder if given a little extra food, so a couple of them arranged for extra vegetables for our soups or for an extra snack during the working hours. George Baker and I volunteered to accompany one of these parties permanently in order to obtain this little extra nourishment and also to escape the dark and dismal atmosphere of the squadrooms.

Contractors paid one yen a day for the men's labour; the Japanese Army kept 90 sen for overheads, leaving our men 10 sen a day. This was equal to about one penny and could be spent wherever opportunity presented itself and so some went to Koreans outside camp for morsels of food. The officers were given the pay of the equivalent rank in the Japanese Army—for a second lieutenant Y70 a month, equal to about £3 10s. 0d., from which 'food and board' were deducted. The fact that majors and colonels received more made no difference since canteen distributions were precisely equal for all ranks, officers or men; it simply meant that senior officers built up greater credit figures in the books. The 'canteen' wasn't a place at all; it was simply a name to cover rare distributions of cigarettes, apples, tangerines, toothpowder and writing paper. Officers received their credits at the end of the war, but few found opportunity to spend them.

The job for which I had volunteered to go daily was in the bed of the river Han. There on a bare, windswept bank of land beside the icy blue river, the first piers were being erected for a new bridge over the river Han parallel to the railway bridge we had first crossed to the city. The river was 400 yards wide, but the flat bank was nearer 600, and bare of vegetation. In the centre of this wilderness stood a frail little wooden hut, which served as shelter and cookhouse. It swayed and creaked before the powerful winds which swept down the river bed and whirled sand into every bowl of soup laid out inside the hut. Amid fiendish winds we pottered about, huddled up in threadbare overcoat, scarf, hat and home-made blanket gloves. It was achingly cold and our faces stiffened so that we could scarcely force open our mouths. But we thought the job worth doing for that extra snack or those extra vegetables in the soup.

Colder than the wintriest day I remember in China, for me the coldest days I ever experienced were in Korea.

By now our men were beginning to want a few words of Japanese for their own purposes. 'How do you say I'm hungry in Japanese?' they would ask.

'O-naka ga sukimashita,' Baker or I would reply solemnly. 'It means "honourable stomach is empty".'

But none of our would-be linguists would bother to repeat the phrase; they would just curl up with laughter.

Singapore ex-Town Hall, 1941. Standing in the city centre about 100 yards from the harbour, it was not damaged in the battle.

Empire days. Visiting officers watch the Loyal Regiment celebrate its 200th anniversary in Singapore in 1941. Later that year, bush hats began to replace topees. (*Straits Times photo*)

The author.

The author, centre, and two other officer-cadets at the OCTU—Officer Cadet Training Unit, Changi, January 1941.

# 13

# Korean Winter

Keijo (Seoul) was then a city of a million inhabitants, a busy industrial and commercial centre, a key rail junction and main Japanese Army base in Korea with acres of barracks in the southern suburbs where our camp was situated. It lies in a valley beside the Han River, with bold raw-toothed mountains on its northern outskirts. Our camp was far from the government offices, the old royal palace and the ancient city gates and it was many months before we glimpsed any of these. Our life began with the flat notes of a Boy Scout bugle call.

We would groan and climb out of our cocoons of blankets, dress, fold the blankets and line up all within two minutes when the Japanese duty officer, splendid in red and white sash of office, accompanied by his duty sergeant and by the POW 'aid officer' and NCO, would make his rounds of the squadrooms for morning roll-call, '*Tenko*.' Each squad leader would report his total, his sick and other duties, the number present and no unaccountable absentees. For a week this was done in English, but thereafter in halting Japanese, which we were all struggling with. For instance, the Japanese for 'Attention' is '*Ki-o-tsuke*' (pronounced kyotskay) but two of our majors were convinced it was 'Trotsky' and shouted that several times a day. Never was the old revolutionary so honoured.

We were also being instructed in Japanese Army drill. The differences in drill were difficult enough for habit-hardened regular soldiers to master, but to learn all the commands in a strange tongue was too much for many and they hid themselves in the middle of squads and followed the crowd. Nevertheless, we were soon standing at attention with fingers outstretched, saluting with the palm facing down and standing at ease with the weight on one foot. The drill we refused to accept was the high-stepping, feet-stamping Japanese goose-step. We made it so ridiculous and protested so strongly that they allowed us to omit it so long as we promised to march smartly outside camp.

Dysentery continued to waste us. All night long men ran down the stairs of our warehouse, half-clad, hoping to reach the *benjo* (as we now called the latrines) in time, but often failing—on the stairs and landings. In the end, most of us, without medicine, survived. But loss of weight continued. We had been weighed on arrival and now, after a month, were weighed again. Men had lost anything from 20 to 85 pounds in weight; those with large frames lost most and appeared all bone and no flesh, with shrunken midriffs and buttocks. Men of compact build lost less and appeared merely scrawny. Now after a month, we were weighed again. There was a further average loss per man of eight pounds. Our colonel patiently explained to the Japanese that unless something was done, *they wouldn't have the pleasure of our company much longer*. So a small improvement was made in both the quantity and nutritional value of our rations and we slowly picked up a few pounds in weight.

Diphtheria now appeared and that plus dysentery accounted for sixteen deaths before Christmas. Luckily, we had good doctors and our senior officer, Lieutenant Colonel 'Bill' Elrington of the Loyals, lean and soft-spoken, was a diplomat who quickly learnt how to deal with the Japanese. Some of his quiet remarks shocked and shamed them and they responded with improved rations or conditions. The young Japanese doctor, a second lieutenant, could of course overrule any diagnosis or treatment prescribed by our older doctors, but after two or three fatal errors he quietly gave them full power while reserving the right, which he never used, to overrule them. A few more drugs and medicines were obtained.

Our leaders requested separate quarters for officers in accordance with the Geneva Convention. These were refused causing Colonel Noguchi, the Japanese commander, to address the officers as follows:

'After one month of captivity I wish to congratulate you on your behaviour and conduct. You have cooperated well and I hereby express my appreciation.

'However, it has been noticeable by your bearing and from a written request from Lieutenant Colonel Elrington that certain fundamental differences of opinion exist between your and the Japanese way of thinking. You ask for separate quarters and back your request on the treatment accorded to prisoners in Great Britain and European countries... I will say in Japan as in European countries the treatment of prisoners is based on principles of humanity. In the East, shortage of materials and different customs makes the application of these principles a little different. You are housed in the same building but in different rooms to your men. According to your requests, you appear to demand the treatment of guests. In Japan we class our prisoners of war and guests differently. As regards your warrant officers, NCOs and men, you appear to despise them. You are arrogant and haughty and my advice to you is to study your men and change your views.

'In the Japanese Army we do not despise our men, but all are members of a happy family. Our officers, especially in the front line, live with their men and are all part of the machine which is controlled by the Emperor and thus are all the children of God.

'England is crumbling. She has been driven out of the East and paralysed in Europe. You are symbols of a land which must be crushed and destroyed for humanity's sake.'

Well, well, we thought, sorry the children of God are not on our side but that was a much better translation. We had a new interpreter, private Ushihara, who had lived for years in California.

# 14

# Japanese News

It was now clear to us that we were being treated much the same as the recruits in the Imperial Japanese Army. Our discipline, drill and punishments were the same, but there was one important difference. We were prisoners of war, captives, the lowest form of life in Japan. The Japanese, we were told, never surrender, and, as up till this time very few had, the Japanese could afford to maintain a superior attitude on the question. Those Japanese who were taken prisoner later in the war were never in touch with their homeland so that this contemptuous attitude was maintained throughout the war. We were almost criminals, almost slaves; we had no rights, not even the right to survive the war. We continued to live only by the grace of the Imperial Japanese Army.

Most of the Japanese we had talked to so far professed to believe that the war would last 100 years and advised us to settle down in Japan. When we laughed and retorted that not only would we go home in about two years, but that the Anti-Axis allies would win the war, they became coldly serious and said: 'Then the Japanese will kill you all. You can be sure of that, we will kill all prisoners.'

We did not take this very seriously until we heard it repeatedly, then we ceased to find it amusing. Stronger evidence of this thinking arose later in the war, and I am certain that if the Americans had invaded Japan, all of the prisoners of war in Japan would have been massacred rather than left in camps about to be liberated.

Settled for the moment in Seoul, one of the first things we wanted was a steady source of news. We asked for English-language newspapers and amazingly soon were given copies of the *Japan Times* and *Japan Advertiser* (soon to be amalgamated as the *Nippon Times*), both printed for the benefit of foreigners in Japan and American-born Japanese. The newspapers were delivered regularly; the Japanese had no need to hesitate; they were proud of the news. But by late 1943 delivery was less prompt and in early 1944 ceased altogether.

The war news in the winter of 1942 was not good. Nevertheless the Axis advances had been firmly and finally halted at Stalingrad, Alamein and Guadalcanal, and we believed that in each of these scattered sectors the tide had turned. But the newspapers were full of fantastic reports of Japanese successes in every theatre of war. There seemed to be a major naval battle every two or three weeks and in each the Japanese claimed two battleships, three carriers and six or eight cruisers thunder-sunk! Pessimists divided all claims by four and believed the result; the optimists believed nothing.

It required much reading between the lines to get a true picture of the 'Greater East Asia War', but the reports of the North African and European battles were more accurate, being the German High Command communiques and Russian, British and American counter-claims. We obtained a clear picture of this war and followed its progress closely, knowing that the Allies had given it priority over the Pacific war.

Those newspapers were interesting psychologically. They told us how Japanese pilots when they ran out of ammunition would 'body-crash' their aircraft against an enemy plane and go to a glorious death, crying *'Banzai!'* (May the Emperor) 'live 10 000 years!' Other planes flew so close to American bombers they were attacking that 'blood from the dying Yankee crew splashed their wings'. One Japanese pilot, running out of ammunition, 'drew his sword and charged the enemy plane and brought it down', and another in the same situation, ' threw two rice-balls at his enemy' which caused the American to swerve and collide with another US plane so that both crashed. Nobody who writes this kind of stuff can resist going farther and having a dead but faithful pilot flying his undamaged plane safely back to base so that it can be used in future operations.

These stories, written with complete seriousness, would often conclude: 'With tears in my eyes, I thought of the great courage of this soldier, which is but an example of the bravery and suffering of all our troops fighting for the Emperor in the Southern Regions'.

Besides graphic reports of current successes, the papers celebrated under banner headlines the anniversaries of all victories. Thus on 8 December, the first anniversary of Pearl Harbor, we were treated to five full pages on the success of that 'glorious surprise attack' and the valour of the dozen naval sublieutenants and midshipmen who manned the two-man submarines which torpedoed the battleships in harbour. They were all now promoted to 'Hero-God' and their ashes somehow recovered and enshrined at Yasukuni, the temple resting place of all Japanese warriors who fall in battle.

In another column, I read how the sole British gunboat left in Shanghai had been sunk by gunfire on the morning of 8 December after the captain, Commander S. Polkinghorn, RNR, had refused to surrender his ship. HMS *Petrel* was flat-bottomed, small and almost defenceless and surrounded by Japanese destroyers and an ancient lightweight battleship, the *Idzumo*. Old Stephen Polkinghorn, for twenty years a river pilot on the Hai Ho, Tientsin, was an old family friend and I was relieved to see he was now a prisoner of war.

A small item told me that the head of the British Municipal Council, the Consul and the 'head of the British forces in Tientsin' had all been rounded up early that same morning and imprisoned. A few months later, a letter from my father confirmed that he had been arrested at 8 a.m. and kept prisoner in the former US Army barracks in Tientsin. The rifles, ammunition etc. of the Volunteers Corps of 110 men were all instantly seized.

On the anniversary of the capture of Singapore, the story of Malaya was retold; there were pictures of the surrender ceremony in the Ford factory at Bukit Timah, the Japanese all in buttoned-up serge uniforms, the British in loose-fitting khaki shirts with rolled-up sleeves. They hardly looked impressive. Turning sadly from that picture, we read the accounts: 'Singapore fortress was entered through the West Gate...' We all rushed about the squadroom with mock earnestness asking each other, 'Who left it open?'

It was interesting to read that it was 'Japan's logical mission to conquer the South Sea, since the Japanese race is the result of an ancient mixture of a Mongol people from the mainland of Asia and Polynesians who arrived in Japan by canoe from the South Pacific'. Further, that 'this was the greatest war in Nippon's history and she was ready to fight for a hundred years to attain her aims: the liberation of all Asiatics from the white barbarians and the formation of the Greater East Asia Co-Prosperity Sphere under Japan's leadership'.

Well, we anyway, hadn't got the impression that Japan treated her fellow Asiatics with much honour, equality or respect.

The English in which these newspaper articles were written had a quaint and distinctive charm. 'Japan,' we read, 'will leave no stone unturned to turn the tables on the United States and Britain.' And again, 'Japan knows on which side of the fence her bread is buttered.' Political and strategic reasoning were not these papers' strong points, they were better employed in complaining about the 'luxury-loving, drunken, ice-cream-eating Americans soldiery' who were said to be seducing most of the wives and sweethearts of the British and Australian servicemen overseas. American soldiers, they wrote, had no spirit, such as the Japanese have; they were lost without their ice cream and other luxuries, they could not possibly win a war.

Eighteen months later, it was not only luxury food that the Japanese complained about, it was 'luxury war' fought by the Americans, using too much ammunition, too many weapons, too many ships to win each battle. It did not seem fair to them to fight wars on such a scale.

Meanwhile, a few officers asked for Japanese grammars with which to study the language. Classes were started, but after five weeks only Baker and I could honestly be said to be studying Japanese seriously. We spent three sometimes four hours a day on it and, strangely, came in for some thoughtless criticism for learning the 'barbaric' tongue of our captors. But our modest knowledge of the language enabled us to bring in items of news of conditions among Koreans and their opinions of the war; it also enabled us to translate war news from scraps of Japanese newspapers, which we did regularly, naming new islands in the Pacific being fought over. Equally important, by omission, one noted place names drifting out of the news as 'Japanese troops swung into action in a new sphere', further north leaving Guadalcanal or Salamaua or New Georgia forever behind.

Professor Ukai, a cheerful young Japanese lecturer at Keijo University, gave us excellent instruction for several months and we progressed well, learning *Katakana* and *Hiragana*, the two syllabaries used to indicate verbal inflections, adverbs and conjunctions, and making our first inroads into the 2000 Chinese characters needed to be able to read a newspaper.

What a curious and difficult language! In a way, it was written in three alphabets: *Katakana* to transliterate foreign place names and proper nouns; *Hiragana* to write verbal inflexions, etc.; and Chinese characters, *Kanji*, to write the bulk of the message. While it is possible to write any Japanese word in either *Hiragana* or *Katakana*, syllable by syllable, only the ideographs can show the difference between words with the same sound. The language cries out for simplification.

As to pronunciation, every Japanese word is made up of syllables—*Mi-tsu-bi-shi*, *Mo-ri-gi-shi*, each containing a vowel. So when speaking foreign words or names the Japanese break them into their own syllables, ending the word with an *ah*, *ee*, *eh* or *oo* sound; thus Wade, *wei-do*, Mark, *ma-ku*. The exception is 'n', which they can sound alone, thus *yen*, *shogun*, and so therefore Thompson, *To-mu-son*, Milligan, *Mi-ri-gon*.

Having taken the monosyllabic Chinese ideographs to set on paper their polysyllabic native language, the Japanese found the Chinese sounds useful for reasons of brevity or euphony. So they Japanised them and retained them; this added a second sound for the same idea. Thus to *yama*, the native Japanese word for mountain, was added *san*, a Japanised form of *shan*, the Chinese for mountain. Somewhat complex, especially as some Japanised forms are less obvious than this example. But there is little doubt that the written forms of the language would profit from simplification.

It was interesting to see how many English words had been added to the language thanks to the strong British and American commercial connections with the country since its rise as a modern power and the later introduction of American sports and films. Here are a few, romanised in the accepted way (and reminding you that Japanese have difficult with *l*s): *gasorin* (gasoline), *basuboru* (baseball), *mairu* (mile), *garasu* (glass), *biiru* (beer), *aisukurimu* (ice-cream), *uisukii* (whisky) and *waishatsu* (white shirt).

A few months later our lessons with Professor Ukai ceased. I had organised some lectures and our colonel, in describing the Loyals' part in the Malayan campaign, had constantly referred to the 'Japs'. The interpreter present reported this. Then someone drew a map of New Guinea for a talk on gold prospecting. This was undoubtedly to illustrate a discussion on the fierce fighting in progress in New Guinea, so lectures were forbidden. Let me put that in a clearer perspective: no lectures or talks of any kind were allowed in this camp in Korea for the last two and a quarter years of the war.

Also the use of the words 'Nips' or 'Japs' was forbidden in Japanese hearing. I

seem to remember our doctor writing a verse for our magazine *Nor Iron Bars*, which
went:

> *You'll be making many slips*
> *If you call these people Nips,*
> *You will certainly get slaps*
> *If you call the buggers Japs.*

We kept asking for stoves and for books. One stove per squadroom was provided
finally in mid-December (and removed in March). It did not warm the whole hall, but
it helped and we could cover our legs with blankets. As for books, a supply of several
hundred came from the International YMCA (not the Red Cross, note). Most of these
came from American schools in Japan, closed since the beginning of the war, and gave
us the opportunity to read some classics most of us had neglected thus far. *Jane Eyre*
and *Pride and Prejudice* were wonderfully welcome and so, to me, were Wilfred Owen's
poems and Plato's *Republic*. A local bookshop also sent in its list. This included some
very old books, years out of date, and among the titles I noticed one by my grandfather:
*With Boat and Gun in the Yangtze Valley* by Henling Wade.

# 15

# Red Cross Inspection

One sunny winter day the Japanese arranged a funeral with full military honours for our sixteen deceased comrades. The soldiers, dead from dysentery or diphtheria, were already cremated and their ashes in little cube pinewood boxes were kept in the camp office. One heard that only part of the cremated bones and ashes were in the box, the rest having been thrown away behind the crematorium—our padre witnessed this. But the funeral was a ceremonious success. Our officers borrowed to make up decent uniforms and a Japanese major general and all camp staff attended. There were a dozen large wreaths standing on tripods, an expensive hearse, and two Buddhist priests in splendid robes, one wearing a mask and carrying a horse-hair whisk. Our padre followed their strange chants with a brief service and the white boxes were interred in the ground and small crosses erected above them. Very correct, but what the Japanese could not understand was that all this energy expended a little earlier might have saved the lives of two thirds of those men. And as for the tangerines and biscuits placed on the altar in the graveyard, they might help a few sick, but when prisoners asked for these delicacies for the living, the Japanese were shocked, refused and the appetising oblations disappeared into the inaccessible world from which they had come.

Nevertheless at Christmas in Korea, the Japanese made a real effort to give us extra nourishment and a holiday so that we could enjoy a break. For lunch they gave us a slice of pork sausage, two potatoes, a can of pineapple, a pound of Hokkaido butter, some white wine and a third of a bottle of beer each. It was all delicious, especially the butter, for our diet was woefully short of fat or oil of any sort and this tasted like pure elixir. An amusing show followed in the afternoon, starring Jack MacNaughton and Gloria d'Earie, which the Japanese enjoyed as much as we did.

Christmas was the one real holiday of the year and in most permanent camps the Japanese provided some extra food and enabled the POWs to enjoy the celebration; it was the other 364 days of the year that were hell.

One day in that cold winter, we heard that a representative of the International Red Cross was coming to inspect the camp. We were elated. Now we would get some real improvements. There were smiles all over camp. But our senior officers were forbidden to speak to him. He spent some time in the camp office, but only fourteen minutes in the camp itself, just the time it would take to climb the stairs to three storeys, glance in the squadrooms, then visit in turn the bath-house, kitchen, sickroom and medical inspection room. All the time he was surrounded by Japanese officers, who blocked any attempt by our seniors to approach the apple-cheeked, shining Swiss doctor. It reminded me of American football. Then he was gone. What sort of a man, we wondered, was this Dr Paravicini, who could be satisfied with a fourteen-minute visit to a camp he had travelled over 400 miles to see, and where he had not spoken to a single prisoner or heard one single complaint or request? We were bitterly disappointed in him and in the International Red Cross.

When I moved to Tokyo in November 1943 I heard that Dr. Paravicini had behaved much the same in every camp he visited in Japan and that no improvements had followed his visits. I learnt that he had lived 30 years in Japan, was married to a Japanese and that his business depended upon Japanese goodwill. How could such a man negotiate with the Japanese with any degree of integrity? As far as any of us could see, he achieved nothing during his appointment as senior International Red Cross delegate in Japan.

In 1944 the news of his death was posted on our noticeboard in my Tokyo camp. The prisoners cheered—and cheered. It was a sincerely welcome piece of news.

In late 1944 Tokyo Headquarter Camp received its second inspection by the International Red Cross delegate. This man was entirely different; he spoke to some of the prisoners and seemed to guess at the truth behind the clipped understatement of the replies made in the presence of the Japanese. He saw all the crippled and dying, hidden in a back barrackroom, and some minor improvements followed his visit.

If I may address the International Red Cross, I entreat then to take great care in the selection of their crucial representatives and to be extremely wary of choosing a man whose wife is a national of the country in which he is working or who is in any way so vulnerable.

All this time we were existing on *daikon* radish and bean sprout soup plus a bowl of rice and barley per meal. Once or sometimes twice a week we had small fish, 'heads and tails' we called them because there was so little between. The *daikon* is a twenty-inch white radish, thick as a church candle, but turnipy or radishy in taste in soups. We lived on them in Korea and Japan. In three years in Korea and Japan, I must have eaten them over 2000 times, and that, dear reader, is gastronomic *hara kiri*.

We also ate vast quantities of seaweed. What is it like? There are several types and the one we gulped in Korea came in long green-black strips. It was packed in bundles without any outside covering and had been thrown about in many station yards and warehouses before reaching us. Our cooks would rinse it, then throw it into boiling water together with a cup of soya sauce to make seaweed soup. The result was a salty soup, floating with slimy yet leathery slips of seaweed. It was an appalling meal. Even hungry prisoners sometimes left part of it. I must have eaten well over 2000 meals of seaweed.

Then there was our self-inflicted hardship. All through Changi and this first winter in Korea, our cooks had no idea how to cook rice. For a year we ate a soft, slushy pap. Cooks insisted on stirring the vats of boiling rice and *never* steamed off all the liquid. In Changi, even our High Command had circulated instructions on how to steam rice, but the officers in authority, especially the older men, voted for pap. They said it was easier to assimilate. Half-true, it is also easy to assimilate steamed dry. This same madness continued in Korea even though the vote was almost even. So for a year we ate like invalids. At times the rice was so soft you could almost drink it. I marvelled at the self-assurance of these Englishmen who thought that they knew better about cooking rice than well over 1000 million Asians. When I got to Tokyo the Americans, thank God, were in command and we steamed whatever rice, barley or *gaoliang* (sorghum) we had as our staple.

To get something to chew, we prevailed upon the Japanese to get us some brownish bread rolls to replace the rice and barley on certain days.

With the spring came the first letters from home. I heard my mother and sister had moved from Miami to San Francisco, where we had other relatives and friends. They were well and happy in a lovely city. I looked forward to returning home after the war via California. My father, meantime, had been moved to a civilian internment camp at Weihsien in Shantung province, China. They had learnt that I was wounded and a prisoner about five months after the collapse at Singapore.

Some letters gave news of German prison camps and we could not help comparing out lot with that of prisoners of war in Germany. They received fortnightly Red Cross parcels, they could study for university degrees, they had plenty of sport and the energy to play it; there was even the possibility of escape in Europe. Men longed to be prisoners of war in Germany. Later, in Tokyo, I saw a photo of a group of British prisoners in a German *stalag*; they were a football team in striped jerseys, muscular arms folded, healthy, smiling. Great Heavens, what a contrast with Japanese prison camps!

From our first days in the 'Hermit Kingdom', 'the Land of the Morning Calm', we had realised that the Koreans were a subject people, firmly kept in place by the Japanese. They were never the equal in any situation of a Japanese. They were ruled and overruled, repressed and oppressed. They had no vote, no representation in government, no voice in the organisation of their country. They could not hold the higher jobs in Korea and they were paid less than Japanese doing the same work. You could see their subject status in their behaviour, their bows, the unprovocative and careful looks in their eyes in the presence of a Japanese. Some had been given Japanese surnames, but it did not alter their status—it just seemed rather absurd to be calling a big, broad-cheeked, Mongol-looking Korean 'Mr Yamamoto'. If they were trusted with arms in a sub-military unit, they had to be prepared to out-strut and out-shout the Japanese, to out-Herod Herod.

The Empire of Nippon had wanted to settle Japanese on the land in Korea to relieve the pressure of population in the Japanese islands. But the few thousands who came soon left the land for the cities and positions of greater influence, the upshot being that Korean immigration into Japan far outweighed Japanese immigration into Korea. We, who had had glimpses of Japanese treatment of the Asians they had 'liberated' in South East Asia, now saw what might be in store for them after 30 years of Japanese imperialism. One could not envy them that fate.

And the Japanese?

All this time we were trying to understand the Japanese better. They often appeared to have an inferiority complex towards Europeans and Americans. Yet they could also be arrogant, superior and contemptuous. Was this simply compensation for the former? I thought not; I believed that this was largely inherent in the world's most homogeneous and insular people, greatly reinforced by a dogmatic education which taught them, not only that the Emperor was divine, but that they themselves were the semi-divine descendants of the so-called 'Sun Goddess Amaterasu' and that the very islands of Japan were of divine genesis.

Because our cultures differed so much, we found them paradoxical, enigmatic. Many thought that they were quite impossible to understand and did not try. But it seemed to me that dissimilar as details of their culture and behaviour were, their main values were much the same as ours: honour, truth, patriotism, industry, family and for many, religious feeling. It was their additional emphasis on 'face', shame and obligation which led to the abrasive discrepancies in behaviour from us. These ideas obsess the Japanese.

One could not accept the opinion, loudly proclaimed by many POWs, that they were uncivilised. But their civilisation included what to us would be a *medieval* attitude to life and to punishment and suffering. 'Death,' the Japanese soldier is taught, 'is as light as a feather.' Therefore they practised callous neglect and witnessed preventable death with a quiet heart, with no misgivings. This was the hardest thing to bear. Having lived long in the Far East, I felt I ought to try to bridge gulfs and explain dissimilarities to my comrades. But for a junior officer there were few opportunities; also, I did not wish to become too noticeable and be singled out for some purpose of theirs which might have consequences verging on the disloyal; nor did I wish to provoke the hostility of our own extreme bigots and xenophobes. I was learning the language—I was *slowly* learning the language—with the aim of widening understanding, but the ferocious conditions in my later camps made progress on any level minimal.

Then came a shock. As winter ended, I suddenly found my vision impaired by a grey cloud which descended, gradually blanking out half the vision of my left eye. I thought

I had strained my sight too much by reading in the miserable light of our squadrooms, so whenever it happened, I dropped my book and lay on my *tatami* mat with eyes shut. This appeared to help as the cloud slowly receded. But one day before I could take any action the blank curtain fell rapidly and left my left eye completely blinded. I was aghast. Was I going blind? Would it affect both eyes? I lay still on my mat and prayed. Twenty frightening minutes passed and light reappeared and the colourless, sightless blank receded.

Our doctors arranged a visit for me to the Japanese Army hospital. I had an examination there, but they prescribed no treatment, merely reporting back that I was probably experiencing some vitamin deficiencies.

'You're telling me.'

Of course, in camp there was not a single injection of vitamin A or B or anything else that could be spared. I simply determined to fight for every milligram of additional nutrition that I could lay my hands on. Curiously—happily—full blindness never returned, though the grey cloud regularly did. The summer's fresh vegetables may have just turned the scale.

# 16

# The Kempei Strikes

Spring comes late and suddenly in Korea. From mid-March we were warned to look out for the first blossom, but the icy winds continued. It was pure Siberia until suddenly they came: first the plum and then the cherry blossom—Japanese cherry blossom; great clouds of the palest pink flowers, five-petalled stars, larger than English blossom and faintly pink. The Japanese proudly told us that the cherry blossom is the emblem of the Japanese soldier because it blooms for only a short while on the tree and then falls at the height of its glory. So with the soldier; death comes at his prime.

After the cherry blossom came the Korean wild azaleas—beautiful mauve and pink azaleas boldly proclaiming spring against a background of brown earth. Korean azaleas are worth travelling miles to see. By the end of April it was full summer. We requested a small farm on which to grow vegetables. The Japanese were surprised by our wish, but made efforts and found us some ex-cavalry lines south of the city which we could use. Farming tools came to us from the International YMCA and very soon we had turned over all the earth, made level beds and were planting the first drills with seed. We planted carrots, leeks, cucumbers, pumpkins, melons, corn, lettuce, tomatoes and Chinese cabbage and later, as these ripened, we enriched our soups, in camp and at the farm, with these healthful vegetables.

No small farm was ever so carefully planned and tilled. It was the sort of area a man and boy might look after in England, but here 28 officers were available for work. It became a model farm and Korean farmers would squat on their haunches on the embankments which surrounded it, watching our activities and our techniques.

About this time, the first Red Cross parcels reached us. They came from South Africa and included some bulk bully beef and sulphur drugs. The latter certainly saved many lives and all of us were greatly cheered by the arrival of good, tasty, solid European food. The Japanese too were doing better now and sold us tins of pilchards, tangerines and cigarettes from time to time. Cigarettes, not for the first time, became a currency within the camp.

One day the Japanese *kempei* swooped on the camp and arrested two young lieutenants from my regiment and an Australian warrant officer and rushed them away to *kempeitai* headquarters. The camp staff explained that these officers had been on duty with a working party at the military warehouse when a Japanese guard had discovered a bundle of clothing with a letter containing war news and encouraging Koreans to have faith in an Allied victory. It was in an obscure corner of the Warehouse waiting for a Korean contact to pick it up, but a Japanese sentry had got there first.

For a fortnight the three officers were grilled by the *kempei*, who wanted to know what other propaganda had been spread, who the Korean contacts were and whether the men had any knowledge of the Korean underground. At the end of this time, they released one officer and the warrant officer, making them swear to divulge nothing of their interrogation. The other officer, Lieutenant Roger Pigott, aged 22, was tried by court martial, found guilty of inciting the natives against the Japanese and of other crimes and sentenced to three years imprisonment.

We were all very sorry for Roger, but thought his behaviour foolhardy. Roger had joined the army in the ranks at nineteen. Several months later he was sent to an OCTU and commissioned. He was very young, enthusiastic and cheery. We had been in the same company at Gillman Barracks and he regularly showed that he thought he knew all the 'old soldier' tricks to get around difficulties or to obtain wanted equipment, passes etc. He had a *Boy's Own Paper* attitude to life; the good chaps always won and the baddies always looked silly and suffered defeat. He carried this attitude into POW camp and obviously saw little risk in writing a letter giving war news (obtained partly by our translating Japanese newspaper scraps) and encouraging the Koreans to hope for an Allied victory. As for the hiding place, some corner of a warehouse bare of everything except piled sacks would do perfectly. Alas, he was caught—and not by some jokey boy's magazine South Americans or funny Germans, but by the deadly serious and ruthless *kempeitai*

In the summer of 1945, just before the end of the war, when he had completed two years, he was returned to the camp at Seoul, an emaciated, silent figure. He was immediately moved into the camp hospital, weak with starvation, pleurisy and beri-beri. He died four days after the end of the war.

Meanwhile at the camp at Inchon (Jinsen), an officer and a sergeant were caught trying to *re-enter* the camp after seeing that escape through the town was impossible. They received eight and six years imprisonment respectively and the two officers who had lent them money for the attempt two years each.

Escape was not a serious possibility in Seoul; the nearest friendly territory, the USSR, was nearly 600 miles away across the most difficult country. How could a European hope to pass unnoticed all that way? We simply had to make the best of our conditions and take heart from the improving war situation: the British and Americans were in Italy and Mussolini had been ousted from power.

The war news was encouraging, even exciting, but we were being initiated into another stage of Japanisation. We now had to bow to the Japanese officers. Our colonel protested and resisted, but soon we were on parade before the Japanese adjutant and being asked to bow 15 degrees stiffly from the waist. We bowed about 5 degrees.

'More,' shouted the adjutant.

We added a few degrees very stiffly.

'More, more!'

Finally he had us all bowing 60 or 70 degrees twenty times in a row.

'Now, we will have bowing on the march,' he said.

For two or three days in September 1943 I had a strange feeling that my father was close by and would appear in the camp one day. This was improbable but not impossible since he was a civilian prisoner in Japanese hands some 500 miles away in North China. In March I had received the first letters to reach any prisoner in Korea—perhaps the first to reach any prisoner of war of the Japanese—and they were from my father, telling me of his arrest on the morning of 8 December 1941 and his internment in the former US military barracks. With him was a platoon of US Marines and the leaders of the British and Americans communities in Tientsin. Since then he had been moved with 1900 other Britons and American civilians to a camp in some school buildings in Weihsien in Shantung province. It was unlikely that he would appear here, even though the whole region from Weihsien to Seoul was under Japanese control; nevertheless the premonition I had was so vivid that I expected to see him daily.

At last the problem of my presentiment was solved. Five parcels had arrived for me at the camp office, where there had been much discussion of the matter though no word was breathed to any prisoner. *Five parcels*! I was walking on air. I had to unpack them in the presence of two Japanese officers but they contained no contraband. Back in the barrack room I found I had 30 small cans of meat, jam, condensed milk, two tubes of toothpaste and two bundles of clothes, mainly socks, underwear and sweaters. Suddenly I was a capitalist, rich beyond the dreams of the average POW.

I offered the food to the mess, but the colonel refused, so I gave nine cans to the worst beri-beri cases in the camp and shared the rest with friends. I was happy that two of those sufferers were game old Aussie Diggers who had fought at Gallipoli and France and re-enlisted in 1939 by reducing their ages from the early fifties to about 39 or 40. The parcels had come from my father though he had not packed them. He had handed the clothing and some money to the Swiss Consul from Tsingtao who had packed and posted them.

During the long, warm, sunny Korean summer besides enjoying our work on the vegetable farm, we accompanied working parties in all directions around Seoul. We found the central business area to be astonishingly modern with tall concrete and stone buildings, thousands of men in suits and typists in short skirts. And yet a few miles away, farmers used wooden ploughs and buckets and most craftsmen seemed to have the most rudimentary tools. I thrilled to see the ancient gates of the city—the South, the West and the North, all in almost pure Chinese architectural style with mighty curving roofs and ornate carved eaves. We travelled in carbide-burning buses or trucks, often with 40 men in an open truck so that the only way to avoid falling off was to cling hard to two or three others, standing swaying round each bend. Every so often, the truck would stop as the carbide fire needed restoking. In wartime Japan, a poker was essential driving equipment. The streets were busy with shops and small industries, making or selling cloth and silk, crinoline hats, bamboo products, pottery, coffins, brasswork, medicines, coalballs, oil, grain and hot meals. On the mud sidewalks, hawkers sold pears, persimmons, apples and watermelons. There was poverty and dirt side by side with these amazing clean white clothes most Koreans wore.

Two or three times, I was in Seoul's main railway station and, since I knew some 680 Chinese characters by now, devised a little game of switching labels on cargoes passing north and south through the station yards. I don't suppose it worked very often, sending something from Manchuria back north to Mukden or Harbin, but once I found a generator labelled for Manchuria and I reversed its direction to Tokyo, writing the characters 東 京 on a new label.

Studying Japanese and getting small insights into the Japanese character, culture and history, I had thought several times that a nation might be surprisingly clever if, instead of treating its prisoners of war as contemptible captives to be worked almost to death, it decided to woo them as friends. Show them some fine historic buildings, some great art, recount to them tales from history, moments of great bravery and the captor nation's way of thinking. I have always found that a fine sight, seen only once, is as easy to bring to mind as a place one has seen 500 times, so why not lock into each prisoner's mind some scenes of beauty and civilisation which he would remember forever and bring to mind at the mention of the name of his captor nation? This could be easy in Japan, where there is much beauty. But it was not to be. It has never been attempted even on a small scale anywhere. It is the idea of this writer alone.

And that brings me to the finest hour I enjoyed in prison camp.

One day in late spring in Seoul, when the weather was as hot as summer, but some trees still bore blossom, a working party of 40 men and one officer, myself, drove through the city to a place known as the Racecourse. It was an exercising paddock near some army stables set in a horseshoe-shaped valley at the foot of the mountains just north of the city. The task was to level a larger area to make galloping more practicable.

After the men got going, shovelling and carrying, working slowly and easily with much joking and ribaldry, sleeves rolled up and necks open to the sun, I went to the stables and persuaded one of the Japanese grooms to let me exercise one of the horses. Twice round the paddock and through the pinewoods on the slope was what he permitted and I enjoyed it immensely. As I handed back the horse, I wondered if the groom would hand it a carrot. If so I might just pinch it.

The Korean guards were as happy and relaxed about the return of summer as everyone else and they allowed me to wander at will. I climbed the hills on all sides of the paddock. To the north towered the splendid, saw-edged mountains which dominate Seoul, their lower slopes green with trees, but the rock above blue in the sun.

After lunch—*daikon* and barley—both sentries and prisoners slept or dozed in the sun. This was *yasume* time, rest time. I walked steadily away from the work party towards a village nestling at the foot of the mountain. I walked over half a mile. This was a long way to wander without permission, but I knew the meal orderlies had walked in this direction to collect water for the tea and I could pretend to be inspecting the well.

The village was neat and unspoiled. The baked mud cottages with their heavy thatched roofs crowded closely together and from the fenced yards I heard the clucking of chickens and the voices of children. The brown earth of the village street was hard and swept clean from each cottage door to the narrow stream on one side. In this roadway one tree had been left to grow and it was a peach tree in full blossom. I feasted my eyes on the details of this scene to take back with me to the dismal barrack.

The Koreans were friendly but cautious. The children gathered round me and stared. I said 'Good morning' in Korean, the only phrase I knew, and they all replied. I explained in Japanese that I knew only those two words and conversation lulled into smiling silence when a sweet vendor came along. I had two yen in my pocket so I bought some sweets and gave them to the children. All the parents thanked me profusely and bowed. I said 'Sayonara' and walked towards the red-pillared temple.

It was a Buddhist temple, too large for so small a village. The curved roof, red pillars and decorated eaves were so purely Chinese I might have been in Peking. There was no one about as I entered, admiring each hall and balcony. I crossed the courtyard; entering the main hall, with a gold-tinted Buddha ahead and pillars and entrances alternating down each side, I noticed three old men in white sitting on the balcony in the sun. Two were very old, with silky white beards, calm faces and serene expressions which did not alter when I approached. I used my single Korean expression on the three scholars and stood by, watching what they were doing.

They had a white silk scroll spread out on the wooden floor and held at each corner with a stone. The oldest man, white-bearded, dressed all in white national dress and with his bald head shining like old ivory, was squatting cross-legged at one end and painting 6-inch Chinese characters on it in a beautiful and accomplished hand. The three men discussed each character before he wrote it and used a sheet of material beside the scroll on which each in turn wrote the next character. They appeared to be discussing styles in calligraphy and demonstrating to each other their preferred way of writing the same ideograph. Time seemed to be standing still. There was no sound but the distant singing of birds and the quiet voices of the three men squatting on the floor in the sunlight.

I tried to speak with them, but they did not understand Japanese. However, I managed to convey to them that I should like to try to write. The youngest man went off to fetch another brush, and on his return inked it and offered it to me. I tried to paint the character 'capital', which figures in the names 'To*kyo*, Pe*king* and *Kei*jo, My strokes were thick and without grace and the ends were ragged. I gasped at their ugliness beside the flowing calligraphy of the oldest Korean. It was like comparing Times or Roman lettering with a whitewash slogan slashed on a wall.

As I watched them practise and write two more characters, I thought, this is a sight seasoned travellers would voyage a thousand miles to see. Three venerable Korean gentlemen in national dress practising calligraphy in a peaceful and serene temple on a sunny spring afternoon. It was one of the most memorable scenes of my life. It was rare, and it was very civilised. What a contrast to the world of military captivity and forced labour only ten minutes away! Was it a dream? Did both these worlds really coexist? I knew that I would never forget this scene—it was one to treasure and remember.

As I walked back towards the paddock, I thought 'Stone walls do not a prison make nor iron bars a cage'—yes, once again that was true—'if I have wisdom in my soul and in my heart am free, Angels alone that dwell above enjoy such liberty'.

Coming over the pine-clad slope into the paddock, the sentry asked me where I had been. I broadly indicated the hillside. What had I been doing?

'Dreaming,' I replied.

'Lazy', he said, but wasn't very annoyed.

# 17

# Transfer to Tokyo

'Rieutenant Wado,' said Old Father Time, the interpreter, 'you wirru go to Tokyo.'

My jaw dropped. 'Rieutenant Ma-ku-no-ton orso.'

I walked back to the squadroom aghast at the news, the surprise, possibly the danger. Stunning as the news was, I had no time to waste; we were due to leave within 36 hours. Six bandsmen, mostly privates, were to be included in the party. We were being transferred 'to do work nearer to our peacetime occupations', which the Japanese knew from captured documents. I was frightened that I was earmarked for writing propaganda and Jack MacNaughton felt the same about broadcasting.

I hurriedly collected addresses, finished the book I was reading, packed a small tin trunk and a bedroll (valise) and said goodbye to friends. I seemed to have collected quite a lot since the day Singapore fell, and I had only recently received two clothing parcels from my father. But... I didn't want to go. Life was bearable in Seoul; we had had five Red Cross parcels each, some bulk bully beef, occasional pilchards from the Japanese and they had promised to try to obtain more butter... I was sorry to be leaving this camp.

Of course, I had noticed that the officers were gradually withdrawing into small cliques, mostly living within ten feet of each other, and neglecting the rest. It was becoming like an English suburban street; you spoke to four neighbours and only nodded to the rest. It was far less chummy than it had been a year ago. While in Tokyo, I might meet Americans with news of the Philippines, news of the Pacific war, navy men, pilots, perhaps British from Hong Kong, all sorts. Yet I was leaving good friends, tested comrades in war and in twenty months of captivity. I began to feel lonely.

The truth was, Colonel Noguchi was an honourable man, not inclined to cruelty or harsh punishments, and Lieutenant Colonel Elrington, DSO, MC, was equally honourable, presenting our case to the Japanese in a calm, quiet voice, which Colonel Noguchi respected. Thanks to the character of these two men, life in the camp was bearable, correct and decent; there were no abuses and a satisfactory discipline.

We saluted our colonel and marched out, *British* drill, climbed into a truck and left the tall warehouse and our pale-faced comrades behind. Inside, I felt lonely and sick, but quickly began to strengthen my ties of friendship with the other seven members of the party, which is the human insurance against desertion or ostracism. Three Japanese soldiers and an officer accompanied us in the train to Pusan. Next day we caught the ocean-going ferry for Shimonoseki on the southernmost tip of the Japanese main island of Honshu. With 120 miles of sea to cross, we wondered about submarine activity—we had already heard of one torpedoing there. With army priority, we boarded first and sat in a huge saloon floored entirely with *tatami* mats. Then the civilians poured in like a damburst and soon every square foot of that saloon held a squatting human being with a bundle, a suitcase or a baby on his lap. One of our guards was a short, bespectacled Nipponese, just like the cartoons. A bandsman asked him, 'How old are you?' The small soldier hesitated. 'In English, five feet,' he replied.

It was night when we arrived at Shimonoseki, where we were met by two first-class private interpreters from Tokyo Headquarter Camp. Both wore the laurel-leaf insignia of the Imperial Guards Division. I thought back to Bukit Payong and the 63rd mile peg near Ayer Hitam, where their comrades had advanced so fast. One was six feet tall and spoke with an English accent and the other was short and stocky with an American accent.

'They ought to be a team,' said Jack. 'Boogy and Woogy.'

We were handed over. I gave the Seoul guards messages to friends in camp which conveyed more than their actual words, notably that the ferry had been guarded by a scout plane. Then we were rushed along 1000 yards of corridor to the railway station, where the two guards left us alone for 40 minutes while they had a meal and sought information. We wondered if Tokyo discipline would always be like this. All around us were businessmen, schoolboys in their Victorian semi-naval blue uniforms and schoolgirls in sailor suits, patient old ladies with bundles, mothers with children tugging their kimono skirts, all too busy with their own affairs to pay any attention to us. It could have been Victoria Station or Grand Central. It could equally have been Berlin or Rome.

After 40 minutes, the stocky interpreter came back joking. He had thick lips and a gravelly negro voice. 'He reminds me of Rochester,' MacNaughton and I said together, thinking of Jack Benny's sidekick. Late that night we caught a small train. The seats were so narrow we were shifting and twisting all night trying to doze off. After some time, I walked to the end of the carriage at a halt and asked the sentry where we were.

'Hiroshima,' he replied.

'Long way to go yet,' I murmured and returned to my seat.

Next day we passed along the shore of the Inland Sea, through Kobe, which I had visited in peacetime, Osaka and Nagoya with its fine medieval castle and past mile after mile of yellow ricefields and villages at the foot of steep, wooded mountains. Occasional Shinto shrines, graveyards and *torii* gates added interest to the views. It was dark before we passed through Yokohama and at Shinagawa station in Tokyo we crowded into the metropolitan electric train and rode with the businessmen and city typists returning to their suburban homes. The Japanese were dispassionate; they neither stared at us nor discussed us. A seat became vacant beside our interpreter. All the Japanese left it to us, according that servile respect that ordinary Japanese civilians then showed to all members of the armed forces. One of the prisoners offered it to a Japanese woman, who accepted it gratefully. The men of Nippon looked on disapprovingly.

Another stop or two and we got out at a small dark station.

'What is the name of this district?' I asked.

'Omori. The camp is very near...on an island.'

Omori—'great forest', but there was no forest now, just narrow streets which I knew in daylight would reveal small wooden houses and shops with fire-fighting water tubs and straw beaters outside every door and paper flags on holidays. We passed some fine, large houses overlooking the bay. The curved tile roofs and tall gateways made me think they were restaurants.

'No,' the private smiled. 'They are geisha houses. Omori famous for geisha houses, but now many geishas doing war work.' He looked up at the dark windows. 'Not so busy now.'

We crossed a canal by a wooden footbridge. This was the island in Tokyo Bay on which stood Tokyo Headquarter Camp. By the light of a single electric lamp, we crossed a grey, sandy waste, lunar in aspect, to the tall wooden walls of the camp and its broad wooden gate, floodlit by arc lamps. Our hearts sank at this unearthly scene. I was indeed 'convinced of fearfulness and became aware of unsavoury results'.

The interpreters knocked and shouted. An armed sentry opened the small door beside the gate and we filed in, across a yard and into an office. We stood in line, feeling depressed and very, very hungry. A prisoner in a leather flying jacket looked in the door.

'Hey, Rochester, when you gonna let these guys go?'

My spirits rose. It was wonderful to hear an American accent again after years among only British and it would mean news of the Philippine campaign and Pacific war.

The interpreter said, 'One, two minutes.'

'Okay. I'll get them something to eat.' Then he dropped his businesslike attitude, smiled and said, 'Hello, fellers.'

The other door opened and in shuffled the Japanese duty officer, wearing full uniform, cap and sash, but loose slippers instead of riding boots. He ordered the camp interpreters to read something and returned to picking his teeth.

It was the no-escape pledge, which we each signed in turn.

'You are now members of Tokyo Headquarter Camp. You must obey all Japanese orders; if you do not, you will be shot. Look after your healthy!'

The Japanese officer left the room and the American POW returned and introduced himself. He was dark-haired, plumpish; he looked like an Italian tenor.

'My name's Lucia. Air Corps. I was in China. Where are you from?'

We replied Singapore by way of Korea and added our names. He was brisk and friendly with a New Yorker's sharpness and wit. He led us to the cookhouse, where we were given some bread and hot tea (milkless and sugarless naturally). The cooks were nearly all British soldiers from Hong Kong. They looked pretty fit—but they were cooks. We ate ravenously as all we had eaten since Seoul 60 hours ago was five small sweet potatoes and two riceballs. Ray Lucia, the prisoner duty officer, then led us to an empty barrack hut where blankets had been made up into beds for us. We felt better; someone had been thoughtful. We rolled quickly into our bedrolls. Our 1200-mile journey was over. This was our first night in Tokyo, the enemy capital.

# 18

# 'Look After Your Healthy'

The next morning at six o'clock a handbell was rung for roll-call. We tumbled out of our blankets, dressed and ran out of the hut into a damp, raw morning. For the first time we saw our fellow prisoners; it was a depressing and discouraging spectacle.

Clad in dirty khaki overcoats, shabby clothes of blue and khaki, hatless and unshaven, they clattered across the yard with bare feet slipped into Japanese clogs and formed up in long ranks. Their scurvy clothes and pallid complexions shocked us. They looked ill and demoralised. The officers looked healthier, but the oppressive and cheerless atmosphere of the camp was easy to sense. They looked at us dully and we wished we had even those thin hessian overcoats from Korea.

The same Japanese duty officer appeared in sash and sword.

'*Nichoko shikan dono ni keirei,*' shouted the senior prisoner officer. '*Kashira naka*' ('To the duty officer salute. Eyes centre').

We all jerked our heads and looked towards the duty officer, who returned the salute and began a cursory inspection of the squads. Each squad leader reported his total, absentees and number present in Japanese and ordered his squad to number. Jack MacNaughton stumbled through this abracadabra for our party of eight. Next day he joined the officers' squad and I was put in command of a barrack.

After the dismiss, we were surprised to see our regimental bandmaster and two musicians running forward to greet us. They had been in a working party transferred to Kobe; somehow they had been moved to Omori. With the bandmaster and two more instrumentalists, our musicians realised they could build an even better band than they had first hoped.

A breakfast of pumpkin soup and a sweet potato came up in china bowls marked with the army star. So the food was different here. Then all the officers and men remaining in camp after the departure of the working parties gathered round us. There were Royal Scots, Middlesex and sailors from Hong Kong, British from Singapore and Java, Americans from the Philippines, Wake Island, Free China and the US Navy, Dutch and Indonesians from Java, Norwegian merchant seamen and various waifs and strays including the youthful British governor of the Gilbert Islands in the Pacific, a civilian. In a separate compound was the crew of an Italian ship, interned since the Italian armistice by the Japanese who did not know whether they were friends or enemies and neither did we and neither did the Italians.

'What was your peacetime job?' we were asked, and when Jack answered, 'Actor' and I, 'Reporter', people shook their heads grimly. We discovered that newspapermen, writers, radio announcers and actors from prison camps all over the Far East had been concentrated in Omori and that the aim was to use us for propaganda broadcasts from Radio Tokyo. A special camp had been set up for the purpose in Tokyo and it was known as '*Bunka*' ('Culture Camp'), a name we learnt to dread from that day forward.

Some of the potential *Bunka* inmates had already been interviewed by four Japanese civilians. As far as I could discover, they had been the chief of the Propaganda Bureau, a member of the Army Press Bureau, a former *Asahi* newspaper correspondent, who knew nearly every journalist of importance in the Far East, and another foreign correspondent. They were intelligent and dangerous adversaries, all fluent in English and thoroughly understanding Western manners of thought and argument. The first of these men, the Marquis Ikeda, had been educated at Oxford and some of the others at universities in California; it would be difficult to bluff them.

I asked a hundred questions. At all costs I didn't want to be drawn into this *Bunka* net. Once there, it was little more than a question of pressure before one was at the William Joyce stage and one would certainly have to answer for it after the war. One newspaperman had been questioned already; it was Gordon Braden, an Australian lieutenant brought all the way from Rabaul, for this interrogation. He told me he had admitted only to sports writing and broadcasting and they appeared to accept this. For broadcasters and actors it might be more difficult and for one newcomer escape appeared improbable.

This was Sergeant Fujita, an American citizen of Japanese parentage, who had been captured in Java. He had been interviewed more than once and told that his blood and race made him a Japanese and that he should work for his true country. Tough, stocky Fujita refused every time. He was completely American in speech and thought; he spoke no Japanese and kept insisting, 'I'm American, American'.

A few days later our interrogation came. A room was prepared and the soft-spoken civilians were seen to arrive. Over a dozen of us were to be questioned. I had decided to say that I had reported only social news and to speak in a slightly husky voice.

My turn came. I quietened a faint palpitation of fear in my stomach and walked in. Three well-dressed, cultured-looking Japanese were sitting in the room, two behind a desk and a younger one well over by a side wall. I recognised Marquis Ikeda at the desk and the *Asahi* man against the wall from descriptions I had been given. The third was the Army Press Bureau representative.

I didn't know what these men knew about me or whether they had read anything I had written. It was possible they had a file on me.

'Mr Wade, have you been to Japan before?'

'Yes.'

'Where?' Ikeda asked and looked down at his papers.

He's got it written down in front of him, I thought. 'Yokohama, Kobe and Nagasaki,' I replied.

'How many days or weeks?'

'Oh no, only three days. I was on a ship.'

'You only stayed three days?'

'Yes,' I lied slightly.

'You were a newspaper reporter in Shanghai, weren't you?' He spoke quietly and casually. If I denied it, he would of course have contradicted me.

I nodded.

He asked me which paper and I told him. Then he asked what sort of things I had reported.

'Oh, cocktail parties, divorces, banquets, bazaars. Social news.' I slurred my words.

'Did you write about the China War or politics?'

'No, not me.'

Only Ikeda spoke. 'Mr Wade, how would you like to learn about something of Japanese history and art and literature?'

'I'm not very interested. We don't see much culture around us. It doesn't seem to have much practical importance.'

He looked at me keenly. 'What do you think of the Japanese?'

I was frankly surprised by this question. What should I say? What I really thought? Or something harmless and noncommittal? Impetuously, recklessly, I decided to speak the truth, 'let him have it'.

'The Japanese are difficult to understand,' I began slowly, thinking. 'They are aggressive, imperialist and militaristic—and they're highly emotional too.' I was warming to my subject; all the subdued emotions caused by knowledge of Japanese expansionism, ruthlessness and atrocity clamoured for expression.

'The Japanese are the Prussians of Asia. They are aggressive and militaristic like the Prussians and, at the same time, they are as emotional as the French or Spanish. This is an unusual combination; it doesn't exist in Europe, but it makes the Japanese dangerous and unpredictable. And, as they are extremely patriotic, it makes them a constant threat. They idolise their army and navy and give them too much power.'

I ended abruptly and thought, either they'll shoot me or they'll let me go.

Ikeda smiled. One of the others pursed his lips, but otherwise betrayed no feelings. Ikeda nodded. 'All right, Mr Wade, you may go.'

I couldn't believe I was getting away so quickly, but I lost no time in leaving the room.

For the next three weeks we were kept in suspense over the outcome of our interviews.

I now had the opportunity to speak with more of the new arrivals—newspapermen, theatrical producers, artists, US Marines with newspaper experience and cases of mistaken identity. From the first morning after our arrival I had been made barrack commander of No. 6 hut in which many of these new arrivals were quartered, and each week more were arriving.

A few of these men were dangerous. They had written anti-American articles for the Japanese press and were believed to be already on General MacArthur's list of traitors to be tried after the war. One civilian was so anti-Roosevelt that the Japanese easily persuaded him to write anti-Roosevelt and therefore anti-US government articles for them. Another strange case was a certain Sergeant Provoo, a blond, good-looking young American who had become a Buddhist priest during a visit to Japan shortly before the war. He was infatuated with Japanese culture and Orientalism and there was little doubt that he would go to *Bunka*. Few Americans spoke to him; he was alleged to have denounced an American officer to the enemy in the Philippines and helped bring about his execution. There were other serious charges as well.

There was a fair young American of great charm, whose father owned a newspaper in Honolulu. 'Bucky' Henshaw, ensign, US Navy, had produced shows at Stanford University. Accompanying himself on a ukulele, he delighted some of us with songs such as 'Maria Elena', 'I'm so Blue When it Rains' and Hawaiian songs. He had more than good manners and charm, he had style and I hoped he would stay in Omori. But when the news came through, Bucky's name was on the list, and so was Jack MacNaughton's, also Sergeant Fujita and Provoo and the anti-Roosevelt writers, all of them. It was a very sad Jack MacNaughton I shook hands with before they departed. 'See you after the war, Jack. You too, Bucky.'

'Country Club Road, Honolulu, any time,' smiled my friend.

In December my squad was swelled again by the arrival of over 30 prisoners from the notorious navy camp at Ofuna, near Yokohama. The Japanese Navy has always enjoyed the reputation of being less jingoistic than the army. This has been true politically (and no navy and army in the world were more deeply involved in politics than the Japanese) and so the navy was regarded as less pugnacious. But Ofuna camp was an atrocity. To it were sent all prisoners captured by the navy, which included all sailors and fliers found in the waters of the Pacific. No Red Cross representative ever visited the camp. The prisoners were told that they were not listed as POWs there and so Lieutenant Louis Zamperini, Army Air Corps, a champion American athlete, was presumed dead after splashing down in the Pacific and an airfield in Torrance, California, named after him, while all the time he had been in Ofuna. In 1944 he was allowed to broadcast to let his family know that he was alive. They had difficulty believing him after over a year's silence.

Al Mead had ditched his aircraft after running out of fuel at the Battle of Midway. Lieutenant Commander Dave Hurt lost his submarine USS *Perch*, and was captured.

Lieutenant Commander Blinn saw his ship, USS *Pope,* sink at the end of the battle of the Java Sea. They all moved into my hut and told me their stories. They were never let alone by the Ofuna guards; they were beaten, forced to exercise and run for hours every day. They were allowed to speak only in Japanese and were starved so badly that they fought for refuse in the garbage bins.

Naturally, the morale of prisoners such as these was far from high. But Commander Al Maher, USN, arriving from Ofuna, became senior officer in Omori and so took over that responsibility within hours. Commander Maher had been chief gunnery officer in the cruiser *Houston,* sunk in the Battle of the Java Sea in 1942. He was in a depressed and neurotic state of mind and his health was poor. The responsibility of senior prisoner officer rested heavily upon him. He had no talent for diplomacy or bluff. He gained little from the Japanese and we believed asked little: more drugs, yes, but books, religious services, funerals, less beating? We believed not. Success in one negotiation can lead to the confidence to attempt bolder requests, but Commander Maher, dark-haired and saturnine, had few successes. Nor could he win the confidence of all officers and men under him. Commander Maher remained the 'broken voiced, broken spirited' leader of the prisoners at Omori until the day I left.

Although the camp was commanded by a Japanese captain, supported by a medical officer, stores officer and NCOs, the day to day management was left to three interpreters, all privates first-class. Japanese officers only visited our section of the camp when they were on duty as officer of the day; all decisions were taken by the three interpreters and they could administer punishment and enforce discipline.

The result was chaos. Orders and counter-orders, 98 per cent verbal, were issued by the Japanese several times a week. No list of orders, except fire regulations, was ever issued to the POWs and the number of verbal orders ran into hundreds. Prisoners were constantly receiving disciplinary correction from one Japanese for obeying the order of another. If both were present, one would generally deny having given his order. This kind of treachery was far from uncommon. The impossibility was to guess which Japanese would give way to the other. It did not always depend upon seniority of rank; sometimes the senior gave way to the junior if the junior had special experience in that sphere. It seemed to depend upon a strange balance between right, responsibility, experience and *personal will*! Not long after this, we saw lieutenants give way to a corporal more than once. As the Americans put it, 'In prison camp you can't win'.

Disciplinary action in these cases usually took the form of a slapping or punching. In circumstances like these, only a strong senior officer could have persuaded the Japanese to coordinate and simplify their orders and fought against the steady deterioration of camp conditions. Many camps, Omori included, did not have the good fortune to possess such a senior officer.

In fact, senior officers did not prove themselves any more able or willing to command men, deal with the Japanese or accept responsibility than the most junior. In Omori, the job of commanding the five barracks, each housing up to 125 men, was the responsibility of one lieutenant and four second lieutenants, while there were always plenty of majors and lieutenant commanders in camp. The cookhouse and labour were also the responsibility of lieutenants and the daily duty officer's role was impressed only on subalterns and captains.

In those first weeks I realised what a difference it made to a camp to have a strong and unified POW command, as in Seoul. In Omori any prisoner could approach the Japanese to make a complaint or a suggestion or to ask a favour. The Japanese merely played off one prisoner or group against another. They encouraged friction between national groups—British, American, Dutch—and above all encouraged discontent and ill-feeling between officers and men. This undesirable situation remained as long as I was in Omori.

Deeply relieved as I was to escape the draft to the *Bunka* propaganda camp, I was not yet out of the woods. Within a few weeks, the *Bunka* boys were back again to interview the latest arrivals, plus some for the second time. On this occasion the main interrogator was a tall, American-educated Japanese with shiny black hair plastered close to his scalp and suspicious, snaky eyes. His hatred of Americans was obviously that of one who owes a debt to another nation and probably feels some inferiority. he shouted, threatening immediate execution to prisoners who said they did not wish to go to *Bunka*. One man was pushed outside the hut, a shovel thrust in his hands, and ordered to dig his own grave. I was 30 yards away, watching. The prisoner obediently dug the sandy gravel, while the interrogator and other Japanese watched him with pistols and swords drawn. When he had dug about fifteen inches deep, the interrogator demanded of him, would he or would he not work for the Culture Camp? The prisoner sadly shook his head.

'Hmm,' the tall Japanese sneered. 'You think you're very brave, don't you? But you are not. You are just a fool. I could kill you if I wanted, but you're more useful to us alive. Go back and work like a coolie. Go on, go back, go back and work!'

Yes, I was lucky to have escaped *Bunka*. I would remain an ordinary prisoner of war, culture-less but conscience-free. I was 'looking after my healthy'.

# 19

# Tokyo Headquarter Camp

Tokyo Headquarter Camp, Omori, was a 70-yard wide compound perched at the north end of an 80-yard wide man-made island in Tokyo Bay. The reclamation was made of sand gravel from the bottom of the bay. Entering the camp through the gate at its head, the administrative headquarters of Tokyo Area came first, then the camp office and medical inspection room, next eight barrack huts, five on one side and three on the other of a central lane, with a small parade ground opposite two of these huts and the bath-house and cookhouse at the bottom end.

The window of the camp office faced down the dusty lane between the barrack huts and it was simple for a Japanese bully to sit at the desk and watch every move in the camp before him. Between the huts and the fences were Japanese style drop-pit latrines and open-air washstands.

Tokyo Area, commanded by a Colonel Sakaba, a stone-faced martinet, administered about 40 camps and there were other groups of camps centred on Osaka, Hakodate in Hokkaido and Fukuoka in Kyushu.

Seven miles north of the camp was the centre of Tokyo, with the docks of Shibaura and Shinagawa much nearer; to the east were only the waters of the bay with no other shore visible, to the south was Haneda airport and the tall factory chimneys of industrial Kawasaki and, beyond, Yokohama. There were many prison camps near the factories of Kawasaki and Yokohama, usually next door to the workplace. On a very clear day we could see in the west Mount Fuji, tall and splendid, her snow-capped peak floating amid the clouds and no surrounding peaks to detract from the unexpectedness of the 12 000-foot pinnacle.

There was an anti-aircraft post at the southern end of the island and in between was the infertile, sandy soil which the officers later farmed.

Five wooden huts, 100 feet by 18, housed the 600 prisoners on double-deck sleeping platforms on either side of a central aisle. A pair of cubicles at either end of the hut provided living space for officers. On coming in from work, the men took off their boots, stowed them under the edge of the lower shelf and then half of them climbed ladders to the upper deck. The men had no more space than the width of their shoulders wrapped in their bedrolls. We were lucky there were not more epidemics. Each man's total belongings were kept on a shelf above his head measuring 16 inches square.

In summer the barracks abounded in fleas and we quickly learnt that fleabites are much itchier than we had thought. Lice never obtained a wide hold on the camp and bedbugs appeared only in the last year. The men did their utmost to keep clean, especially as many of them worked in coal, and they more than once dumped a lousy companion and all his clothes into a boiling bath.

I had a great admiration for those men—NCOs and privates in Omori. They were a particularly tough and resourceful bunch. Grimy and pale as they were, they never lost their good spirits and humorous outlook on life. And the Japanese never ceased to wonder at the cheerful humour of their strange foe. Defeat, prison camp, starvation, beatings—none of these things got them down for long. The smile would vanish for a while, but it never failed to come back.

The majority of the prisoners of war in Omori at the end of 1943 were British troops from Hong Kong. They had been sent to Japan in the first draft. At Shamshuipo camp in Kowloon, the Japanese had suggested that the British get rid of their 'undesirable' and difficult men. The British Army jumped at the chance and so soldiers with poor conduct sheets, men who were 'bolshie' and men who had been resisting the Japanese and British orders in camp were listed. Naturally, the command did not send their most able or popular officers with this draft; no, it was a soft-spoken solicitor, a missionary doctor aged 60 and some naval warrant officers. It is also worth notice that these 'undesirable' elements contained most of the men who had refused to sign the no-escape pledge for the Japanese. In other words, the 'Undesirables' included many men with a strong sense of duty and the courage to face the consequences of their conviction. They were as proud of the title 'Undesirables' as their fathers had been of the description 'Old Contemptibles' and their brothers of the title 'Desert Rats'.

The Americans in Omori were from the Philippines, part of the army that fought so courageously in Bataan and then made the 'Death March' to prison camp at O'Donnell, later moving to Cabanatuan. Their morale was not as high as that of the British. They were depressed by the coolie standard of living to which they had plunged; they missed the material comforts of their normal life and they were more shocked by the idea of surrender and capture.

Americans are used to a higher standard of living than the British and found it hard to adjust to this dirty, hungry Asian level. Also, the Americans had won all their wars and been reared in the creed of victory: victory in business, in sport, in war. To people like this the early reverses against the Japanese came as a great shock and they felt the ignominy of their position more deeply than our men, especially as the surrender was to the unloved Japanese.

To the British troops, most of whom were regulars, life in prison camp was not much harder than life in poorer homes in parts of London, Glasgow and Lancashire.

The barracks were crowded, there was no beer or women, but the discipline was not watertight, beatings were quickly over compared with fatigues and guardroom sentences and there was no cause for envy since no higher ranks enjoyed a better lot. Losing early battles in a war was not unusual, the important thing was to win the last one. This is not a generalisation about British and American prisoners of war throughout the Far East. It describes Tokyo, where we had some of the toughest and most independent British from many units, while the Americans were more truly representative of a citizen army. I think their average age was younger and they had had less army service.

The officers at Omori were a motley crew. There were American Army and Air Corps officers from Bataan, US Navy men from the Philippines and the Asiatic Fleet, 'Flying Tigers' from Free China and later many young pilots and bombardiers from B-24s based in Northern Australia, who had been shot down bombing Balikpapan oil wells in Borneo, Rabaul or the Japanese bases in New Guinea and the Solomons.

The few British officers were from Hong Kong or Singapore and included white-haired David James, aged 63, one of the two senior Japanese interpreters in Malaya. Captain James had lived much of his life in Japan since the age of three. He was utterly fluent and I think sometimes shamed the Japanese when they spoke crudely and with the utmost impoliteness to us. I found out that he, playing for Kobe, and my father, playing for Shanghai, had met in several interport football matches in 1911–13. As we had no newspapers, we sometimes took the scraps of Japanese papers to Captain James and asked him to translate the news. James always refused absolutely, but months later I learnt that this was his public stance. Any newsprint that came direct to him, he would study and then pass out the news through one trusted officer, who would never name James as the translator. This was the only way that he, a translator, felt safe in a rumour-mongering motley camp.

Because James appeared to refuse to cooperate, Lieutenant Commander Blinn, USN, and I used to attempt the translations of newspaper scraps brought into camp. We were expert at picking out words like 'cruiser', 'destroyer', 'aircraft carrier', 'sunk', 'damaged', 'bombed' and other military phrases, also all the place names in the Solomons, New Guinea and central and south Pacific. Later, as the Japanese searches for newspapers, contraband and 'spying' materials grew, I threw away more and more Japanese-language reference material and more rarely took on translations.

Individual experience of the war interested me deeply. For months I went from person to person listening intently to the details of officers' and men's experience of the war. I had the idea that since the Japanese had not selected me for *Bunka*, they would in due course send me back to Seoul. Of course, this was misguided; to the Japanese I was now just another POW in Omori and would stay there. But I heard and committed to memory many men's tales, thinking to repeat them accurately to my former comrades in Korea.

Thus I heard the whole story of the defence of Hong Kong and the fine performance of the Middlesex Regiment and some of the Hong Kong Volunteers, of the destruction of over 20 out of 35 B-17s at Clark Field in the Philippines hours after word of the Pearl Harbor attack should have reached all concerned there, of the horrors of the 'Death March' of 65 miles from Bataan to O'Donnell camp during which over 1000 Americans and Filipinos were bayonetted to death *en route*, of the build-up of troops in Australia and what life was like in Hawaii up to and including Pearl Harbor day, of the search for the Japanese carriers at Midway and where the 'Flying Tigers' were based in China. It was all raw history and the more one knew the better one could guess at the strategy to come to wind up this Pacific War.

In those early days, the officers often gathered in one bunkroom, fifteen or more in a 6 by 10 foot cubicle, lolling everywhere, with a kettle of green tea for warmth, swopping stories and tall tales for a few hours. But soon after, this was forbidden, visiting ended, and one of the things I most resent about our bullying NCOs was that they prevented us enjoying this harmless social dialogue.

I was glad that there were Americans in this camp. I had always got on well with them since my early schooldays in China. I had American cousins, aunts and two uncles who were commanders in the US Navy. I found that if you knew a little about their home state—even the names of two cities and one product—you were on good grounds to create a friendship. If you added to that some familiarity with American history these grounds were further improved. I also listened a lot and absorbed a great deal more about their way of life. It often fell to me to explain the British to the Americans and the Americans to the British, even to the extent that some Americans were uncertain of my nationality.

(A year after the war, I received a letter from the US Department of Defense stating that POWs had listed an American Lieutenant Wade in their camp. Was I this person and could I help them with this enquiry? I replied that I was British but thanked them for their enquiry which I found pleasing.)

Soon after arrival in Omori, Major F. H. Frankcom, of Army Education Corps, Singapore, handed me eight letters. They were from my mother and sister in San Francisco and some were only five months old.

I could scarcely believe my luck. This was the most wonderful moment in prison camp. I read them all immediately. My mother and sister were well and quite enthralled by San Francisco. I got the impression that funds were a bit short but they missed no opportunity to see theatre and art. My sister was a private secretary and my mother devoted a lot of time to British War Relief and other charities. I deeply missed my sister, with whom I had always had a very close and confiding relationship. I really yearned for the day when I would see them both again.

I thanked Peter Frankcom profusely. He was tall, urbane, Oxford-educated.

'So come and work in the post office,' he said.

I now looked in at the post office for the first time. It was set in the front half of an empty barrack hut with the lame and disabled sitting in the rear half, sewing scraps of

Four lieutenants of the Loyal Regiment grinding rice for flour in Changi POW camp soon after capture (author at left). The camera was later buried until 1946.

*Cinderella*, the 1944 Christmas play, being performed for Japanese foremen (*fus* and *hancho*s) in the bath-house. Sergeant Watanabe standing at right in total control.

Liberation, 7 September 1945. A planeload of POWs from Naoetsu arrive in Okinawa. Front row from second right: author, Lieutenant Theo Lee, 'Doc' Sandy Barrett, Lieutenants John Abbott and Louis Zamperini, Ian McDonald. Standing third from left: Ken Firth, fifth from left Corporal Harold Brisby. Standing below door: Sergeant Dale Williams.

A US Navy carrier fighter buzzes Omori camp on its island in Tokyo Bay, August 1945. Five of the central huts housed 600 POWs. (*US Navy photo*)

'Some corner of a foreign field.' The burial of the ashes of seven British prisoners of war following a formal military funeral in Seoul, Korea (then known as Keijo), December 1942. Colonel Noguchi in full uniform at end.

fur together to cover Japanese army packs. Five officers wearing mitts to keep their hands warm and with blankets round their legs were seated at different tables with rudimentary home-made pigeonhole racks in front of them, sorting letters. They had home-made trays with a 'knitting' needle piercing eighty or more cards, on each of which was inscribed a prisoner's name, unit, place of capture and present camp. Letters for prisoners of war, which had been very slowly sorted by Japanese students working at the Propaganda Bureau, now came to Omori where Frankcom had promised to sort and return them sacked to the Japanese quicker than our hosts could perform the task. It was remarkable that he had been able to persuade the Japanese that a few prisoner officers could undertake such a task, but undoubtedly this was not considered very honourable work and the Japanese hadn't needed much persuasion to transfer this labour required of them by international law.

Neither the Japanese Red Cross nor the army gave the prisoner officers one single indexing card, rack or pigeonhole to create this post office. Nor even wood and nails. The entire thing was improvised from the scant materials around the camp and used cigarette packs from the Japanese camp staff. Major Frankcom asked for and received lists of prisoners in every camp in Japan. These lists were always out of date, so the information on the envelopes was all we had to guide us. This always included rank, unit and country of capture. We would then send it to, say, Changi (Malaya) or Cabanatuan (Luzon); if it returned in a few months it might say 'moved to Thailand' (or Borneo or Manchuria) and a date. We would then direct it accordingly and hope. Once it said 'Moved to Japan' we would check the name against our lists and try to locate his camp.

Individual index cards were created for every prisoner, including new names of, for example, a pilot shot down in the Pacific only a week or two before. Sometimes a letter went to four destinations before finding the right one—and this took many months.

Sorting was done by at most nine officers at a time. I, for example, handled all Ws, Ts and Ds and sometimes Ys, checking against my cards, adding new information and then writing the next destination to be tried on the envelope. Every couple of months after much begging by Frankcom, the Japanese post office would send to collect the 70 to 100 mailbags we had filled since their last visit.

This was without a doubt the most useful work done by any prisoners of war in the Far East. We supplied tens of thousands of prisoners with over half a million letters. But in May 1944 a single Japanese second lieutenant, named Kato, decided that the whole exercise was simply an excuse to sit around and drink tea and gossip. For several months after that the whole world's mail to all POWs in Japanese hands was handled by one man, a Norwegian ship's captain named Karlsen, until the Propaganda Bureau again took back mail for overseas and Karlsen handled mail for the camps in Japan.

In return for our labour, we considered it our privilege to read open letters. But it was surprising how little general news we gleaned; a Derby winner's name, the potato glut one year, an occasional joke and that was all. One officer's wife, who sent four or five cards to her husband, seemed to be spending a lot of time in Mayfair; she constantly mentioned several nightclubs and three or four young officers who were escorting her. We used to shake our heads and wonder if that marriage would last.

We even received six letters from Japanese prisoners of war in the United States. Such men, the Japanese often told us, did not exist, yet here was indisputable proof. Peter Frankcom handed these letters over to the senior interpreter without comment but with a challenging expression and the latter snatched them and hurried away.

By about April 1944, the Japanese realised what a vast amount of information Major Frankcom had about their camps. He knew the total in every camp in Japan, Korea and Manchuria, he knew the incidence of death in each camp, how many were removed to hospital and how many came back! Several times Tokyo Headquarters, finding gaps in their own paperwork, were forced to come to him to discover the whereabouts of a prisoner. This entailed considerable loss of face and perhaps engendered fears that we might be able to organise some sort of resistance, so they gradually curtailed the activities of the post office and left it all to Skipper Karlsen, shivering alone in a hut without a stove.

Several months later, we read the news that the Japanese were sending parcels to their prisoners of war and civilian internees in America and elsewhere. The parcels would contain some pickles, sweets, a writing brush, some poems and a flute. Very Zen. We all laughed scornfully, but thinking it over later, I comprehended the thinking of a less than rich Asian nation with limited resources interested in the spirit of their lost brethren faraway and inwardly approved the Japanese action. It was the thought of a Japanese prisoner playing a flute and the motive in sending the flute that influenced me.

# 20

# 'Undesirables' and Others

My thoughts were concentrated so much on the danger of *Bunka* and broadcasting for the Japanese and, otherwise, on hearing all the war news I could possibly absorb, that for the first six weeks I paid little attention to the work the men did for about nine hours each day outside camp. They marched out each morning at seven o'clock and returned each evening from five o'clock onwards—over 400 men, leaving only officers, sick and disabled and, say 60 men on *yasume* or rest. The latter spent most of their free day asleep, wrapped in their blankets, except for an hour or two washing and mending clothes.

The jobs were at four railway yards, Shiodome, Shibaura, Onagigawa and Sumidagawa; at Mitsubishi, a warehouse, Tokyo Sempaku, unloading colliers and the Beach, shovelling sand—the worst.

The important thing about the jobs to POWs was that they gave access to food and food could be pilfered and eaten or brought back to camp to sell or exchange. The sturdy 'Undesirables' from Hong Kong, the first prisoners to reach Omori, had cornered the best workplaces: Mitsubishi, where there was always sugar to be brought home to sweeten the tea of the Mitsubishi workers, their friends and anyone else who could pay the price for a bowl of it; Shiodome and Shibaura, where *anything* might pass through the railway yards and prisoners often smuggled back dried fish, egg powder, tobacco leaf, wheat, rice flour and whalemeat. The Americans had access to almost as great a range of foods at Onagi and Sumidagawa. Once there was a huge shipment of dried coconut at Sumidagawa. As the days passed and the men ate coconut all day on the job and then brought more home at night, we in camp could watch the healthy improvement in their skin; instead of being dry and *mat*, their faces became oily and shiny, like rosy cherubs in comparison with the rest of us.

These perks at the jobs was what kept our men healthy and gave them their undoubted supremacy over the discomforts and punishments of prison camp and their resilience in the face of all trials and reverses. The amount of contraband smuggled into Omori was astonishing; I think it could have filled the hold of a barge. The Mitsubishi party of 28 men would smuggle an average of ten pounds of sugar a day. In two years that means about three tons! Sugar was the constant medium of exchange at Omori and the mainly Scottish lads of the Mitsubishi party were known as the 'Sugar Barons'.

One day a man offered me a dried fish—a salmon—for fifteen cigarettes or a shirt and three cigarettes. I asked to see it, whereupon he put his hand inside his shirt collar and drew out a fish 22 inches long which had been lying flat against his chest and held in position by his belt.

If you watched the men undressing after returning from the jobs, you would see white Japanese-issue socks filled with sugar or grain, the ends tied off, come slipping out of sleeves, inside legs, flat against the belly, the small of back, even under the caps of crafty POWs. Some men even wore extra large boots, marching and working all day, to bring back half a sockful of sugar in each boot at night. Tobacco leaf was even easier to smuggle and, when the Americans came across pure grain alcohol, some of them filled their water bottles with it and readily poured out a few drops to show it was colourless. A dozen times, Yanks came back to camp reeling with drink and twice at least dead drunk, propped up by a comrade on either side through all moves and searches.

'*Byoki*,' his comrades would say. 'He's sick.'

That night there would be sounds of revelry as contrabandiers drank 'tea royal' liberally laced with 190 proof pure grain alcohol. On Christmas Day 1943, five officers and I had the tastiest drink of three and a half years when we mixed an eggnog out of egg powder, Red Cross milk powder and 'alky'.

Naturally the Japanese foremen and guards did not stand by and watch this pilfering going on. Any man caught stealing was beaten up by the *fus* (company guards) or *hancho*s (senior foremen) and the matter often reported back to camp and the disciplinary NCO. So a man might get punched or kicked four times for one sortie. If extensive stealing was reported back to our disciplinary corporal, he would come back before the working party (of anything between 40 and 150 men), and lash out at each man in turn as they stood helplessly at attention. Some toppled like skittles but the majority just threw back one leg to maintain their balance and returned to attention.

Before leaving the workplace each evening the prisoners were searched by the Japanese foremen and any contraband seized. Arriving back in camp another search was made and more guilty men punished. Often the guards ordered a strip search. Then each prisoner had to strip to his underwear on the parade ground and allow his garments to be investigated. And we, sitting inside the barrack huts waiting for supper, would hear the thud of punches and the familiar screams of angry Japanese.

The brazen impudence of some POWs should be recognised. Such men would risk all and bring back a complete haversack full of sugar—say ten pounds in one stroke. The good psychologists would choose a day when many men had been caught and punished at work to bring home their most daring haul, guessing—usually correctly—that the Japanese would not expect such defiance on such a day.

Once the boys at the Shibaura docks found two crates of chocolate. They hid both crates in a corner and all day visited the spot and wolfed chocolate. This was dangerous; hiding one crate out of a consignment of twenty was one thing, but hiding the whole freight was asking for investigation as some Nipponese somewhere would have the bill of lading and would make enquiries. But chocolate was so rare... Eventually the *fus* discovered that the consignment was missing and accused the prisoners. They searched high and low through the docks, and when at last they did discover the crates, they found them nearly empty. They shouted helplessly and vainly at the POWs, but slowly they were persuaded to eat the rest themselves and forget the matter, marking it down on their records as 'Loss due to enemy action'.

At Shiodome station one day, a group of prisoners came across some personal baggage belonging to the German Ambassador, Herr Stahmer. This was too good an opportunity for British troops to miss. They tore the trunks and suitcases open with their loading hooks, ripped up the clothes, threw in some mud and oil and some written slogans—'We'll get you, Nazi', 'Love from Winston'—and sent the baggage on its way to the embassy.

But although the Omori boys did occasionally get away with some striking hauls, they paid for what they pilfered with black eyes, broken eardrums, chipped and missing teeth and years of slavish toil. The hardest and heaviest work in Japan and Korea was given to the POWs because, even on the poor diet they were fed, they were better and stronger labourers than the Japanese and Koreans. Through rain and snow and the hottest suns of summer, they jogged along in the quaint coolie trot they learnt from the Japanese and worked nine hours a day, nine days in a row, having their *yasume* or rest on the tenth. And, one should remember, that each man in the Tokyo railway yards loaded or unloaded with his bare hands *25 to 30 tons* a day!

But if they were sent to the beach there was not a morsel of food in sight and all they did all day was shovel sand.

One might have thought that in prison camp, where all men lived on level terms and all goods were distributed exactly evenly, that it would be natural for a socialist system to develop; but it was not so. Though we all appeared to be equal there were disparities between the relative value of each man's personal property, and it was from the trading possibilities engendered by those differences that a capitalist system developed. Where most shirts were cotton, the man who owned a flannelette shirt owned *two* shirts and could at any time exchange it on those terms; or if he preferred demand one cotton shirt, a pair of socks and half bowl of rice. Trading and especially dealing in food was not allowed in Seoul, but in Tokyo anything and everything could be traded. The Americans believed strongly in the freedom to trade and would never have dreamt of restraining it. At Christmas, 1943, after American Red Cross parcels were distributed, trading immediately began and at the end of it the Americans had most of the coffee and the British had most of the corned beef. The distribution was three parcels between five men, less than one parcel each. Lieutenant 'Hank' Hankin, US Army Air Corps, and I drew an Invalids package, full of orange juice, rusks, cocoa and only one can of meat whereas the ordinary parcel had six. We had to trade furiously for days to try to make good that deficit. In prison camp, as elsewhere, luck played its part in comfort, discomfort and even survival.

Of course, it can be said that some men must have lost in such free trading, but each deal was a voluntary arrangement, satisfactory to both parties even though a bystander might see a loss for one party. Market values of all items rose and fell each day; the opinion expressed by one or two doctors that the small can of liver paste was the most valuable food in the package made it possible for traders at one period to exchange that eight-ounce can for a twelve-ounce can of bully beef plus two cigarettes. Value is a relative and fluctuating thing and most of the prisoners in Omori found bartering such fun that they even slowed down eating in order to continue trading, for which, of course, they needed the currency of exchange.

Sugar, however, remained the permanent currency in our society and so the 'Sugar Barons' had most of the best overcoats and thickest sweaters in camp and each had his retainer cleaning his boots each evening before roll-call and washing his shirts and underwear.

What about sex? I have regularly been asked, quite early on, in conversations on the war. Japanese sociology students from a university visiting the camp asked the same question. 'Starving men don't have sex urges,' we replied and this was true. The vast majority of us had no sexual or indeed homosexual experience of any kind during all those years in captivity. We simply had no desire. All we craved was food. It was said in Omori that one or two hungry young men had offered themselves but I never heard of anyone taking up the offer and I left POW life at the end of the war almost entirely convinced that there had been no homosexuality in the camps I'd been in.

The saddest thing about Japanese prison camps was the sickness and death of so many young men. They died of beri-beri, diphtheria, pneumonia and malnutrition, and so many of those deaths could have been prevented. When I arrived in Omori our doctors were short of good medication and so there were several deaths; in 1944 larger supplies of sulfa drugs, including sulfathiazole and sulfaguanadine, came in through the Red Cross from America and the deaths decreased. If the working men fell ill, they usually recovered thanks to the illicit food they had consumed on the job, but when the weaker men fell ill the scales were tipped sharply the other way. Whoever the man was, if once he fell ill and gave up the struggle mentally there was little hope for him. A terrible thing was to see a man whose chances of recovery were fair, throw in the towel and say, 'I don't want to get better—what's the use? Let me die.' We had a few Indonesians who went like this. 'I am going to die,' they said, huddled in their blankets and, in a few days they did.

The most serious cases were removed to Shinagawa Hospital camp, which had half a dozen POW doctors and two Japanese. There were many deaths at Shinagawa and recovery was difficult because the Japanese placed all sick men on half rations, reasoning that as they were not working they did not require a working man's diet. We fought this reasoning successfully in most work camps, but in Shinagawa it prevailed.

In that camp there was a Japanese Army doctor Tokuda, a bow-legged, moon-faced gentleman with large round spectacles who tried many experiments on his numerous weak and sick POWs. He tried injecting soya bean milk direct into the bloodstream. It didn't cure. He and his junior doctor in Omori practised a hundred times the 'burning treatment' for vitamin deficiencies. In this, sufferers from beri-beri were laid out and little heaps of rice polishings (containing vitamin B) placed on their chests, thighs and hips and then set alight. The hope was that some of the vitamin B would enter the body through the burn and bring about a recovery. (Dr Tokuda was tried as a war criminal after the war and hanged.)

There were no ceremonial funerals in Omori. When a prisoner died the body was hidden away in a small back room. A day or two later a poorly dressed Japanese of the despised *eta* class would arrive with a pushcart and a plywood box about the size of a tea chest. The body was to go into this box. To do so, the man had to break the neck and bend the head forward, break the legs and force the knees up to the chin and cram in the arms. Much hammering and bone-cracking could be heard as he compressed the large frame of a dead POW into the small cubic box.

Omori was not a pretty place. We had men who had lost most of their toes through beri-beri and some who were still shedding them. Illness was a thing to be feared and there developed a tendency among the fitter prisoners to shun the sick, much as animals do. They feared not only the disease but the state of mind of their stricken comrades and feared contamination by either. Life in prison camp was nasty and brutish; what we fought for was to prevent it being short.

It wasn't that the well deserted the sick; in fact, they quite often gave them presents of stolen food; it was just that they hated to watch men *lose*, and these men who ceased to fight were losing. One of the American officers in Omori put into simple words the ideas I had been thinking less pungently.

'Don't let the Japs beat you,' he said. 'The bastards are trying to kill you, so don't give them that satisfaction. Keep living. The most important thing is to get home, so don't try to be a hero and don't be a fool. Don't stick your neck out; just keep living and don't let them beat you.'

Joe Mills, a friendly, dark-haired, stubborn Southerner and a second lieutenant, knew exactly how to go about surviving. He had been left for dead in the dysentery morgue in a camp in the Philippines. The filthy hut was littered with dead bodies. He lay on a blanket on the stone floor suffering from a twisted intestine and dysentery. One day a Japanese doctor walked through and kicked Joe to see if he was alive.

Joe swore. 'Why the hell don't you operate on me instead of leaving me here to die, you uncivilised bastard? And what's so funny?'

The Japanese had begun to smile. He didn't understand English but he understood Joe's blazing desire to live. He decided to give this prisoner a chance of life. He operated on Joe, making a twelve-inch incision in his belly and straightening the gut. When he returned to see his patient a few days later, he seemed surprised to find him alive.

'You....strong,' he smiled, still amused, and for the first time ordered a little special food for his patient besides soft rice.

Looking at Joe Mills, you knew that he would come through.

# 21

# Corporal Watanabe

The same week as I arrived in Omori camp, a young Japanese corporal also arrived to join the camp staff. His name was Corporal (later Sergeant) Matsuhiro Watanabe (Wa-ta-na-bi) and no one noticed him. He was quiet, amicable and harmless; he spoke with prisoners about the United States and Europe, which he hoped to visit after the war. He seemed to admire the West. He was intelligent and well-educated. Then one day a barrack commander shouted 'Gangway' at the corporal's approach and Watanabe took it as a warning to those engaged in unlawful activities, flew into a temper and struck the barrack officer repeatedly, also two or three of the men. Everyone was so surprised that several tried to soothe him.

Suddenly Watanabe found himself noticed by the prisoners; he saw new respect in their eyes and from that moment he became a tyrant in the camp. He would look for trouble: sidelong glances, smirks, poor salutes, slowness to obey an order, etc. Then he would lash out with his fists, bubble saliva at the mouth and leave prisoners doubled up or flat on the floor behind him.

Up to this time a dark-skinned, stumpy private named Kuriyama had been in charge of discipline in the camp and he often ordered men, even whole barracksful, on to the parade ground where he made them do press-ups for half an hour.

'Down-u! Up-u! Down-u! Up-u!' he would shout. 'No. 2 barrack bery dirty!'

He often hit men cheating on the exercises with his clog or kicked them and sometimes had sentries lever their stomachs off the ground with bayonets. But after several weeks of Watanabe's furies, the camp authorities realised that the corporal engendered more fear and they put camp discipline in his hands.

Kuriyama did not particularly bully officers, but to Watanabe they were his meat and drink and the average officer received ten or fifteen times the punishment of the average man. The reasons for this were not far to seek. Watanabe was the spoilt son of a wealthy Kobe family. As he told us, he had a beautiful home with a swimming pool in the hills behind Kobe, unlimited money, an adoring mother and he had led a dissolute student's life. He had been educated at Waseda University in Tokyo and then worked for *Domei*, the Japanese news agency. When called up by the army, he had immediately taken the examination for a commission. He had failed and resented this deeply as his brother and brother-in-law were officers. So the army made him a corporal, spared him service overseas and settled him at the age of 27 in a safe berth in Tokyo Headquarters POW camp. Although of the wrong rank, Watanabe was a typical member of the 'Young Officer' clique, believers in *Kodo*— The Imperial Way—an extreme patriotic association which dominated first army, then national policy. He was proud, arrogant and nationalistic, while sheltering an inferiority complex over his failure to become an officer, which he tried to crush by brutality and quick anger.

Watanabe was a good-looking Japanese of about 5 feet 7 inches, with a large head and strong face which gave the impression that he was much more heavily built than he was in fact. I was surprised how light his body was once it was stripped of uniform and jackboots. His hair was clipped close

Sergeant Matsuhiro Watanabe, the tyrant of Tokyo Headquarter Camp, Omori, and Naoetsu, notorious for his paranoid beatings of prisoners. A drawing by the author.

to the skull but never actually shaved. He had bold, black eyes which seemed to burn like boiling tar when he was enraged and his lips were curving and at times rather feminine. When in a fury, he would shout in an impassioned and powerful voice and use the most impolite forms of address to us, in a language which has four or more degrees of politeness for every phrase. Being shouted at continuously is something of which most Western people have little experience and this alone was sufficient to cow some prisoners.

We often speculated on Watanabe's power in camp and wondered how and why he had been given so much authority. He frequently gave orders contrary to those of more senior Japanese and forced them to withdraw and see his orders carried out. On two occasions the most humane and understanding Japanese officer in camp, 'Gentleman Jim' Lieutenant Morigishi gave permission after evening *Tenko* for the new YMCA gramophone to be played. The first time Watanabe charged up to the officer without saluting and demanded to know why his orders had been countered. Within moments he turned round to us and announced triumphantly, 'No music'. The second time, Morigishi, hearing no music from the camp, returned to the office to discover why. Watanabe, lolling in his chair, replied without standing up or saluting. They argued for two minutes after which Morigishi left and we continued to have no music.

Was it that Watanabe was a secret member of the *kempeitai* and therefore could overrule officers and NCOs senior to himself? Or was he a member of the Black Dragon Society or some other powerful patriotic secret society and this made him feared? Such societies had exercised great power in modern Japan; by terrorising politicians and assassinating cabinet ministers and even premiers they had sought to keep Japanese governments from straying from the path of imperialist expansion. Since we could obtain no more information, we were inclined to accept one or other of these theories.

It is not altogether rare in the Japanese Army for the decision of the junior on the spot to be accepted rather than that of a senior in less close contact with the situation; also, all orders in the army are traditionally direct commissions from the Emperor and the soldier is allowed considerable scope in their execution so that the spirit as well as the letter of the order is obeyed. Bearing this in mind, it becomes easier to understand that once Watanabe was made 'Disciplinary NCO' at the end of 1943, he might claim that any order concerning the prisoners was subject to his veto. But it is still difficult to understand how he was allowed such absolute and despotic powers and was never restrained. From December 1943 onwards, the moody temper, actions and broken English words of this man became not only the daily but the hourly subject of our conversation.

The first time I was slapped by Watanabe was for insufficient water in my barrack's fire buckets. The second and third times were for telling a lie—and he wasn't altogether wrong. Half-truths and covering up were our staples in replying. Another time he made me stand at attention outside my barrack in February for four hours without a coat and then eat my meal cold. Most of my offences concerned my barrack and its 100 men and the correctness of our equipment. They also stemmed from wrong behaviour by the men, such as not having a gargling bowl, having dirty boots, not saluting properly, making too much noise and, later, not bowing to him fast enough when he entered the hut. 'I was lookin' the other way, sir. You gotto have effing eyes in the effing back of your effing head for him.' This soldier and I took our slapping— hard with extended arm on either cheek—without recrimination. And to think, in Seoul, an officer had slapped me hard on both cheeks for not seeing him on top of a twenty-foot mound of sandbags and so saluting late, and our colonel had objected to the Japanese and they had sought to hush up the incident. Happy Seoul.

Although most men in camp and especially officers felt his fist, Watanabe reserved special venom for two officers who had lived for many years in Japan and so knew how badly he was behaving. Sub Lieutenant Lewis Bush of the RNVR had been a writer and lecturer in Tokyo until he went to Hong Kong to join the navy. He had been brought to Omori as a likely recruit for writing and broadcasting Japanese propaganda. Bush was especially vulnerable to pressure as his wife was Japanese and was being held prisoner by the *kempei*. The authorities tried to force both the husband and wife to broadcast for them by exerting pressure on them alternately and reporting to each the misery and sufferings of the other. For some inexplicable reason the pressure was sporadic; both held out and Bush managed to evade *Bunka*.

One evening Watanabe shouted that he was going to kill Bush, then punched him into semi-unconsciousness in the dust. He picked up a stirrup pump full of water and slammed it down with both hands towards Bush's head. The POW had just enough sense to move his head so the fire extinguisher missed him, otherwise he would probably have been killed. Screaming with rage, Watanabe lifted it to aim another blow, when the Japanese doctor rushed out of the office and seized him by the arms and dragged him away from his helpless victim. Watanabe was bundled into the office and calmed. Bush was bruised, swollen and bleeding and scarcely able to walk.

Watanabe's other prey was David James of the Intelligence Corps, who had lived 25 years in Japan and belonged to one of the most respected foreign families in Kobe, Watanabe's own home town. James had even been a liaison officer with the Japanese Army during the Russo–Japanese War of 1904–5. He was 63 years of age and small of build; in every way a man a young Japanese should respect, yet Watanabe discovered him standing at ease while the rest of us were at attention one dark evening and then proceeded to beat him and punch him until the old man collapsed on the ground. Twice he had to pick up his white-haired victim in order to continue the punishment, knocking him flat each time. None of the other officers made a move, such was the power of our disciplining and fear, but many must have felt as I did, sick with myself, sick and unworthy at having stood by and not moved a muscle to prevent such ugly brutality. Captain James was confined to bed for three weeks after this incident, but happily, he survived prison camp.

Does it seem strange then when I say that this Japanese non-commissioned officer, Matsuhiro Watanabe, was one of the three or four most influential people in my life? But it is true and I would not deny it, because it shows the terrible consequences of such power. This demonic tyrant had greater influence on me than any schoolteacher, employer and most friends. For eighteen months he ruled my life for 24 hours a day; I was never beyond his call and I saw him every day—sometimes nearly every minute for sixteen waking hours—and so had to rule all my actions according to his mood and whim.

Many former prisoners of war will understand this, also many men and women who have spent time in concentration camps—that one's peace of mind or misery, one's very life, can depend on the temper of one's tyrant.

# 22

# Officers and Men

Officers had requested to be allowed to farm vegetables on the empty land outside the camp gate, and in March 1944 this barely profitable work began. Only captains and below took part, under Colonel Pike of the Air Corps and 'Flying Tigers'. This wrenched eight regular post office workers from that occupation and slowed down sorting and forwarding there. We began to dig the loose, soft sand of our island and scatter seeds. But poor soil like this required fertiliser. Exactly, and that's where the *benjo*s came in. The Japanese provided two-foot wooden buckets and dippers and indicated the pit latrines.

How we had fallen! Up until this time *benjo*-emptying had been a punishment for thieves and insubordinates; now it was the daily work of officers. At first we thought it disgusting and degrading. Watanabe and the other Japanese enjoyed watching our expressions as we set about the task, so we quickly learnt to deny them that satisfaction and by the summer could smile lightheartedly and talk about any topic, even food, as we swung along with a large tub of nightsoil suspended on a pole between two of us. Watered down, the manure was poured into the long trenches we shovelled outside camp and later dug in, or else spread round the roots of young plants. We grew sweet potatoes, cabbage and peanuts.

Over 100 new prisoners arrived from the Philippines. Lean, hollow-cheeked and sad of eye, they told more tales of Cabanatuan and O'Donnell. Several still wore palm-leaf hats. I sighed. I knew the feeling; in prison camp you never threw anything away, not even bits of banana or nipa leaf. Three officers moved into my barrack. Soon after, Second Lieutenant Kato became camp commandant and he moved the entire Mitsubishi squad of 'Sugar Barons' into my hut. I could see that wasn't going to work well: rich privates and impoverished officers in one hut.

Watanabe immediately showed the new boys who was god in these parts. Night after night he had them bowing and saluting 30 or 40 times in succession to his command, '*Keirei*!' One night he decided that all officers needed this practice as well and so from eight o'clock till eleven we were all standing outside shouting '*Keirei*!' every three seconds and bowing to a spindly tree.

Kato's rationalisation of the camp was logical. Each work squad was in a single barrack; they no longer assembled from four or five huts. Each man had his *yasume* (rest), on the days of the month with the same final digit as the last figure in the POW number on his breast. So on the 7th, 17th and 27th of each month you expected to find only men with numbers ending in 7 on *yasume*. Anybody else would be suspect and had to be ready with an explanation. Pleased with his reorganisation, Second Lieutenant Kato surprisingly gave us a film night later with short documentaries on the castles of Japan, wildlife in the mountains and some industrial factory.

Meanwhile Watanabe continued tightening the screws on us. At first, as disciplinary NCO, he had demanded that we all spring to attention when he entered a barrack or cubicle and shout, 'Good morning, Watanabe *San*'. He soon tired of this; perhaps to him as well as to us it sounded like a schoolroom. Now we had to leap to attention, shouting *'Keirei'* ('Salute!') and then bow for as long as he kept his hand at the peak of his cap. Next he began confiscating any excess of clothing or blankets that officers had, while our kit and papers were searched 'to see if you are spying.' So much for two parcels of clothing from my father; little of that remained and now I gave away several more vests and pullovers. (The tin trunk and bedroll with which I arrived in Tokyo were long gone.) All we were allowed, like the men, was clothing to fill the storage space on one shelf above the head of our bedspace.

Next we were ordered to salute every Japanese—NCOs, privates, sentries, everyone. I wasn't surprised; in the Japanese Army every soldier salutes every superior, including NCOs and even other privates in certain circumstances. If Watanabe called any of us from the office, we had to shout *'Hai!'* ('Yes!') and come running. This applied to our men as well, but it happened far, far more rarely with any single man, whereas one officer might be called two or three times in a day. The men felt some disgust at the sight of an anxious-faced officer, shouting *'Hai!'* and clacking his clogs up the lane to the camp office. It did the harm to officer-men relations that was clearly intended.

Finally, Watanabe ruled that every time we were within sight of the window of the camp office, we had to salute it *in case* any Japanese were inside. This meant that every time we walked from one hut to another, every time we went to wash clothes or fetch food or see a doctor or go on parade or even step outside our barrack hut we had to salute the blank milky panes of the office window.

It was little wonder that the men used to say that they were glad to get out of camp for eleven hours each day and how they could feel the tension and misery of the camp atmosphere the moment they re-entered the gates. The tension in the camp became so great that two American officers requested to be allowed to work with the labouring troops outside camp in order to escape this endless persecution. Permission was granted.

By questioning, Watanabe began to realise that although officers did not mind working in the post office or farming vegetables for the camp, they did object strenuously to working for the Japanese at docks and factories. As soon as he comprehended this, he tested his power to break that resistance. He ordered Captain

Brice Martin of the US Army out to work with a working party. Martin, a tall young Texan with a strong sense of duty, refused.

'But I *order*!' Watanabe shouted.

'I'm sorry. I can't do it.'

'Why you can't do it?'

'It's against my duty as an officer and it's against international law.'

Spitting and spluttering, Watanabe shouted, 'I don't care for international law. Japan does not care about international law. Japanese Army makes its own law. You must go to work at Onagigawa.'

Captain Martin still refused, so Watanabe reported the matter to Second Lieutenant Kato.

Kato, who was at least as emotional as the average Japanese, quickly lost his temper and sent for Martin. The above dialogue was repeated in the camp office, then Kato lashed out at Martin. He rained blows on his head, his body and his back and kicked him on the legs and in the stomach. Once he had him on the floor, Kato kicked and jumped on him until Martin was unconscious. Then Watanabe, seeing Kato's temper was beyond control and that he might kill Martin, dragged the body out of the office— Watanabe of all people, who had once been dragged away just in time from a semi-conscious victim of his own!

For a week afterwards Martin was confined to bed with huge bruises all over his body, two black eyes and a hideously swollen face. He limped for weeks after that and it was four weeks before even Japanese would pronounce him fit to work and he went out to Onagi.

The night of the Martin beating all officers were called on parade and Watanabe read a written order requiring five officers to work the next day. I need hardly say that I was one; the other four were Americans.

'Howardo, Rusha, Wado, Tusken, Hinson,' he shouted and we stepped forward. 'Japanese order you will work.'

So we joined the Shibaura squad the next morning, went by truck to Tokyo's docks and spent the day carrying 40 kilo sacks of rice back and forth. But not the day after; the principle having been established that we could be made to do any kind of work, the example was terminated.

We were a bit stiff the next day, but I thought I wouldn't mind *one* day in Shiodome. That was a railway yard right in the centre of Tokyo, not far from the Ginza, or perhaps Sumidagawa (*gawa* means river). When I first heard that name I thought of Hokusai's woodcut, *The Bridge Over the Sumida River*. But art and civilisation were far away from Tokyo No. 1 Prison Camp.

Three or four of the more senior American officers were now complaining about the discipline of the British troops and the way they answered back. This had been partly brought to a head by the lifestyle of the 'Sugar Barons' in my barrack; each 'baron' had his 'batman' who washed his dishes and his clothes, cleaned his boots and did his night watches as fire picket in return for a bowl of sweet tea each evening and a spoonful of sugar to spread on his *gaoliang* or barley. Worse still, two of the officers living in the hut had begun to ingratiate themselves with the 'barons' and were suspected of doing occasional chores for them. When an American officer had accused a 'baron' of this, he had told him 'to bloody well mind his own effing business.' (I tell you the 'barons' were the toughest, lustiest, hardest boiled characters in camp—not only my 'barons' but their equals in other working parties. I had only recently heard that a Shiodome group brought back flour, egg powder and milk powder and had a *cake* cooked for them in the pre-dawn fires of the cookhouse. 'A *cake*, for Chrissake,' officers said. 'A *cake*!')

To the American officers' complaints, we tried to explain that British troops were very independent and found difficulty in obeying orders from officers not of their own unit. This excuse should be nonsense, yet there is a grain of truth in it. It seems to me that, thanks partly to our healthy native independence, British discipline tends to stand up less well under the unusual strain of prison camp where there is no longer any power to back an officer's commands than the discipline of American and Australian troops. Certainly this was true of Omori. With the threat of the 'glasshouse', the guardroom cell and pay stoppages removed, the troops with the greater sense of comradeship between officers and men stuck together better in prison camp and maintained better discipline.

In Omori we had British and American troops and later over 40 Canadians, while in my last camp there were about 300 Australians. After living closely confined with all of these for many months, I formed definite opinions on how well their discipline stood the test of prison camp. It seemed to me that the Australians came out best, well ahead of the rest. A sound fraternity and harmony between officers and men survived all strains and crises. The officers always addressed the men by their first name while the men usually replied with a 'Sir', but deeper than that, there was more genuine comradeship and friendship between them than in the other cases without any condescension on the one hand and sham respect on the other.

We had one Canadian officer (Wing Commander Len Birchall, RCAF, who patrolling south of Ceylon had radioed the only warning to Colombo of a powerful Japanese fleet approaching and was then forced down; his signal saved Ceylon from complete surprise). But the obedience of 40 or so Canadians in my hut to the commands of a young sergeant major was so noticeable that I seized upon it to help me run the barracks. Sergeant Major Bill Laidlaw of the Winnipeg Grenadiers, short and lightweight as he was, was the best NCO I had under me in prison camp and the only one who could obtain results every day and give more than personal cooperation.

The Americans seemed to grumble and obey, moving rather slowly. The British troops often sounded close to mutiny and their first reaction to a command was to disobey it. They often remained where they were, lying on their blankets; fifteen minutes later they might arrive to do the job or else join you if you set them an example and started it yourself. Once separated from their own unit and their own officers and senior NCOs, British troops assert their independence very strongly and feel that they have to take orders from no one.

It was difficult to command men in POW camp, especially in mixed camps like Omori; there were no sanctions whatsoever with which to enforce orders and the men knew it. They also knew that in a barrack of over 100 men the chances of their being singled out for a beating were slight. For a barrack commander the chances of a beating were extremely high; that was why no officers ever agreed to take over these posts while Watanabe, the most notorious bully in all Japan, was in camp. I was a barrack commander throughout Watanabe's reign in Omori and was beaten up scores of times because I held that post. I was also punched scores of times for doing something wrong personally or for no reason at all. But although I often grumbled about the post, I never asked to be relieved of it because I felt tested by the responsibility, I didn't believe that most of the officers could do it any better and I thought I had something to learn from this task of winning obedience from undisciplined men without the aid of a single sanction.

I decided that the only way to win their cooperation was by becoming a friend. This suited my personality and was not hard to attempt and though I would not pretend to more than partial success I made many friends and managed to maintain uneasy order. The other barrack commanders all seemed to reach the same decision and adopt similar methods—and they were a South African second lieutenant (Rees), two American Air Corps second lieutenants (Tusken and Martindale) and an older British lieutenant (Abbott). It seems fair to say, therefore, that this was the only way to command men in Omori, and although the senior officers often reproached us for being too 'pally' with the men, once these barrack jobs had been harnessed to the most junior officers in the camp, none of the more senior ever volunteered to relieve us of the responsibility.

The reader must have wondered if any protest was ever made against each successive enormity of Japanese behaviour. The answer is yes, although some were very half-hearted weak protests from our Senior American Officer; but the Japanese had only to . start shouting 'Japanese orders must be obeyed!' and threatening to cut our rations and argument ceased. And we had long, long ago ceased mentioning international law.

Surveying his empire one day and thinking how happy he was there, Corporal Watanabe must have decided that we needed a camp song. He ordered songs to be written. About four were attempted and my setting of topical Omori words to a cheerful song used in musicals in Changi won—but Watanabe forgot to give me the prize of twenty cigarettes. Here, with apologies to the composer is 'The Omori Camp Song':

*There's no reason*
*Why this season*
*Shouldn't be a gay one*
*While and after work is done!*

*'Bishi', 'Domi',*
*'Nitsu', 'Nagi',*
*Beach and Camp Employed*
*And one and all and all like one,*
*Just sing:*

*Cheer up and smile,*
*Cheer up and smile,*
*Sing your troubles away.*
*Greet each Omori day*
*In the right way,*
*March on* Tenko *every morning, smiling and gay*
*Smiling and gay,*
*And keep that smile all the day,*
*Everyday*
*'s a* Yasume
*If you wake up and smile*
*Cheer up and smile*
*Cheer up and smile and be gay.*

(In 1943 the word 'gay' had no double meaning with anyone, anywhere.)

Sometimes in the barracks at night as the men sat waiting for *Tenko* and I stood at the door ready to make the report, one or two of my irrepressible 'barons' used to softly sing the song.

'Don't sing that foolish song,' I would say.

'Och, but it's a guid song. I think it's vera clever,' one of them would protest.

'Remind me to recommend you for sergeant, Ward, when we get out.'

Yes, relations between officers and men were on a level, democratic friendly basis that shocked our senior regular officers, but made me sure that I preferred to spend my POW time in a camp with mixed men and officers, which is more of a cross-section of ordinary society, than in a highly rank-conscious all-officers camp. Officers, among themselves, were inclined to be a little more quarrelsome, a little more discontented, a little more *nationalistic* and a little more maddening than the men. The more mixed the society the saner it is. Undoubtedly some of the simplest and most unimaginative men contributed as much to our sanity as the most intellectual. Perhaps they were right, too? They weren't so full of worries and they were pretty good at smiling.

# 23

# New Prisoners and Tojo's Visit

The torrid Tokyo summer with its months of sunshine made life more bearable although brutality and bullying continued to increase. Omori was now known as the 'punishment' or 'disciplinary' camp for Tokyo Area and recalcitrant officers from branch camps were sent to Omori for treatment by Watanabe. Four or five American medical officers came because they had objected to Japanese diagnoses and treatment or had disobeyed orders about medication and operations. Two of them, Doctors Al Weinstein and N. Kaufman, were not allowed to practise their profession, but instead had to wash 30 pieces of clothing each day for Watanabe's inspection. He also had them emptying *benjos*, washing windows and punched then so hard that we almost became accustomed to their black eyes and to Doc Weinstein's graty, throaty voice after he had received a hard punch that damaged his windpipe.

The camp became more and more full; 40 officers and a few men arrived from Ofuna, the navy camp. Many junior officers had to vacate the bunkrooms and I received about 36 officers in my barrack hut. For the next five months I, a lieutenant, was in command of one lieutenant commander, four captains and 31 subalterns, all except for six or seven of whom were senior to me. The officers were more cooperative than many men, but I had trouble getting some of them to do their share in cleaning the place. One man did his full share and was ready to shoulder responsibility in maintaining order. He was Captain 'Sammy' Samson of the US Army, a first-class officer, soon to be placed in command of one of the American barracks. What most of us had to achieve by chummy friendship, Samson could achieve among the Americans by the authoritative tone of his speech and his steely glance. He was one of the best officers I ever met.

Many of these new officers were B-24 (Liberator) pilots and bombardiers shot down in the gigantic struggle which was moving, month by month, north towards Japan. They came from Rabaul, New Guinea and Borneo, Tarawa and Saipan. We now heard that Midway had been an important victory. We also heard, on 7 June, that

D-Day had succeeded in Europe and that the Anglo–American advance in Normandy was progressing well.

Many of these officers had been in the United States as recently as the previous December, so the Americans clustered around them to hear details of life in wartime America, which many had not experienced. But we soon found that we were better informed on the general progress of the war than these men who had been wrapped up in their own squadron and area activities. When we could name the whole Russian utmost line of advance as Polotsk, Minsk, the Pripet marshes and Bessarabia, our new prisoners were telling us that the Russians were in Warsaw. We soon exhausted their war news and asked for details of life in the United States at war.

'Tell us everything. What are they doing? What are they saying? When do they think the war will end?'

'Well, you know there are lots of new airfields and army camps?'

'*We don't know nothin'*, brother. Start again.'

'Well, there are new airfields everywhere, big army camps, long troop trains, busy shipyards, all the world and his brother training as pilots in Texas, girls in uniform...' And places and names would follow.

'What new movies are there?' someone would ask.

'Oh, they made one called *Bataan* with Hedy Lamarr as an army nurse...'

Everyone laughed.

'Imagine that! Hedy Lamarr in Bataan and I never knew it!'

'.. and one called *Wake Island*, where everyone is killed so they call it the Alamo of the Pacific.'

Again laughter.

'I'm from Wake,' announced an unshaven survivor in faded khaki, 'and quite a lot of us got out alive.'

'What are the new tunes?'

'Gosh, let's see. "Pistol packin' Momma", "Brasil!"...'

'Let's hear it. Let's hear it.'

And the newcomer, who is tone deaf, wobbles through it. Silence follows.

'I don't know all the words... oh, there's a new singer. They had a poll and he turned out top favourite.'

'*Above Bing?*' everyone exclaimed, deeply shocked.

'Yeah. Sinatra's his name. Frank Sinatra.'

There was silence. Men looked at each other. There was not a sign of recognition.

'I just can't believe it—more popular than Bing,' one old-timer said, shaking his head.

'Oh, I forgot to tell you about the best movie of the bunch, *Casablanca*. It had a wonderful tune in it. I'll...I'll try to sing it.'

Pained expressions came to our faces as we watched this shameless music-lover prepare to massacre another song. Diffidently he began in the middle:

*'And when two lovers woo,*
*They still say I love you,*
*On this you can rely.*
*The world will always welcome lovers*
*As time goes by.'*

'You mean like this,' Hank Hankin interrupted and proceeded to sing verse and chorus. We all stared at him open-mouthed—Hank, from Bataan, April 1942!

'So that's where you've been going nights,' someone said.

'No,' Hank laughed. 'It's an old song, popular about 1929. I just remember it, that's all.'

But I'm telling you, we watched Hank after that.

Our news service was improving now: the number of Japanese and Koreans repeating war news to us had increased; they reported radio news, showed our men newspapers, sometimes in English and they translated. News scraps were still smuggled in, enabling us to confirm place names in areas fought over. Rome had been liberated, D-Day in Normandy had taken place, but of equal interest to us was the capture of Kwajalein and Eniwetok, important Japanese naval bases in the central Pacific. Probably Truk and Saipan would be next and Saipan was within bombing range of Tokyo. And north of New Guinea, the Americans now held the western end of New Britain and were probing towards the invasion and liberation of the Philippines. We completely approved the American island-hopping strategy: it left entire Japanese garrisons or armies vitually disarmed and impotent on islands bypassed by the American advance. It meant the war would be shorter.

We kept well-informed and our appreciation of the general strategy was stimulated by seeing some of our forecasts later fulfilled. I remember, later, Lieutenant Commander Blinn and I both selected Okinawa as the next target after Luzon and Saipan and as the projected invasion base for Japan.

New prisoners with their information also served to refute pieces of Japanese news which some of us had begun to accept. Thus one of the newly arrived officers was from the aircraft carrier *Saratoga*. When the Japanese asked the name of his ship and he told them, they refused to believe it. Twice already the Japanese Navy had claimed the sinking of the USS *Saratoga*. They slapped him and shouted and even pleaded with him, but he insisted, 'Well, if you want to believe you've sunk her, believe it—but I just flew off her'.

Some of the new aircrew who came in were crippled either by beri-beri or by amputation as in the case of Fred Garrett, a crisp-haired, slow-smiling Army Air Corps officer with a Western drawl. When his B-24 crashed, his foot was almost severed from his leg. The Japanese garrison of Tarawa, the target island, threw Garrett into a prison cell and kicked his leg until he passed into unconsciousness with pain. The first time a sentry did this, Garrett, who happened to have a pair of handcuffs attached to one wrist, swung a blow at the face of the Japanese. The handcuffs whirled round and made it a double blow and the sentry was knocked out. As punishment, the Japanese kept visiting him to kick his broken leg. Finally a Japanese doctor decided to amputate as gangrene had set in. Garrett was laid out on a table and held down by five Japanese while the doctor, without using any anaesthetic, sawed off the leg halfway up the thigh.

In Omori Fred Garrett was an inspiration with his friendly manner and ready smile. As any prisoner who was there will testify, Garrett only had one leg but there was more 'guts' in him than in most men with two. What had we to complain about beside men like this?

'Wado,' said Watanabe one day. 'I want you to make a camp newspaper.'

I said I had no news and no access to any.

'Ah no. Not a newspaper with news, a newspaper with *no* news—only stories and jokes. Many jokes, eh? Make all men laugh.'

I protested and exaggerated the difficulties, but he was insistent; this was his brainwave, it proved him benevolent. He promised paper, pencils and the use of the mimeographing machine. I was unhappy about the whole project because it might lead to my being considered once again for *Bunka*. (They had been around seeking volunteers to broadcast messages to their families.) I found that not one of the men who had escaped *Bunka* and had writing experience was willing to risk a word. So I wrote the entire copy myself, condensing a story from Dickens and another from some other published writer which I would acknowledge ('Not me, Marquis Ikeda, I can't write original stories') and some really pitiful jokes and produced the first issue in two weeks.

I thought of calling it *Oosh!*—the way Watanabe said '*Yoroshi!*—Good!' when he was satisfied with one's explanation for action or inaction. It so often meant no beating this time. Several senior officers deplored my idea; they thought it would send him into a temper by mimicking his manner of speech and keeping Watanabe pacified was everybody's business. But I stuck with it and Watanabe did not see any sly joke at his expense and approved the title.

The newspaper came out once—fifty copies mimeographed. Then, the novelty being over, *Oosh!* died a natural death.

Watanabe's gesture of interest in our welfare may have followed certain foreign criticisms which had been quoted in the Japanese press. A month or two after President Roosevelt and the British Foreign Secretary had publicly denounced the Japanese treatment of prisoners of war in their hands, Omori received an unexpected visitor—General Hideki Tojo, the Prime Minister. Fortunately he had not given the camp authorities notice, otherwise the cleaning up and beating up that would have preceded his visit would have left us all punch-drunk and limp.

We just suddenly saw him walking through the camp; a short man in a grey tweed raglan overcoat with a large shaven head, black-rimmed glasses and a poker face. I was awed by the sight of the war leader of Japan, the man who gave the order to attack Pearl Harbor, to attack Singapore, Hong Kong and the Philippines, the man who cast 90 million Japanese into war, who ordered the invasion of the Dutch East Indies and Burma, Borneo and New Guinea... I stopped and stared. It was difficult to connect this small figure with the billion deeds that stemmed from his decision—invasion, battle, murder, torture, rape, the sinking of ships, the massacre of innocents, cruelty. I stared at him as just another man. I *could not* connect him with my imprisonment at Omori, with the imprisonment of hundreds of thousands of men in camps all over the Far East and Pacific, but he, more than any other single soul was the cause. He had initiated their suffering, starvation, beatings and disease and the deaths of so many of their comrades. It *was* because of him that I was in Omori! And *all* these men here running to and from the bath-house—it was bath night. Some of the men, carrying little khaki towels, were smiling; we all felt our best on bath nights; a week's grime was washed away in the benison of hot water. So some men smiled as they ran back to their huts; three or four even smiled at him! These were the fit, their day's work was over, they were glowing from their weekly bath. It didn't balance out or make proper sense. I felt sure the appearance of these men, lean though they were, must give Tojo a completely false picture of POW conditions. He would probably go back to the cabinet with a totally false impression of our conditions. And he left after seven or eight minutes in our part of the camp, with, I feel, this misleading picture in his mind.

Does anyone who visits a controversial place for eight minutes *want* the truth about that place? Did Tojo? Did Dr Paravicini of the International Red Cross in Seoul?

Tojo's visit did not bring us better food, nor did a visit by Prince Tokugawa, the head of the Japanese Red Cross. Soya beans however were sometimes mixed in with our *gaoliang* and we were glad as they helped to stave off beri-beri; sometimes we had seaweed or squash pumpkin, lily root or sweet potato leaves in our soups and one rather horrible dish was cow's entrails, looking like rubber nail-brushes or slices of garden hose. If what was called a meat soup appeared, we knew that this meant that six or seven pounds of meat had been added to the soup for 600 men.

But unappetising and unpalatable as our food was, the flies seemed to like it. At the height of summer, flies in Omori swarmed about in clouds, settling on blankets, bowls, walls, ceilings, everywhere. It looked as if barrels of sticky raisins had exploded in each hut. Just behind each hut was the pit latrine, with excrement, crawling with maggots, open to the flies and not far away was the cookhouse. The Japanese saw nothing wrong or dangerous in our sanitary arrangements; their only offense against flies was to swat them and never to destroy the grubs or try to prevent the eggs being laid. They seemed not to have heard of the use of lime or of burying food waste and nightsoil deep. Each summer there was a half-hearted fly-swatting campaign and ten semi-invalids would be permanently employed to swat flies in the cookhouse. But this summer, 1944, there was a bigger fly-killing contest.

Each barrack commander was ordered to see that every man had a fly swatter and that men made special efforts to kill flies. These were to be collected and produced for the Japanese medical sergeant's inspection. Watanabe turned it into a competition with the prize of cigarettes for the barrack that killed the most.

The first evening we five barrack commanders appeared at the medical room each with a half-palmful of flies on a scrap of paper. The flies were weighed and the scores set down. 'Not enough,' cried the medical sergeant. 'Must kill more, much more.' Watanabe tightened his lips and snarled 'Double, must *double* tomorrow.' He also said he would inspect fly swatters.

That evening every man in camp searched madly for cardboard, bamboo, string, slivers of wood, anything to improvise a fly swatter, but we were so short of materials to make anything that when Watanabe inspected my barrack that night there were men with swatters made of paper and straw and two men each with a kind of cat-o'-nine-tails—they said they were going to *whip* the flies to death!

By now the spirit of the competition began to infect the men. After all, the prize, Watanabe promised, would be 300 cigarettes. In a 'fight them on the landing grounds' speech, I urged my men to greater efforts. That evening in most barracks the last safe refuge of the flies—the ceiling, was vigorously attacked. Stooping on the upper shelves the men held six-foot bed mats across the gangway space and, holding the two ends, rhythmically beat the mat against the ceiling all the way down the hut. Vast quantities of flies were killed in this way and their greasy remains poured into empty boxes. At the weighing that night my barrack moved smartly into the lead.

The competition was to last ten days and by now rivalry between huts was intense. Men made efforts to bribe the medical orderlies into saving the dead flies from the night before and smuggling them into their barrack for use again the following night. The struggle for dead flies became so intense that the senior POW medical orderly had to bury them at dead of night in order to avoid being seen by unscrupulous competitors. And my barrack's lead was increasing.

Other barracks began to complain that my men were cheating. It was alleged that we were soaking our dead flies in oil so that they would weigh more. This charge, so far as I knew, was quite unfounded. However, once or twice among what appeared to the lay eye as being roughly similar heaps of flies, the one from my barrack was found to weigh more than the others. The other barrack commanders looked at me with mean suspicion, but it was too fatuous to deny—oil was almost worth its weight in *tobacco*! Our lead was running away from the others; it just seemed that they were bad losers.

'Och, they've got more flies in No. 6 Barracks than any of the others.'

'Sure, they have; their flies are fed on sugar.'

'Aye. That probably makes them heavier than ours. Ours don't get much but the old *daikon*.'

'You bet.'

Each night I carried my shiny flies to the sickroom and the Japanese sergeant spread them out on a newspaper to see that there were no chips of wood or fine gravel hidden amongst them as some barracks had attempted, then he would pour them into the scales and solemnly weigh them, writing down the weights achieved. At the end of the competition my barracks led handsomely and Watanabe handed me the cartons containing 250 cigarettes.

I continued to deny that my men had broken any of the rules of the contest for some time until one sidled up to me one day with a leer and said: 'We sairtainly pulled a fast one with them flies and oil, did you no think so, Mr Wade?'

# 24

# A Day Under the Terror

As the summer passed, Watanabe's furies became more and more frequent; sometimes they lasted almost two weeks. The nerves of everyone in camp were torn and raw-edged. The atmosphere was charged with fear. Every move of 'The Bird' (as he was harmlessly called in case he should overhear) was reported immediately in every corner of the camp; every word he spoke and every action he committed was known to each of the 600 men over whom, so he often said, he had complete power of life and death. All power corrupts; absolute power corrupts absolutely, and Watanabe had enjoyed unbridled power over us since the beginning of the year. He lost his temper quicker now, more often now and with more destructive effect; he was a maniac, glorying in the terror he knew he could create in the hearts of the prisoners of war in his charge. There was no need for him to control his most savage impulses for he had often been congratulated by his officers on his most effective iron rule, and they would never fail to turn their backs when they saw him beating up a prisoner. Watanabe was a demon, drunk with power and conceit, who exploded into paroxysms of rage and then vented the full fury of his wrath on defenceless prisoners.

A typical day under 'The Terror' begins with the ringing of a handbell rousing the long rows of dormant figures in the barrack huts. Wearily they drag themselves out of their blankets and dress, fold their blankets and pile them in the approved manner and then slip into wooden clogs and shuffle outside for roll-call.

'Don't forget your gargle cups!' someone shouts, but the habit is so strong that few forget. The difficulty is finding a pair of clogs: once, long ago, the Japanese issued a pair of wooden *geta* to each man in camp, but since then many have been lost and there are never enough to go around. So there is a scramble and some curses, but two minutes later everyone is lined up on the parade ground awaiting the Japanese duty officer. In winter, while waiting a few warming exercises are done, but in summer we just wait.

The duty officer is rarely late and the ceremony is brief: '*Kashira naka!*' ('Eyes centre'), '*Naorei*' ('As you were'). The Japanese officer goes to each squad leader, who gives his total and absentees then shouts, *'Bango!'* ('Number!') and the squad numbers off. *'Jiko roku mei, shushin,'* ('Six men sick'). *'Ichi mei shigoto'* ('One man working'), *'Ijo arimasen'* ('All present or accounted for'). The ceremony ends with another salute to the officer then the order to 'Gargle' is given. Water is poured into each man's cup and we gargle with plain water 'to protect our health'. Once we were provided with a potassium permanganate solution, but now, as with many Japanese habits, the empty form of the ceremony continues after its value has disappeared.

*Tenko* over, we rush back to our barrack hut and change from clogs into boots while the 'dishers-out' are apportioning the *gaoliang* and soup with scrupulous care into white bowls laid out on the narrow serving tables in the centre of the aisle. Several hungry-eyed figures superintend the process and see that the 'solid' in the soup is fairly distributed and that the dishers-out don't steal a mouthful as they serve.

'Okay, any complaints?'

One of the lean and hungry men points out a few bowls he considers have been short-rationed. Minor adjustments are made, then, 'All right, boys, take it away!'

Everyone collects his bowls, white china bowls marked with the Imperial Army star in blue and with the owner's number scratched on the side, and sits down on his bed-space to eat breakfast. Some pour the *gaoliang* into the soup, but most people find it more filling to eat the grain dry. It is much coarser than rice to digest. The 'barons' sprinkle sugar on part of their *gaoliang* and eat it as a dessert. The meal is quickly over. Mess-tins have already been filled with cold *gaoliang* with a few vegetables on top; this is the working ration to be eaten at midday. The workers put their mess-tin into their haversack, throw in a spoon (it is years since anyone had occasion to eat with a knife and fork) and some clothes they plan to wash out at the job. A few white socks to carry home contraband are added and the prisoners' chief weapon for tapping sacks of food, a short piece of bamboo tubing, sharpened at one end, known as a 'shoot' or 'flute' or even 'fiddle and flute'. Armed with one of these, a prisoner can stab it into a sack of sugar and drain off a sockful in a few seconds, then pull it out and leave no visible mark on the sack.

In the bunkrooms the officers would be talking about Watanabe.

'He kept Birchall standing at attention outside till ten-thirty.'

'Well, Fukujima had Carlo and Meado walking round the galley holding on to their ankles for half an hour—some oil for the Jap officers' fried veg was missing. Meado says it will be in our soup today.'

'Good old Meado.'

'I think the Bird should get the duty today.'

'Oh, for God's sake, don't be such a damned pessimist.'

It is nearly six o'clock now, an hour after *Tenko*, and the men are gathering in their work parties on the small parade ground. The Japanese civilian guards, the *fus*, are there, each in his semi-military uniform of olive green and his cloth cap marked with the badge of his commercial company. They each carry a haversack and a wooden sword—a replica of a samurai sword in its scabbard, but all made in one piece of wood. With this they show their rank, 'defend themselves against the prisoners' and, unofficially, administer punishment.

They are a strange assortment of beings: small, spindly, emaciated, many are ex-servicemen, others are victims of Japan's main scourge, tuberculosis, but one or two are by contrast paunchy and pink-cheeked. They all have nicknames which describe their outstanding characteristic: 'The Rat', 'Donald Duck', 'Skeleton', 'Goering', 'Efficiency', 'Shakespeare', 'Sweetie Pie' and so on. They scurry around on spidery, puttee-bound legs and push and prod the taller, long-suffering prisoners into ranks.

'*Bango!*' they shout.

The men count off in Japanese, '*Ichi, ni, san, shi, go, roku...*'

'*Bango!*' they command again. Three or four times this happens; they never get it right first time.

The *fu* notices a lazy worker in his squad. He pulls the big prisoner out of the ranks by his coat and sends him off to the Beach squad, then runs over to the POW labour officer and asks for the lazy one to be struck off his gang and demands a good, strong worker. Joe Mills sends him off to choose someone from among the spares. The *fu* runs his eye over legs, build, muscles. He selects the best of the bunch and drags him back to his squad. '*Bango!*' More numbering.

The Japanese sentries arrive with their rifles, bullet pouches and khaki mess-tins and form up in the middle of the square. The *fus* form up behind them. The Japanese duty officer in his red and white sash arrives and the senior Japanese on parade gives a hoarse shout.

'*Kashira naka!*' ('Eyes centre!').

All heads and eyes click stiffly towards the immaculate olive uniform of the Japanese officer. He salutes easily. 'Working parties ready to leave.' 'Permission to march off.' Soldiers and *fus* double back to their squads and the prisoners curse or chuckle when they see which *heitai* and *fus* have been allotted to their gang. Raucous commands and the squads turn right.

'*Mae su'met!*' ('Quick march!'; 'My cement' the Aussies called it) and the squads march off, heavy-booted, a man here or there joking in Japanese with the *fus*.

Once they are gone there is quiet in the camp. Officers and camp employed are washing their dirty dishes, completing their toilet at the open-air wash-benches or sweeping and tidying their rooms. Watanabe's POW batman or *toban* returns from the NCOs' quarters and reports that the great man seems to be in a quiet mood today. He hasn't asked for his best boots to be polished so he is obviously not going into town today.

The sick drag themselves up the dirt lane between the huts to morning sick parade. A story comes back that one of the Japanese soldiers has reported sick with VD.

A Yank says, 'What do you have to do to get that?'

'Hell knows. He says he got it from something called a woman.'

'Oh, I remember them. Kinda soft, aren't they?'

It is nearly seven o'clock; the gardening officers have their boots on and are snatching the last few minutes before going on parade to read.

'*Maher!*'

Everyone recognises the voice. The Bird is up. Commander Maher, USN, our senior officer, clacks in his clogs up to the office. Someone looks out of the door of my hut and sees Watanabe standing in the camp office, hands in pockets, staring down the lane between the huts. You can see right into the office as the window frames have been removed because it is warm.

'*Kura!*' shouts Watanabe at the top of his voice. Everyone in camp stiffens for several seconds—cooks in the galley, doctors and orderlies bending over the sick, men shaving, men sweeping, sick men sewing pieces of fur. They listen for a few moments and find out as soon as possible who is 'catching it' and why, then they continue with their business, with occasional glances over the shoulder.

'Oh hell!' says the officer who peeped out of the door. 'He saw me.'

'Course, you idiot, why do you have to look. You knew it was him.'

'I just wondered what he was doing.'

'You better go and face it or we'll all get it.'

One of the men entering the hut announces excitedly, 'He's put on his cap and he's coming out the door.'

Just then Colonel Pike shouts 'Gardeners!' and the officers who work on the vegetable gardens run out of their huts to parade facing the office window. They salute Watanabe as they run past him. He pays no attention, he has his eye on the door through which a head poked out to watch him. He storms into the hut with a clatter of clogs.

'*Nanda?*' he shouts. 'Who was spying? Who look out the door?'

The officer who did it is just inside the door, waiting for this inevitable retribution.

'Me, Watanabe *San.*'

'*Bukero*! You spy on me, eh?' and he cracks his fist into the officer's face. The prisoner staggers.

'*Ki-o-tsukei!*' ('Attention!'), Watanabe screams. 'Why you do?'

'I was just looking to see if the gardeners were on parade. I didn't hear the shout and I thought...'

'You thought, you thought...You *lie*! You *spy* on me. That only you do. *Kanero!*' His lips curl as he spews out the last word with contempt; like *bukero* it means 'priest' and the insult is in the fact that priests are celibate and therefore by implication impotent.

I am in line with the gardening officers facing the office window. Colonel Hal Pike of the US Army Air Corps faces us. He is a six foot three burly pilot of about 34 with thinning blond hair, an ex-football player.

'Don't look round,' he says without moving his lips. 'He's out of the hut now, pushing Benjy about.'

We soon hear the clip-clop of Watanabe's clogs as he approaches. Every prisoner in Omori can distinguish between the sound of Watanabe's clogs and that of anyone else's. He is a lazy walker; he drags his clogs, he is slovenly yet confident. Japanese clogs reveal character. He stands silent behind us and watches us from the rear. One officer grows nervous and moves his head slightly to try to see the Bird. Watanabe sneers with amusement, slaps him on the ear and then comes to the front of the squad.

Pike shouts 'Keirei!' We all salute and study Watanabe's expression.

He salutes and, keeping his hand at his cap, glances at each face down the line. We notice the wet and slightly withdrawn lower lip and the glinting eyes. Yes, he's in a dangerous mood again. He lowers his hand at last. We lower ours at a command.

'This morning there is one field to hoe, one to weed and some cabbage to pick,' Hal Pike explains the program.

'Oosh,' says Watanabe. 'No! Empty benjo and dig air raid shelter. Understand?'

'Yes, Watanabe San.'

More salutes and we march off smartly with the Bird's eyes on each of us as he tries to detect the slightest sign of refractoriness or impatience. If he sees anything but the blankest facial expression he calls out the man's name and punches him for having 'a bad attitude' and then leaves him standing at attention for two or three hours. We breathe a sigh of relief as we turn the corner of the office and pass out of his sight.

As we pass the 'front office' we see the windows wide open to the sunshine and the prettiest Japanese typist sitting at her machine facing the compound. Every one of us is looking at her—the prettiest girl we have seen in Tokyo, perhaps the prettiest we have seen in two or three years. She is round-eyed and pink-cheeked and her black hair is, of course, arranged in Western style. She wears a coloured blouse and is probably eighteen. She looks up and smiles at us. We all grin back.

We collect our tools: spades to dig the trenches and buckets, poles and dippers to empty the latrines. The sun is pouring down hot, beneficial rays and we take off our shirts and work naked except for brief shorts and shoes. I am on benjo dipping. Well. I don't mind; it's easy work. We all choose our partners—someone about the same height so that the pole won't slope and the bucket slip down towards you, and no one with a jaunty, bouncing step that sets the bucket rocking and splashing.

Bob Tusken, a good-looking young pilot from Wisconsin, comes with me. I like to talk with other people about less frustrating subjects, but today I'll just talk with Bob about women. In midsummer a prisoner of war's fancy tardily turns to thoughts of love.

Each time we pass the typist's window, I smile at her and perhaps Bob does too—I can't see his face. She smiles back, every time.

'Wado, I think you're doing pretty well with that gal,' says Bob.

'I think so, you know. All I need is an opportunity.'

But it never came. Once I handed her a couple of flowers I had picked and asked her her name. It was Yukiko—'Snow Child'— and another time I met her in the corridor behind Watanabe's office. 'Let me kiss you,' I reeled off my long-prepared Japanese sentence. She blushed and hid her face, then padded back to her own office with a backward smile. No, Yukiko was not quite my speed.

As we walk through the camp with our tub suspended between us, remembering to salute the blank face of the office window, we notice two officers standing at attention in different parts of the camp and immediately sense the tension in the air. We ask one of the men on *yasume* what has been happening.

'He caught Mac reading and Doc Berry sunbathing. He's in the leather shop now.'

Reading, sunbathing, writing notes, playing patience, doing nothing, doing almost anything except working on *benjos* or polishing boots was a crime. Suddenly we hear distant shouts of '*Keirei!*' repeated every few moments. The convalescent sick in the leather workshop are being practised in saluting. Then we hear a nearer cry of '*Keirei!*' followed by another still nearer. From these shouts we can plot Watanabe's course across the camp; he is between Six and Four barracks now. '*Keirei!*' shouts someone close behind us.

'*Keirei!*' shout Tusken and I with apparently fanatical zeal and salute with our free arm. He won't risk a quarrel with us because of our bucket; he doesn't like coming too near.

He acknowledges our salute and slip-slaps past in his clogs with his eyes fiery and one corner of his mouth compressed with anger and impatience.

'Oh, brother, there's trouble coming from him today,' says Bob with conviction.

When we pass through the front gate once more and are emptying the contents of our buckets into a furrow between two rows of sweet potatoes, we report all the developments to the other gardening officers, digging and covering. On our way in, we report to the officers squaring the crumbling trenches inside the camp, but they know it already and can add the news of the last five minutes: Watanabe hit one of the sick men limping out of the sickroom for not saluting smartly and cut his knuckles on the man's teeth.

'He's in the MI room now getting his hand dressed.'

'Bastard! I hope he gets blood poisoning.'

'Not a chance,' drawls one of the Americans too sensibly; we like our wishful thinking.

'I still think we ought to put ground glass in his food,' says a British officer.

'Hell no,' replies an American. 'They'd detect that. All the doctors have to do is to shoot him full of dysentery and diphtheria germs. That would finish him off, but they won't do it.'

There is a moment of thoughtful silence.

'Getting near chow time,' says a Yank.

'What's for lunch?' I ask.

'Cow guts.'

'Oh, good...'

'Oh, shut up!'

'Well, it's better than *daikon*.'

'Tell us some other time, bud,' says Bob Tusken. 'Here comes Hal.'

We put away our spades, bucket and poles and form up, right turn and march to the camp office. Colonel Pike obtains permission to dismiss just as the cooks shout 'Come and get it', and we disperse to our bunkrooms for lunch; it is about a quarter to twelve. The lame soldier, whom three of us pay five cigarettes a month for washing our dishes every day, carries in our little wooden buckets, one of *gaoliang* and one of gut soup; then a kettle of green tea. The meal is carefully divided and we eat. I keep half my 'rice' for a dessert; I have a tangerine peel and a little sugar, so I dice the peel, add two spoonfuls of sugar, moisten it and enjoy a wonderful orange pudding.

One of the men pokes his head in the door and says, 'The Bird's got the band.' This means the duty NCO's armband.

'Oh, God!' we exclaim.

'He's working up into a beautiful temper and he's got the duty as well,' says Hank Hankin, my room-mate.

I hurry with my orange pudding in case he should come by. Sugar is contraband. We all cast our eyes over our clothes on the shelf to see that everything is tidy. Of course it is; it always is; it has to be.

After the meal, we fill up with cup after cup of hot, milkless, sugarless tea. We should now have an hour's rest, but we must never appear idle. We bring out a pair of shorts or socks and a threaded needle, ready to pretend to be doing minor repairs if Watanabe comes in, but what we really get on with is a novel.

There is silence as everyone reads.

A nervous-looking officer from another bunkroom opens the door.

'Where is he? Have you seen him?' he whispers.

'Oh, for God's sake stop worrying. Get hold of yourself. We don't know.'

'I...heard he was around, that's all.' He closes the door gently. We curse under our breath.

'Boy, I wish the men would bring in some real news today,' says Vic Howard, my other room-mate. He's short, neat, foxy.

'I wish the Bird would get leave to go home to Kobe,' I say. 'I'm sure his mother is dying to see him again.'

'Yes, that would be *oosh*. Remember the time he took a party to Zentsuji? Four wonderful, glorious days!'

'Yeah, I remember it. I also remember that he went on a tear for a week after he got back. There were cracked jaws and broken eardrums everywhere..' Hank Hankin begins to sing softly:

> *Take me back to my little grass shack*
> *In Zentsuji.*

*That's where I want to be,*
*Beside the Inland Sea.'*

'I don't think that Zentsuji would be all that great for lieutenants,' I say. 'They'd have us cleaning *benjos.*' I also remembered Katyn Forest, where 14 000 Polish officers were executed. If you concentrate officers in one place, you can also easily eliminate them all in that place.

The sudden shout of '*Keirei!*' shocks us back to Omori. We slip our books under our blankets and pick up our 'alibis'. I look out of the bunkroom door.

'It's only a sentry.'

In the barrack room I can see a young two-star *heitai*, his bayonetted rifle at his side, bowing in response to the bows of prisoners on holiday. The soldier's face looks blank, but serious. I know that he has been taught to believe that at this moment he is the main pillar of the Japanese Empire as he bows on behalf of the Emperor to these respectful inferiors.

The private second-class walks slowly through the barracks looking at the vari-coloured kits lined up on the shelves above the sleeping platforms. Some of the British troops have folded their jackets with the brass buttons, polished with toothpowder, gleaming in a neat horizontal line. Pure bullshit; camouflage that bluffs inspecting officers so that they do not look at the sugar, 'flutes', skeleton keys, tiny war-maps hidden behind.

Soon the cry 'Gardeners' rings out once more and we double out as if to a fire and within ten seconds are all lined up in two ranks outside the camp office window. Watanabe, sitting at his desk, has witnessed the whole insane charge to get on parade. He calls out the name of the last officer to arrive and says, 'Why you late?'

There is no answer to this. The man wasn't late; somebody has to be last to arrive.

'I'm sorry, Watanabe *San.*'

Pronouncing his words slowly and venomously, Watanabe says, 'Be *careful*. If I see you have bad attitude, I will punish. I have the power *daro*. From today I will watch.'

For the next two days that officer makes sure he is not last on parade nor shows any sign of laziness and so someone else receives the warnings or the blows.

We notice that Watanabe is wearing the red and white armband of the duty NCO and that there is a piece of plaster on his right fist—not enough to prevent him using it. We march off and when we approach the front gate, we notice that the latest American officer prisoner, who is being kept in solitary confinement until his news is at least two months out of date, is taking his exercise. In floppy, fur-lined flying boots and accompanied by a Japanese private he is walking around the yard in a small circle. On the back of his leather flying jacket is the red and blue Chinese Nationalist flag with the American star as well as the Chinese sun in white on blue: a 'Flying Tiger' from China. We grin at him and he winks back.

Halfway through the afternoon, Watanabe comes clattering out to the garden in his clogs. He passes some orders to 'Pike-u' and soon we are putting away our implements and parading outside the front office with firebuckets full of water and rags to wash the office windows. This, like repairing the sea wall or building a pig-sty comes under the general heading of gardening. As we wash, we strain our eyes hoping to read an English headline on a newspaper inside the offices, but there are none. So we just give the Japanese typists wicked looks and they all scamper off to the powder room to chatter and to giggle. Whatever the Japanese do, they can't stop us looking at the women exactly as we please.

Five o'clock arrives at last. It's been a long day gardening. We parade outside the office and ask Watanabe's permission to dismiss. He inspects the washed windows first, then returns and says we must pick ripe cabbages first before we fall out. As we march off to do this job, the first working party arrives back in camp. Dirty, coal-stained and ragged, they come swinging into camp in good spirit, their tanned faces smiling and their boots crunching the sandy gravel with a rhythmical tread. Smiles, nods, winks pass between us as we wait to pass through the gate.

'I hope they've got some news,' one or two people say.

It doesn't take us long to pick two sacks of cabbages so we are soon inside the walls once more, showing them to Watanabe. He says *'Oosh'* and the meagre cabbages are handed over to the cooks.

As soon as we are dismissed we make for the men who are most reliable in reporting news in the parties already back in camp. We find one, a stocky Royal Navy petty officer, eating real jam on real biscuits. Between mouthfuls he gives us the news. There is still fighting around Caen and Brest; the Russians are still advancing and have captured Brest Litovsk, and the Japanese claim there is still fighting on Saipan. We think Saipan's in the bag already. Most of us think the European war will be over by December or January and that Japan will probably make peace a few months after that. General Tojo is already out of office and the moderates are gaining power. There is more and more whispered talk of peace among the Japanese and the whole Japanese war machine is creaking. There are practically no merchant ships left to supply the forces in the south and their troops in New Guinea, New Britain and Burma have been living off the land for a year or more. Low physical grades of recruits are being called up and there is much evidence in industry and communications of improvisation. The news is cheering. One more winter, that's all.

I return to my bunkroom and clean and brush my boots—Watanabe is always hot on boots. The Mitsubishi 'barons' arrive late and there is trouble. The *hancho* reports that eight men were caught stealing sugar and that one man was caught taking a padlocked metal door off its hinges. Watanabe charges out of the office and roars at the 'barons', then goes down the line swinging a resounding blow at each man in turn. They come in rubbing their jaws.

'What happened today, Quinn?' I ask a quiet-spoken private from Edinburgh.

'Och, we all got caught—couldna get away wi' it at a'. It's becoming harder evera day. I think I'll transfair to the Domi.'

But he doesn't. The 'barons' always find a way. By unhingeing doors, climbing slippery chutes, entering skylights and other almost superhuman dodges, they continue to bring in the sugar and to be the capitalists of Omori.

Supper arrives and everything is forgotten as we make the most of a short and unsatisfactory meal. We hear that the uncle of one of the *fus*, an old retired petty officer, has been recalled by the navy. He is 59 years old. Once, our American friends told us, Japanese warships used to steam straight past Japanese survivors swimming in the water, making no attempt to save them. Now in 1944, we receive indications that the Japanese Navy is desperately short not only of ships but also of trained men.

After supper I wander into the barrack and warn the men that the Bird has the duty and will probably inspect boots. They can't stand a lecture on the subject so I simply announce it once. I hope that one of the 'barons' will offer me a cup of sweet tea, but this doesn't turn out to be one of those rare days. I talk with an ex-waiter about Soho and then the news comes in that Watanabe is in a bunkroom in No. 3 barracks and that the officers inside are standing to attention while the Bird looks wild. Before we can discover what they have done or not done, we hear the shout, '*Shokos* outside! All officers on parade!'

There is no hesitation; all officers pour out of their huts and race for the office. We line up in fours facing the office window. One American officer is standing by the office door facing us. Someone whispers one word in our ranks, 'Blankets.'

Watanabe throws open the office door and stalks out in his slipshod but purposeful manner. We can't see his face clearly but his voice will tell us all.

'*Keirei*,' shouts the senior officer and we all salute.

The Corporal salutes, then in an enraged howl, 'All.. officers... listen.' His voice is thick with rage; I can imagine the vein standing out on the side of his neck.

'Hinson break Japanese order. Hinson cut Japanese blanket to make boots.' So that's what it was about. 'You.. you cannot break Japanese order. If you do, I will punish. I will punish bery strongly. All blankets belong to Japanese Army. You cannot cut property of Japanese Army!'

He was strangling with rage; Hinson was guilty of sacrilege.

'Hinson!' he shouts. Sedgie Hinson, a tow-headed, boyish artillery captain with a turned up nose and a deep Mississippi accent, doubles from the door to Watanabe, halts close to him and throws up his arm in salute. Watanabe jerks back his head as if he had expected a blow.

'Ah, you want to fight?'

'No, Watanabe *San*, Ah was just salu...'

'*So-o-o*, you want to fight! You want to fight me, eh? Good! All right, we will fight. You and me. American and Japanese soljer.'

Watanabe unbuckles his belt and sword and belt clatter to the ground. He throws his cap after them. This is an old favourite routine of his; we know every word of it. 'Now,' he cries , 'I am not Corporal Watanabe, I am ordinary Japanese. You will see how Japanese solja can fight. Come we fight. Come! See if American solja as brave as Japanese.'

'Ah don't want to fight, Watanabe *San*.'

'Hah! You don't want to fight?'

'No.'

His voice rises once more to a scream, 'Then you must *obey Japanese order*! If you *will*, you can *do*!'

For a long minute he stands and glares at Hinson, while we all stand by as rigid and motionless as a row of bottles. Then he turns and picks up his cap and belt and puts them on. When he speaks again his voice is somewhat quieter.

'Officers must *not cut* Japanese blankets. If I find, I will punish.'

He stares at us for several moments. '*Oosh*,' he grunts and clatters off into the Office.

'*Keirei*!' shouts the senior officer. We hold the salute till Watanabe has quite disappeared, then we dismiss to our huts.

'Phew, that wasn't so bad,' say one or two officers, smiling with relief, but we all realise that we had better hide all blanket boots even if they are obviously made from civilian blankets. One more crime has been added to the ever-lengthening unwritten list.

'What happened?' some of the men ask.

'Nothing,' we reply. 'No one hurt. Hinson standing to attention.'

We return to reading or tea drinking. Twenty minutes later, the sliding door of our bunkroom is hurled open with a bang and a grim, martial Watanabe in polished boots and gaiters steps into the room. We had just heard he was coming, but it is always a shock when he slams open that door because its panes are of frosted glass and we can't see through it. Our stomachs turn over with that involuntary clench of fear. We leap up, shouting '*Keirei*' and bow. He salutes. He is fuming like a volcano about to erupt.

'Officers have bery bad attitude,' he commences. '*Bery lazy*! What you do today?'

We each tell him of our sewing buttons and repairing torn clothes. I throw in some barrack duties as well. He grunts and looks at our possessions. Suddenly he steps up on to the sleeping platform in his boots and studies our kit neatly piled on the shelf. We are anxious as he does this as we each have one or two extra garments which we don't want to lose. I also have a Japanese dictionary buried under my clothes which I would rather he didn't find. He turns and looks at the walls of the room. We are all praying that he won't discover our secret cupboard, which lies behind a movable panel. He looks straight at it and hesitates. Our hearts are in our mouths. Surely his eyesight isn't sharp enough to pick out the faint fingermarks and scratches! Then he unhooks a US

Army waterbottle that is hanging on a nail high on the wall. He unscrews the cap, lifts it towards his face, then shakes it instead. There is some liquid in the bottom.

'Water?' he asks and hands it to Vic Howard, a short American flier who is reaching for it.

'I'll empty it,' says Howard eagerly and takes the bottle.

'*Nani?*' Watanabe squeaks. '*What?*'

'I said I'd empty it.'

*Smack*! Watanabe lands a blow square in Howard's throat. Vic staggers back.

'*Bukero*! You have bad attitude. *Cheeky*! *Understand? Cheeky.*'

'Yes, Watanabe *San.*'

'Take care,' he warns. 'Japanese orders *bery strict*. I am *bery strict man*. I have my duty. You *must obey.*' He turns on his heel; and leaves the room.

Vic swears. 'What the hell was that for?'

'You didn't stick in enough Watanabe *Sans,*' I say.

'Son of a... I'd love to fight that bastard. I'd give two years of life to fight him *now.*' We all feel like that, but we know what would happen if we struck back. There is an Omori prisoner named 'Martha' Rae in gaol now for striking back at a railway foreman. A big, quiet Scot who was deliberately provoked into striking back and he'd been sentenced to two years.

'Anyway,' Vic Howard adds, 'he didn't find the alky.'

'Alcohol?'

'Yes, there's half a cup in this canteen. I thought I'd moved it all but I must have forgotten. I'm gonna drink it right now.'

We laugh with relief and Vic gives us each a sip.

It is fifteen minutes to evening roll-call, the chief parade and inspection of the day. The three *tobans* for the day sweep the earth floor of the barrack, empty ash-boxes and fill kettles for gargling. At five minutes to roll-call a bell is rung and we are supposed to take up our positions and not move or talk till *Tenko* is over about 35 minutes later. Watanabe usually makes his private inspection of each barrack shortly before the Japanese duty officer, but today he walks in even before the five minute bell.

As he enters the barrack room there is a tremendous shout of '*Keirei!*' by the men who first catch sight of him. Everyone in the hut spins round to face the door and bows—men standing, men sitting in circles on the bed-spaces, men kneeling on the upper decks; about 130 men bow to the corporal. The roar of conversation ends abruptly. Every man holds his pose while the Japanese corporal salutes and slowly passes his eyes over 130 statuesque figures. If he sees a muscle moving or someone peeping at him from below their brows, he rushes at the man like a demon and slaps or punches.

'Position for *Tenko*,' he roars and men scramble to collect their bowls, do up jacket buttons and then sit or kneel in position in two long rows on either side of the aisle. Visitors from other barracks slip out of the door, saluting the corporal as they go. The front rank on each side sits on the edge of the platform, hands resting on their thighs, and the rear rank kneel to attention behind.

'*Oosh*,' says Watanabe. 'Show me your gargle cup-u.'

A hundred and twenty men pick up 120 cups and hold them up. No one is without.

'*Oosh*,' says Watanabe and strides out of the hut, followed by shouts and salutes.

The officers who live in the bunkrooms are lined up in the corridor just outside their rooms and they kick their heels waiting. 'The Marionette has the duty,' someone says.

The Marionette is a short, smiling Japanese pay corps officer from the reserve, whose jerky movements have won him this nickname. He is mild and unimportant. Watanabe takes no notice of him at any time and when they are on duty together it is the corporal who is in virtual command, giving orders, making his own inspections and dispensing punishment, while the doll of an officer stands and waits like a puppet whose strings have been dropped.

In the distance we hear Japanese soldiers repeating the *Reihai*, homage to the Emperor and intoning their duty: (1) loyalty and fidelity, (2) honour and politeness, (3) courage and bravery, (4) truthfulness and good faith, (5) frugality and simplicity. They face towards the Imperial Palace and bow. Once or twice I thought, we don't need that daily, but perhaps in Malaya we needed just a touch of that. We had little spiritual motivation.

I am wondering what sort of things Watanabe is inspecting tonight, when Petty Officer 'Corny' Cahalane of the Royal Navy, a great big, boxing Irishman with an open red face and a voice like a siren, darts to each barrack door with the warning while the Japanese are inside another hut.

'Bharrack commander,' he calls to me. 'He's in the divil of a mood. He's blitzing brooms, foire buckets and cut blankets and you're supposed to have two *tobans* detailed to clane everyone's boots...'

'What's that?'

'Two boot *tobans*, who're supposed to have cleaned all the boots in the barracks. Wroite their names on the bhoard, you know.'

He is gone and I hasten to warn my barrack. I must check my allotment of brooms...

'Pay attention, men. The Bird has thought up a new one. From now on there are two *tobans* on duty each night who are supposed to clean everyone in the hut's boots. I know it can't be done. All you have to do is clean your own boots as you do now, but these two are supposed to be responsible and if you forget they'll be in trouble, so don't fail them.'

While the men groan at this new stupidity, which everyone knows will provide Watanabe with many excuses for punishment in the future, I ask the private who keeps the roster of the night picket duties for the top two names on his list. It takes him time to find them and I can hear the shouts as the Japanese reach the next barrack, but finally he tells me.

'Okay, Marable and Lewis, you're the *tobans* for tonight. You've cleaned everybody's boots.' I turn to my clerical assistant and tell him to write the two names on the picket list and also add a couple of names to yesterday's list, kept on the clip board for reference.

'Who shall I put down?' he asks maddeningly.

'Anybody, it doesn't matter. Work off the roster in the future but put any two names now.'

Next I ask the men to hold up the barrack brooms; I am pretty sure I'm two short. Seven months ago the Nips issued five bamboo brooms to each barrack but, of course, half of them are worn out or lost now. The brooms are produced—three of them, each with only a dozen twigs left in the head.

'I've got a bit of bamboo, sir,' says one man. 'We can make one.'

'Oh, good, make it.'

And while the Japanese are inspecting the last barrack before ours a couple of my sturdies are manufacturing an extra broom, using two twigs extracted from each of the old brooms. They tie up the last string when Corporal Watanabe, in belt and sword, with his chin thrust out like Mussolini, stamps into the hut, shouting *'Tenko!'*

*'Keirei!'* the US lieutenant commander shouts and bows.

The Marionette enters, his head twitching, and salutes. The reports in Japanese are made to the duty officer by section leaders while Watanabe strides about the barrack looking for men not staring straight to their front. Suddenly Watanabe shouts at a man for moving his eyes; no one else moves and the recitation to the officer continues, while we are all thinking of Watanabe. When the reports are completed, the ceremony so far as the duty officer is concerned is over, but for Watanabe it is just the beginning.

'Barrack commander!' he calls.

*'Hai,'* I shout and approach a little nearer.

'How many fi-ya bucketsu?'

'Six, Watanabe *San.'*

He shouts to the sentry with bayonetted rifle who accompanies the parade to count them. The soldier reports that there are six.

'How many men cut blankets?' he addresses the barrack as a whole.

There is complete silence.

*'Answer* me, *hai* or no, which men cut blankets?'

'NO, WATANABE *SAN,'* the men roar in unison.

*'Oosh.'* He points to two men in different parts of the barrack. 'Show me.'

The men dodge out of the ranks to their sleeping spaces and unfold their blankets, holding them high to show that no edges have been cut.

*'Oosh,'* Watanabe grunts and turns to me. I wonder if he is going to check brooms. The Marionette evidently thinks it is all over because he starts to walk out, but soon stops short.

'Wado, who are Numbah Six Barrack boot *tobans?'*

I name the two men. Watanabe asks them if they have polished all the boots in the barrack. 'Yes,' they reply, eyes steady. Watanabe then orders each man in the barrack to hold up his boots for inspection and when they do so, he walks up and down the aisle inspecting them.

'Wado, where you write name of *tobans*?'

'Yes, here.' And I show him the picket list with the two additional names added at the bottom.

'Everyday like this?' he asks.

'Yes, Watanabe *San*.'

He turns back the page and I pray that the two men have been warned. There seems to be another page attached to the board underneath this one...It will have *no names*, I.... He drops the board and spinning round cracks a stunning fist into my face. I stagger back and sit on the laps of the men sitting watching. As I rise he lands two more punches, left, right, on my head. I am too dizzy to think, my face burns with heat and I feel a bruise on the back of my head where it bounced against a pillar.

'*Kiotsuke!*' he screams. As I straighten up, a burning rage floods up inside of me. It would be easy to fight back now; it is difficult to hold oneself, but I want to go on living...

The next blow I watch all the way; from near his right trouser pocket I see his fist swing up to the side of my jaw and it rocks me.

'Come!' he shouts and I follow him out of the barracks, weak in the knees and thin and palpitating in the stomach and not seeing and hearing everything.

I wait in the dark, shivering from cold and apprehension while roll-call is completed. Then when the dismiss is shouted, the Japanese officer hurries away and Watanabe marches past me.

'Come,' he snaps.

We go through the camp office past Hinson still standing at attention and enter the NCOs' quarters and his room. I close the door and stand with my back to it, while he takes off his belt and sword, making petulant whining noises at me all the time. I notice that he has a Western-style bed. He picks up a *kendo* sword—a four-foot, two-handed weapon made of strips of bamboo tightly bound together and used for practising sword fighting in the Samurai fashion.

He whirls it above his head with both arms outstretched and cracks it down on the top of my skull. Then he swings it like a baseball bat against the left side of my head, then the right. My ears are ringing and my cheeks stinging. He is not tall enough to exert the maximum force so he jumps onto his bed, plants his feet firmly apart and towers over me. He reverses the sword and hits me instead with the solid wooden handle, this side, that side, left, right, beating, crashing, smashing it down on my head while he roars and curses me and I feel numb in the head and dizzy and aching and everything is black and red. He goes on and on—Japanese never know when to stop—and his temper is still far beyond control. His face is inflamed with fury and brutality while I hunch my head into my shoulders and raise my arms to ward off the blows.

'*Kiotsuke!*' he screams and I have to straighten up again. About 36 times he hits me with all his strength and at the end of it I am reeling. No helmet or bamboo armour for me as in real *kendo* fighting, I'm bareheaded. He stands panting, a giant silhouette of doom.

'You *lie*! You *lie!* You don't obey my order!'

He pants for a few moments, his lips curling with anger.

'*Kanero*! *Bukero!*' and a string of furious, complaining Japanese words follow. With an oath he throws down his wooden sword and draws his steel one from its scabbard. He advances towards me, the steel flashing light. He holds the point against my throat, and whispers threateningly, 'If you lie, if you break Japanese order, *I will kill*'. His eyes are blazing.

I have tamped myself deep into the corner of the room to evade his blows, but I manage to contract my neck even further at the touch of the point of steel.

'Yes, I understand,' I mutter.

He lowers the shining sword and runs it back into its scabbard.

'You are... *bad*. Why you lie? When I say "everyday like this?" you say "Yes!" Why you lie?'

I can hardly think in my stupor. What can I say? That he is always forcing those of us in authority into positions where, if we tell the truth he beats us for breaking some *imagined* order, and if we lie we are beaten if we are found out—but the chances are even that we will get away with it. It is no longer a question of simple right or wrong; it is right to escape punishment, it is wrong to be punished, just as it is right to live and wrong to die, right to be well and wrong to be ill. To a captive, survival is right. Survival is the great truth whatever the means, and a lie is no crime.

'I... try to obey all your orders,' I murmur.

'*Nani*? But you do *not* obey! You lie. You lie, eh?'

'Yes.'

'If you lie, I punish. I hate lies. Do not lie to me. I can tell when a prisoner lies because of my mind. I am not foolish.'

'No, Watanabe *San*.'

'One month... one month I gave this order and you disobey me. All right, Wado, if you disobey me, we will see who will win.' And here he patted his sword, lying on the bed.

'No, I obey.'

He grunted, '*Oosh*. Go.'

I walk out into the night and back to my barrack. My ears are singing, my face is battered and aching and my jaw clicks each time I move it. Lie and be punished, tell the truth and be punished; as the Americans say, 'You can't win'. My mind keeps going back and reliving the last half hour and until I fall asleep I see that towering figure on the bed brandishing a long sword in two hands with a face distorted like the great statues of warrior guardians in a Chinese temple.

I can feel my cheeks beginning to swell and my head is so tender I know there will be bumps tomorrow, but there is no blood showing and the mirror reveals no black eyes so the rest of the camp will probably think that my punishment could not have been very severe. I sigh; no one is interested in the details of your beating-up. I make my bed and crawl in before Lights Out and pray that Watanabe won't visit us in the night. As I drop off to sleep, I think: He forgot to check brooms; there'll be trouble about them one day.

# 25

# B-29

Except for the beating up with the *kendo* stick, that 'day under the terror' could have been any day in Omori during the year 1944. I was slapped or punched about 350 times altogether, but the *kendo* stick working-over happened only once. To me, standing at attention for four or five hours without an overcoat in winter was as bad as a short beating. I really feared catching pneumonia, but I think because we were *always* cold in winter and the barracks had no heating that we ran little risk of sudden transfers from a higher to a lower temperature.

In my first winter in Omori, one of the British troops from Hong Kong, a congenital kleptomaniac, was caught stealing a Japanese officer's silk shirt. We knew his punishment would be severe because he had been found *wearing* the shirt and that added insult to larceny, nevertheless we were shocked when the Japanese camp commandant ordered him to be tied to a tree in the open for three days and nights. For some reason this man, Gunner Mansfield, was clad only in pyjamas. For three days and three nights in the bitterest mid-winter, he was tied to the tree. Each day when the working parties marched out they expected to see him frozen stiff and dead, but there he would be, slumped in his ropes, alive; and each evening when they returned, there he would be, gazing through his glasses with a faraway stare, apparently not giving his plight a moment's thought. I think that was why he survived: he simply did not feel any fear for his health.

The Japanese thought him mad and the best that we could call him was eccentric. He had a solemn look and staring eyes. *Five* times he stole Red Cross parcels from the padlocked Japanese storerooms. Once he stole two crates, each containing four 9-pound parcels, climbed two fences, passed through the Italian compound and then buried the cans under his hut. When the theft was discovered, the whole camp was searched and prisoners as well as the Japanese scrabbled in the dusty gravel around the huts to find the buried treasure. A dozen empty cans were found and slightly more full ones.

The Japanese were exasperated; they locked him in the guardhouse cell, a cubicle with wooden walls, no windows or electric light and a door of stout wooden bars. It happened that some of the large consignment of Red Cross packages in the camp at that time were stored in the guardhouse under the noses of seven Japanese sentries, day and night. With a dexterity which even the accomplished pilferers of Omori recognised as the work of a true genius, this prisoner stole *sixteen* more Red Cross parcels while confined to this cell. He consumed the contents, hid every tin or cardboard container and finally went to civil prison without leaving any clues. When the time came for another distribution and the theft was discovered, the Japanese were enraged. These parcels had been packed in outer cardboard crates and bound with steel hoops, yet not one tell-tale wrapping had been found. Later prisoners confined to the cell found one clue. At floor level near one corner were the words: 'Food, help yourself, lift here', and inside the wall were the contents of about three parcels plus instructions on how to dispose of empty cans in another secret cupboard.

A year later this prisoner returned from gaol and soon after was caught once again—stealing parcels.

The first time this man stole Red Cross parcels, most prisoners in Omori were indignant; they considered that he was stealing from them. But later they realised that these losses made no difference to the meagre number of packages issued to us, because the Japanese were taking a very large share for themselves. We could see them throwing away unmistakeable wrappers, carrying bowls of bulk cocoa and sugar between huts or even trying to wash clothes with cakes of American cheese. We knew they made the senior officer sign for more parcels than we received in order to cover their tracks and once, we knew, Watanabe took 48 parcels for his own use.

Forty-eight parcels was four times the number I received in 43 months as a POW and infinitely more than some prisoners in Thailand and Burma ever got.

One sunny day in November 1944, at exactly noon, we looked up from our 'farming' and saw a four-engined, graceful silver plane flying high overhead, leaving long vapour trails behind her.

'B-29!' breathed one of the American pilots.

'One of *ours*?' we gasped. 'A Flying Fortress?'

'No, a Superfort, a B-29. See the tail?'

The Japanese too were staring.

The plane circled over Tokyo and was on its way out over the bay before the first siren sounded. There had been one raid on Tokyo before this, on 18 April 1942 when the Doolittle raid bombed the capital, lost some planes and flew on to Free China. The survivors of the planes shot down had been thrown into prison and later three were executed. There had been a terrific outcry at the time. The Japanese had truly believed that their capital was immune from foreign attack and yet they and above all the Emperor had been grievously and intolerably insulted by this attack. It had been a high point in anti-American hatred, and we wondered how they would react now.

Some guns opened fire, but the silver giant flew safely away to the east.

The excitement this event caused is hard to imagine outside prison camp walls. This was the first visible evidence most prisoners in Tokyo had seen of the mighty forces pressing powerfully to their rescue and to victory. Many had begun to believe the pessimists' estimate of 'Golden Gate in '48' as the date of final victory. Now here was proof to substantiate the arguments of the optimists and show that B-29s could fly the 1300-mile journey from Saipan and return safely. (We all knew it was from Saipan, captured four months earlier, that these planes came. Most Japanese had no idea where they had come from.)

More reconnaissance flights by two or three Superfortresses followed and the air-raid sirens would sound only a minute before the planes circled the capital, the guns would throw up little puffs of white smoke far below the bombers, which then majestically sailed out to sea.

The camp staff tried to pretend nothing important had happened, but they sometimes looked discomfited or embarrassed. The Japanese workers at the docks and railway yards were impressed by the calm way these American bombers flew over the heart of their Empire and were shocked at the feeble Japanese opposition.

'*Ima takusan Beikoku-no hikoki kuru-daro-ka*?' ('Now many American aeroplanes will come?') they asked nervously and our men promised, '*Thousands.*'

Within days 'B *ni-ju-ku*', B-29, was on the lips of every Japanese in Tokyo; twenty-nine became an ominous number, full of significance and danger. At roll-calls the prisoner who shouted *ni-ju-ku* (29) would shout it louder than his neighbours calling out *ni-ju-hachi* (28) and *san-ju* (30). It made the soldiers angry, but not even bayonet prods could wipe the smile from POW faces now.

The first raid with high explosive bombs was carried out by nine B-29s in formation. No shells or fighters came within half a mile of them.

During November and December 1944 the raids intensified. It was astonishing how difficult it was to see the fighter planes darting in to attack the bombers. At 30 000 feet one could clearly see the four engines, the boomerang-shaped wings, the nose, the high tail, but the Japanese fighters were like tiny silver bullets, usually only visible when their fuselages reflected the sun. The Zeros were now attaining the altitude of the bombers and their tactics were to concentrate on the last planes and on stragglers. From our island we had an unimpeded view of the entire sky (we also believed that word had reached the Americans on the situation of our camp).

One afternoon we witnessed the impossible: a late B-29, far behind its fellows straining to escape a horde of buzzing Zeros. Over the bay it gently slipped into a wide descending spiral.

'Come on, you beauty, you can do it,' every prisoner prayed.

We rushed to the fence and watched the end of the drama through knotholes. A parachute appeared and moments later the silver giant curved into its last spin and slipped under the waters of the bay. One of our champions was gone. A pair of Japanese fighters made dives past the parachute figure and we heard the fire of their machine guns. We watched in agony. The parachutist also disappeared in the waters of the bay.

The Americans now sent in low-level night raids by only one or two bombers to keep the city awake and the defence guessing. Larger night raids followed and we would look across the bay and see the red glow of fires in all parts of Tokyo and in Yokohama to the south.

Our air-raid drill was to remove all windows from their frames, leaving a gaping, 80-foot void in both sides of each hut through which the wind whistled coldly or, when the local alarm sounded, to drop into the slit trenches dug between the huts by the gardening officers. The barrack fire party, consisting of the barrack commander and ten men armed with two stirrup pumps, six fire buckets and some highly inflammable straw brooms for beating out fires, had to stand at the hut door constantly at the ready. Because we too needed sleep at night, we often took several minutes to gather at the call 'Fire parties'.

In December came one of those rare occasions when Watanabe, now a sergeant, was granted leave to visit his home. We knew he would not return full of brotherly love because Kobe was receiving its share of destructive raids, but we expected him to be away for four days. With our tormentor away, the raids going well and the Philippines completely liberated, we were full of hilarity.

The night of the third day was stormy; rain poured in torrents, flooding the trenches and spreading pools across the parade ground. I was in bed enjoying my third undisturbed night in succession. The local alarm sounded but nobody moved. Suddenly we heard 'The Voice'—the one and only, unmistakeable voice of our bully and tyrant, Watanabe. Every barrack commander leapt out of bed, hundreds of officers and men too. I plunged my feet into my boots, pulled battledress trousers over my pyjamas and dashed outside, calling to my men and pulling on my overcoat and cap. My fire party staggered out sleepily one by one to see a bristling, demonic Watanabe in steel helmet, brandishing a naked sword and shouting. I was two men short. Watanabe swore, punched me on the jaw, punched the two late arrivals and charged to the next barrack. More roars and more punches. We stood in the rain in the dark, wishing we had more clothes on and wondering why he had come back early.

Frenzied and furious, Watanabe called out the rest of the prisoners in camp: a party to remove documents from the Japanese office, one to salvage stores from storehouses and another to salvage rice from the cookhouse. Soon the whole camp was standing to attention in the drenching rain while the paranoiac, with sword drawn, was strutting up and down, cursing our disobedience and calling us all 'priests'.

Now we practised the salvaging of stores and documents, while the fire parties were made to rush to different parts of the camp and fight imaginary fires. For two hours we added the thin jets of our stirrup pumps to the torrential rain on roofs here, there and everywhere, refilling our pumps again and again. All our clothes were sodden, our faces and hair too and our spirits thoroughly chastened. When finally dismissed, we staggered back into our barracks steaming wet and miserable. We knew our clothes would still be wringing wet next day and Watanabe would still be furious. As I slipped under my blankets on the hard floor, wet-haired and cold, one of my room-mates muttered, 'We don't make much money, but we have lots of fun!'

During January and February 1945, large day and smaller night raids were made every day without interval. Several hundred B-29s (finally a thousand) took part in the daylight attacks, flying in waves of squadron formations and disappearing into the smoke over the capital, then re-emerging twenty minutes later to return to base. The anti-aircraft barrage was tremendous; we saw three or four bombers crash over Tokyo and more limping homewards far behind their squadrons with one engine streaming out a feather of white smoke while Japanese fighters lunged at them repeatedly. We also saw twenty or more fighters disappear in a momentary puff of flame and no one parachuting to earth. That was not surprising; we had always heard that the Japanese sacrificed protective armour to manoeuvrability.

Only days before the end of the year, Watanabe took a party of officers into Tokyo pulling three light carts. He had permission to collect wood from destroyed houses in order to build a hut in camp. We pulled the carts through miles of city streets, many showing bomb damage, from Omori, through Shinagawa up towards Shinjuku. There seemed no reason to go so far, except that it pandered to Watanabe's vanity. Every half mile he would jump onto a concrete water tub outside a house, shout '*Keirei!*' and have us salute him as we passed. He would stand on the tub, with lower jaw stuck out, looking very like Mussolini on his balcony and would return our salute and eye us carefully to see that each officer was according him the correct courtesy. The citizens of Tokyo would gape at this modern samurai.

Reaching our destination, we found that a broad swathe of houses had been torn down to make a better firebreak and our wood was to come from this demolition. The Japanese were ruthless about this precaution; all over Tokyo a network of long fire lanes, 100 yards wide, had been cleared to prevent fires spreading. Every single house in these lanes had been razed to the ground and the occupants ordered to live with friends or leave the city. Piles of wood and loose timber were everywhere.

After the great earthquake and fire of 1923, Tokyo had been reconstructed with canals widened, new canals and additional firebreaks created. Now, with American fire-bombing just starting, more and larger firebreaks were thought essential.

The Japanese showed no signs of hostility towards us, though we had heard that they attacked some B-29 crewmen who landed in the city by parachute. They were all working hard, clearing debris, busy with their own business. The women were all in khaki or blue *mompei* (dungarees) and padded jackets with hoods. Not one kimono was in sight all day. The men, most of them, were in the khaki semi-military uniform which was so much a part of the wartime Japanese scene. There were also families, all with blue bundles on their backs and a suitcase or two, leaving the city for safer areas.

In February and March the Americans made incendiary raids with the intention of burning the city to the ground. Every fire engine in Tokyo was fully occupied day and night and hundreds of fire-engines, fire-pumps and fire-carts from the provinces were brought to the capital to join in the overwhelming task. Our men going to and from their work would see these rattle-trap old fire-cars, antiquated equipment, rattling and back-firing along the Keihin Road and breaking down everywhere, but all gamely doing their duty in the battle against Japan's age-old enemy—fire. Speeding by in their army trucks, the prisoners would give the Tokyo firemen an ironical cheer and the sweating, tired Japanese would look up and swear and sometimes grin.

We were sure Omori camp would never be hit and, later, many Japanese believed this too, for whole families came and camped along the outer sides of the camp walls. But other prison camps in Yokohama and Kawasaki and still others in Osaka and Kobe were burnt out and the prisoners sent to improvised camps in industrial districts like Sendai and Niigata in northern Honshu.

By February and March, communications were rapidly breaking down in Tokyo; most of the tram and bus services were out of action and the electric railway service was frequently interrupted. All over Tokyo city workers walked to work, climbing over debris, factory staffs lived in their factories in order to carry on production, organised volunteers fought fires and tended the wounded and refugees camped in the streets and ruins unable to tear themselves from the city in which they had once owned a little wooden house before the holocaust.

From what I have already said, it is obvious that the Japanese behaved under bombing much the same as many other men and women have behaved under bombing. From what our working parties told me, it appeared that the Japanese were long-suffering, obedient and brave. A million had already left Tokyo and more would follow. They did not dispute this order from their government, nor did they dispute the demolition of many houses to make firebreaks. One day we would recognise that not only the people of London and Chungking and Stalingrad had been brave under bombing, but those of Berlin and Tokyo as well. All men and women are capable of bravery. The pity is that nationalism divides us. Perhaps a true internationalism and cosmopolitanism will one day supersede our bickering and jealous nationalism. Perhaps it will not be too long before all of us on this small planet realise that we are one, and that our true nationality is Mankind.

# 26

# Christmas Joke

Before the bombing and burning of Tokyo had proceeded very far, Christmas was in the offing. Since August we had been preparing a pantomime for this our one permitted celebration of the year. *Cinderella*, we decided, would be a super production with better songs and lines than ever before. The British were in a minority in the camp, but we persuaded the Americans to agree to staging a pantomime. It took a week to clear up the misunderstanding over the word 'pantomime', which the dictionary clearly states is a 'dumb show'.

'But it's a fairy story!' said Maher and the other American officers.

'No, no, we'll write it and let you approve it.'

So a script was drafted and songs and comedy indicated and the Yanks agreed with enthusiasm. A Welsh RAF corporal, Glyn Bowen Jones, who had produced several prison camp shows would produce and he and James Bertram, a New Zealand correspondent caught in Hong Kong as a Volunteer private, would write it. Bertram, a Rhodes Scholar and probably the leading Far Eastern political observer in Japanese hands, had also arrived in Omori as a potential *Bunka*-mate. He was lucky to escape. I tried to develop a friendship with him, but he was extremely cold to all officers. As a private, he was made to do manual labour and I think he decided for reasons of political orthodoxy to restrict his friendships to members of the working proletariat.

The script and above all, the songs—topical lyrics to well-known light operatic arias like 'Velia' and 'Only a Rose'—were a great success. Band Master Austing arranged the music, the mainly Loyals band performed, both Cinderella and the Prince were played by Americans and Wing Commander Len Birchall, RCAF, was an entertaining Buttons. We had rehearsals every few nights, Watanabe permitting. Everything was fine except for costumes; we had only two ship stewards' white jackets and one hooped football jersey. Cinderella would probably appear at the ball in a khaki shirt and off-white sheet as a skirt. Among 600 men there wasn't a single garment that wasn't khaki, white or blue.

A week before Christmas we warned the camp office that our play would be a failure unless we could find some costumes. Someone there remembered that years before the camp had loaned a few POWs to appear in extra film scenes shot connected with the surrender in Singapore. Watanabe was persuaded to approach this film company. Within 72 hours, 40 rich and beautiful costumes of velvet, lace, satin and serge with a general Ruritanian hussar flavour were delivered. The brillant colour of these costumes was a sensual delight to our eyes; we caressed the luxurious materials with appreciative hands. So delighted were we with the gift that we tended to credit it, hopefully, to a new generosity in Watanabe.

The pantomime was a brilliant success. It played once for the Japanese staff, *fus* and *hanchos* and once for the camp. The Japanese talked about it for months afterwards and probably still remember it, as I am sure they still remember the cheerful, hard-working rascals who worked for them for so long and brightened their lives with their unorthodoxy and daring.

Christmas, in the shape of Christmas cards, had landed me in serious trouble with the Japanese weeks earlier. I had drawn some Christmas cards for friends in camp and had placed then in envelopes suitably addressed. I spent much care on the envelopes. I copied the post office cancellation stamp of the man's home town, crossed off his military address in Malaya or the Philippines and scribbled forwarding instructions like 'Moved to Japan, Nov '43' and finally, I copied the camp's censor's stamp, a long red-ink stamp of ten characters reading '*Tokyo Prisoners of War Camp Headquarters*'.

In a search, Watanabe discovered one of these envelopes among one officer's possessions. He showed it to Lieutenant Kato and immediately there was a tremendous excitement in the camp office. Watanabe asked my explanation. He was in a good mood, wondering perhaps where this would lead.

'Wado,' he said. 'Bery serious. You understand, eh? You draw Japanese Army censor's stamp. Japanese Army bery strict. You make big mistake. Lieutenant Kato says you must go to court martial for spying. Why you do it?'

'It was just a joke. I made an imitation letter for a joke to give my friend at Christmas.'

'Ah! Joke, eh? Kurisimasu joke?'

'That's right. Christmas joke.'

'Ah, *so desu-ka*.' Smiling happily because he had understood the workings of a Western mind, Watanabe returned to the office to explain my case. Kato and Tokyo Headquarter Office didn't take it so lightly. They asked me again and again if I was attempting serious forgery, if I was spying. I had only just realised that the stamp probably included the character for 'Censor' or 'Approved', which I hadn't considered while copying it. I had to act 'dumb' as the Americans say, but my palms were sweaty. I stuck to my Christmas joke answer and Watanabe supported me. Finally Colonel Sakaba, the Tokyo Area Commander, decided that the case need not go to court martial. I was pointedly warned not to copy any more Japanese signs or stamps on pain of long imprisonment. I was handed over to Lieutenant Kato for punishment and he made me empty latrines for ten days—easy!

Christmas was over. We returned to work with fond memories of greasepaint and footlights. Suddenly on 30 December, came the unbelievable news that Watanabe was being transferred to another camp. We could hardly credit it; it was too good to be true. After fourteen months at Omori as our ever-present disciplinarian and tormentor, Sergeant Watanabe was finally and definitely going. How many hundreds of beatings there had been! One older lieutenant commander had turned white-haired in that year. Two officers had asked to be treated as privates and laboured daily with the working parties to get away from camp and from him. And now, in a flash, he was gone.

Within two days Commander Maher announced to the barrack commanders (four second lieutenants and one lieutenant) that he was going to appoint more senior and slightly older officers to these posts. We asked why. He said that we were 'too junior, too inexperienced and too familiar with the men'. We replied that we had not been too junior for up to fourteen months and so why change now? He repeated his reasons more rudely. I said to him that we had taken a lot of rough and a lot of beatings for fourteen months and I thought things were going to be easier now and I was ready to take the smooth with the rough. He refused to talk further.

The next day we were ordered out of our cubicles and an American naval lieutenant took over my barrack. For two weeks or so the new barrack commanders barked orders and acted as if they were in peacetime barracks. But then they understood their lack of sanctions and they became more relaxed, friendly and persuasive with the men.

# 27

# Steel Mill Camp

Near the end of February 1945, the Japanese had some important news for the 70 officers in Omori. We guessed we would hear of transfers to other camps. Well, as long as it wasn't 4B camp—Watanabe had transferred to 4B. We paraded and the names of officers and their destinations were read out. I kept hearing the dreaded 4B. Mead...Samson...Tusken were all going.

'Wade... 4B.'

I gasped every breath out of my body. My shoulders sagged and my head bowed. I just could *not* believe it. Fate *couldn't* play such a trick. I was going to Watanabe's new camp. Why me? Good God, I'd had Watanabe longer than anyone! Just two months respite and now Watanabe again. This was the end... the very end.

People were milling around, talking. We had dismissed. Why me? my mind kept repeating. Why me? And there was no answer. If anyone had handed me a pistol I would have shot myself. All that evening I was in the pit of utter despair. No inner strength, no spiritual faith could conquer my hopeless depression that night.

Next day fatalism dulled the pain and I packed my kit and said my farewells. Officers bound for other camps offered a word of sympathy but could not conceal their joy at escaping our fate. The officers staying in Omori were busy planning new improvements. That night we climbed into a truck and left Omori for the last time. We drove through deserted streets past bombed and incendiarised houses and shops to Shinagawa station. The same short seats in a familiar small train and we sprawled or curled up to try to sleep.

In the morning we saw we were in the snow-covered mountains, the high central backbone of Honshu, and bound for a small port called Naoetsu (Now-etts) on the west coast of Japan, opposite Korea and Vladivostok. All morning we descended the snowy white mountains with black streams, black rocks and huts making charcoal drawings of the scene. The sky was blue, the sun shone and the snow sparkled and glistened. We heard that snow could be three metres deep in Naoetsu. It was obviously still there.

We arrived at the station and saw two Japanese guards with rifles and three Aussies in short, threadbare overcoats there to meet us. The overcoats were exactly like the ones we had worn in Korea, except for wispy goat fur collars. More relics of the war of 1904. The Aussies smiled and waved.

'How's the Bird—Watanabe?' we asked.

'Oh, he's a proper bastard. He's crunched a few of our fellows. You had him in Tokyo, didn't you?'

'Ha, I'll say we did! Fourteen months we had him.'

'My word!'

We picked up our kitbags and walked to the front entrance of the station. It seemed to be blocked with snow. It rose like a wall in front of us, but looking left we saw steps cut into the snow leading up to roof level and a sliver of blue sky. We climbed the icy steps and arrived on top of a huge cake of snow filling the street up to the level of the eaves of the houses on either side. We could look down into bedroom windows. People walked about on this ice cap and when they reached their destination disappeared down the crevices in front of each house. It was as if a giant frosted cake were sitting in the town, a cake that fitted loosely in its tin.

'My God, it isn't this deep all over the countryside, is it?' we asked.

'No, it collects in the streets and keeps falling off the roofs. In the fields it's only about five feet deep.'

Deeply awed, we heaped our baggage onto the sledges the Aussies had brought with them and then helped pull them towards the camp, slipping and slithering on the ice. We had been thinking about spring in Tokyo and now we had slipped back to mid-winter and the longer cold of the west coast of Japan.

After a mile we crossed a bridge without parapets over a frozen river. A cold wind whipped off the sea just 300 yards to our left. Ahead was a roof rising above surrounding roofs. That was the camp. Most of the town lay behind us. A mile beyond the camp we could make out the smoking chimneys and dark snow-free roofs of the steel mill.

Sixty men had died in this camp the previous winter. We had heard that snow drifted onto the sleeping figures at night. The barrack was a tall two-storey warehouse, 100 feet by 50, all of wood with a corrugated iron cladding front and a tile roof under deep snow. When we entered the building minutes later we saw that each squadroom was only separated from the rest by partitions, leaving a gap above, so that heat was quickly dispersed throughout the whole building.

We halted outside the camp office, footsteps sounded and out came Watanabe in cap, belt, sword and boots and his most Prussian manner.

'*Keirei!*' We saluted.

He saluted, giving a series of little bows as he faced the left then the right of the ranks before him. Lieutenant Commander Fitzgerald of the US Navy, our senior officer, reported to him.

'*Oosh!* You are 4B camp now. I am commander here. You must obey all my orders. I want make this camp *just like Omori*.'

We walked into the warehouse, groaning, '*Just like Omori.*' What a prospect!

But a crowd of Aussies greeted us. Most of them were in overcoats; they were pallid and thin. They joked and asked about the Tokyo bombings. We climbed a staircase to the upper floor and noticed gaps and holes in the wooden flooring all the way. The Aussies told us they had stripped well over a ton of wood out of the building the previous winter to add to their fires. Looking up we saw the underside of the roof 25 feet above, supported by thick blackened beams.

There were only four officers in this camp, two doctors and two lieutenants with plenty of duties to perform. Three hundred men worked either day or night twelve-hour shifts. The three of us who had been in Omori long enough to know Captain Sandy Barrett, AAMC, spoke to him now. We found a pale, tight-lipped Sandy, who for two years had been the only doctor in this camp and therefore on call 24 hours a day. For the past month he had been assisted by a young American doctor brought there in anticipation of the usual increase in sickness and death in winter. Sandy Barrett, because of protests he had made to the Japanese about deaths and conditions in this camp, had been sent to Omori for a month for disciplining. The two Australian lieutenants, Theo Lee and Allan Campbell, handled between them all other duties such as duty officer, stores, labour and canteen officer and they each had a full day. Both proved to be conscientious officers, devoted to their men. Most of these men were from the 2/20th Battalion of the AIF in Malaya and so there remained with them the familiarity and loyalty of a unit. Some of the NCOs actually tried to help the officers with their responsibilities.

We were shown an empty squadroom behind a canvas curtain. Instead of a raised platform for sleeping, one slept on the floor on a pelt of loose straw. The upper deck was partly hidden from view by a low balustrade. The fifteen newcomers appreciated all these features in a glance and, remembering Omori where Watanabe usually hit the men nearest to him, we made a rush for the ladders and in a minute all fifteen of us were on the upper shelves and had staked our bedspace. Our hosts looked at us askance. Then we started arguing; we quarrelled for minutes before conceding that Watanabe would insist on filling the lower space before allowing anyone on top, so all except two moved down and I got a terrible place just where one's glance first fell when one swung aside the sailcloth curtain on entering the room.

At *Tenko* that night, we all paraded in our squadrooms. Waiting for the Japanese inspection, the Aussie duty officer shouted 'Start your *yushaws*!'

We watched with astonishment the sudden strange contortions of the Aussies. They imitated the arm and body movements of a man standing rowing in the Oriental manner while crying '*Yushaw! Yushaw!*' with each stroke. Deadly serious and no smiles. We almost giggled; it was quite funny.

'Come on, you might as well get started,' cried the rowers, a shade testily. We joined in, mocking the exercise. '*Shaw-yu! Shaw-yu!* sang one American officer. 'Whoops!' I cried. 'I caught a crab!'

Though snow did not seep into the building, terrible draughts did and there were few stoves. The sickroom was the largest room in the building and was always full. The Australians had persuaded the Japanese to put a ceiling over this room and its neighbour, which we used as the officers' room, library and mortuary: 60 cube pinewood boxes bearing the ashes of dead Australian prisoners lined one wall. A month later these were removed to a Shinto temple.

About five o'clock each evening the night shift climbed out of their blanket cocoons for work and soon afterwards the day shift returned to camp. The men's faces were white and haggard and their eyes sunken in bruise coloured hollows; none of them ever saw the sun except for moments at lunchtime on day shifts. They were thinner, paler and sicker than the Omori workers and they never had an opportunity to steal themselves a morsel of extra food. The food in camp was terrible too: *gaoliang*, *daikon*, seaweed and some roadside weed we called 'sticks'.

I felt intensely sorry for these cheerful Australians who had had to spend two grim winters in this nightmare camp. They were so game and sound and reliable still; they faced the world with a united front, their discipline was uncorroded and they were not as ruthless as the mixed prisoners of Omori had become.

Outside our barn were storesheds for grain and vegetables, latrines, a brick cookhouse, the camp office and soldiers' quarters. In a corner of the snow-filled yard an Aussie prisoner daily dropped a few vegetable tops and peelings down a black hole in the snow. There was a pig down there surviving winter, we hoped, in his igloo.

On bath-day, once a week or ten days, we marched to the Nippon Stainless Steel factory for this rite. In this way I gradually visited most parts of this vast agglomeration of blast furnace sheds, machine shops, foundries and mould shops threaded with narrow-gauge railway lines, scrap-iron heaps and dumps of metal and coal on all sides. Outside, one could always hear the hum of the blast furnaces, the clash of tools on steel, the whistle and shunt of locomotives and the diminishing chain of jolts of a line of boxcars being bumped. Inside the lofty sheds was that fantastic world of vats of molten steel, white hot, red hot or cooling grey, of travelling cranes, flashing carbides, splashing steel sparks and open-mouth furnaces roaring like fiery dragons. In this inferno, the slaves condemned to serve these monsters, Australian, Japanese and Korean, danced feverishly with glistening bodies or shielded in filthy rags, stoking, feeding, heaving huge metal gobbets to and from the flaming gullets. To me it looked like a ballet of hell, a fiery cavern where puny dwarfs danced to an orchestra of clamouring fire and crashing steel—brilliant, all-devouring, frightening.

Behind the furnaces were water tanks and hot water and there we bathed and the Japanese washed their clothes. There, beneath the towering furnaces and vats, in the glow of the brilliant ovens and amid all the din of industrial production, we would scrub each other's backs in the sulphurous water, dry and dress in the warmth and hang our towels to dry before hot furnaces. It reminded me of bathing as a small boy in a tin tub before the kitchen fire in a farmhouse with towels hanging by the coal stove and fully dressed people walking about making cocoa or boiling extra water.

After the bath we would go to the POW workers' rest room, where the men had regular twenty-minute breaks. There they would be stretched out on the benches, licking salt and pouring cup after cup of boiling green tea into their parched bodies and wiping their faces and chests with dirty cloths. How did they keep working like this, I often asked myself? What was the fuel fed into these human machines to keep them labouring? I knew what: it was the same wretched cattle grain *gaoliang*, *daikon* and seaweed we'd survived on for years with the very occasional fish and the so-called 'meat soup' with five kilos of meat for 350 men. What a staggering exploitation of human bodies and beings!

# 28

# The Australian Camp

A camp where 60 men had died in two years was no health resort. It compared sadly and bitterly with either Omori or Seoul. Further, we were into Japan's fourth year of war, when shortages were increasingly biting. I determined to learn the character of this prison camp and its guards so as not to be caught off guard.

Talking quietly with Theo Lee, Allan Campbell and, in rare moments, when he could spare time from the care of the sick and injured, Doc Sandy Barrett, I learnt that things had looked promising at first. When the Aussies arrived in Naoetsu in December 1942 they had been housed in an ex-school building where they found blankets laid out per man, also Japanese khaki uniforms and boots to work in. A whole week was devoted to medical inspections, form-filling and practising Japanese commands and counting. But once work started, this promise of reasonableness faded.

The camp lacked its own water supply; all the water had to be brought in in buckets on sledges from a well a mile away. And it was doubtful that the water was pure because three-quarters of the men suffered from diarrhoea. Work meanwhile began in the Nippon Stainless Steel factory, making sheet steel, lengths and mouldings and also at Shinetsu Chemical works. There they manufactured carbide metal silicon into the large dry cell electrodes used in electrical furnaces. Both were heavy and relentless work and, on a near starvation diet and in deep snow and intense cold, the men steadily lost weight, many suffering from pneumonia.

As some protection against snow and rain, the Japanese provided traditional peasants' rice-straw cloaks to be worn overall. These were of thick straw with a tie round the neck but no front. As long as you kept bent over and working, you were protected from snow or rain, but if you straightened up your front was unprotected. Prints by Hokusai and Hiroshige of peasants working in the fields in such cloaks came to mind, but picturing tall, rangy Aussies garbed like this was almost beyond imagining.

It was in the first April, 1943, that the Australians moved to this present camp, an ex-warehouse with no heating but a better water supply. Their colonel, A. Robertson, had just died of meningitis and malnutrition. He had been a good leader and was much mourned. He had often protested to the Japanese NCOs about the lengthening of work shifts and enforced running to and from work, but every attempt to have an interview with the camp commander, Lieutenant Ota, was refused. Instead, Colonel Robertson was himself made to run four miles every morning for about two months leading to his final illness.

This lengthening of work shifts was a pernicious trick. The original nine-hour day was lengthened to ten hours, then twelve-hour shifts were introduced; before long, men were working sixteen-hour shifts and on occasions eighteen hours, and doing this for as much as 110 days without a single rest day. Once five men were made to work for 23 hours straight. Add to this doubling a mile each way to and from work and you got utterly exhausted, worn-out prisoners wasting away under the strain and an easy prey to any disease.

'Suddenly,' said Sandy Barrett, 'men began to die at the rate of two a week, sometimes three. It looked as if pneumonia and pleurisy on top of all our other ills and deficiencies were going to knock us off like flies. But the quality of our food was not improved and, as you know, the sick got only one-third ration.'

'*One-third!*' I exclaimed. 'In Shinagawa and most camps it was a half, but one-third! How did anyone recover?'

'We managed to give them a bit more, but it was—just impossible. Twenty-eight men died that year.'

'And 32 last year—1944.'

'Christ, what a camp!' I muttered.

Some of these deaths were from industrial accidents or punishments. One man was blinded by a splinter of steel but was not allowed even one day off work. Another, George Beale, got caught in a coke escalator which cut up his stomach and cracked his pelvis. They tried to wire it together, but he died on the operating table. He had just worked a *24-hour shift*! (That's a world record, George Beale. Others may equal it, but no one can beat it.) Many men were punished by making them stand to attention for hours without overcoats in the snow; one man had to do this utterly naked. And sometimes the whole camp was called out in the dark to stand to attention without an evening meal till midnight.

A digger named Downie, a bull-like, square-jawed fellow, accidentally scorched his coat on a stove. Sergeant Shibano, an enthusiastic punisher, struck him about twenty times across the face with a heavy belt, next stood him in a snowbank with the snow up to his mouth, then pushed him into the guardhouse for 'severe guard house punishment'. This meant only two riceballs a day as food and no blankets at night. It was to last for ten days. Blankets were got to him after five nights, but work in the steel mill on two riceballs a day was too much; he collapsed ill and was sent to Shinagawa Hospital camp, Tokyo. Few expected to see him again, but he was a survivor; a few months later in his battered slouch hat and part-Japanese, part-Australian uniform, he walked back into Naoetsu.

'You haven't heard about the coffin racket,' said Theo Lee. As deaths mounted about November 1943, two Japanese privates, Yanigizawa and Sekihara, were noticed as being particularly harsh and cruel to sickly prisoners. Several times they forced these light-duty men to stand impossibly close to red-hot fires until they collapsed and then thumped them. At least one POW died. It was then discovered that Yanigizawa had filched the contract to make the pinewood boxes for prisoners' ashes from the local carpenter and was receiving 13 Y per box. He had organised himself a vested interest in POWs' deaths and fifteen had already died. How many deaths would be attributable to this treatment must be left to War Crimes Tribunals to decide after victory, but these two Japanese names were carefully memorised to be reported.

There was one other thing about this camp that caused me some anxiety. All the Japanese here had a tendency to inflict bizarre punishments on the prisoners. A favourite was to line up the Aussies in pairs and order them to fight and punch each other. If they did not punch hard enough, the guards would kick them or butt them with their rifles. I could just picture the guards giggling as they watched this display. Blood was expected and the guards would hit out brutally if no blood was being shed. At times the POWs were obliged to do press-ups in the yard with onlooking Japanese giving encouraging kicks during the process; or they were made to run round and round the yard for an hour or scuttle round on all fours assisted by kicks or blows. Men would be severely punished for failing to align their boots exactly, for not catching enough flies in an evening or for failing to use a blanket on the hottest nights. The punishments in Naoetsu camp were so frequent, wanton and bizarre that I was alarmed at the possibilities. Perversion is something to beware and to fear and these guards were perverted. I said to the Aussies that we must do everything possible to end this addiction to fanciful and perverse punishments.

Paradoxically it seemed, Watanabe had unwittingly improved the situation of late by insisting on carrying out most punishments himself. Now, with more punishments to handle, he dispensed swift discipline with a hard left, right to the jaw, quickly finishing the matter. I hoped—we hoped that things would not slip backwards.

# 29

# Another Farm

The finest thing about Naoetsu was the splendid range of mountains lying east of the town. In winter these mountains were deep in snow and from our barrack we had an unimpeded view of every slope leading up to the highest peak. In the morning the snows would be tinted with rose, then the glowing sun would appear over a white shoulder turning the white to gold. All day the snow sparkled brilliantly with soft blue shadows until at dusk the slopes were spread with

> The blue and the dim and the dark cloths
> Of night and the light and the half-light.

Many of us drew inspiration from those cool, free, enduring mountains. Humour and comradeship kept most of us sane; beauty alone could do the same for me. The tallest peak in the range was Mount Miyoko, *Miyoko San*, clothed all year in snow, clean and pure, and far, far aloof from the neglect and callousness which was our bitter daily diet.

Soon after our arrival, Watanabe told me that he had especially requested Tokyo Headquarters for five particular officers: Samson, Mead, Abbott, Tusken and me: Samson to command the gardeners; Tusken and me as experienced squad leaders and gardeners; John Abbott, the barrister from Hong Kong, to keep statistics; and Mead to be cookhouse officer.

I had suspected this when I first studied the composition of our party. It was evident that Watanabe had chosen some of his trained and tested 'lieutenants' and omitted any officers he despised. None of those who collapsed before his fist ever hit them—not that it did them much good, they got punched anyway—and none of the officers who requested to be sent out with the working parties. I was forced to the conclusion that he respected us. He had punched and slapped us many times, but we had continued to carry out our duties and not shrunk from his punishment.

Al Mead went straight into the kitchen, John Abbott took over equipment control and the rest of us, nine Americans, one New Zealander and I, became gardeners under

'Sammy' Samson, a US artillery captain and the ablest officer I met in prison camp. Stubborn, tough, self-confident and decisive, he looked at times like the British comic papers caricature of an American with his rimless glasses and trilby with the brim turned up in front. But what those caricaturists miss (and perhaps what many British people fail to notice in Americans) is the firm mouth and not-easily-fooled eyes. If they probed deeper they would glimpse a mind untrammelled by cautious tradition, a mind that can 'think big' and build industries and fight wars on a scale still beyond the comprehension of most Europeans. Think how fast the Americans fought their way 4000 miles from the Solomon Islands to Tokyo Bay—in under three years. Most British can't see beyond bright and unusual fashions, an embarrassing openness and an accent they find funny. Which is a pity.

Lieutenant Commander Fitzgerald, being senior to any of the Australians, took over the post of senior POW officer. 'Fitz' was bulldoggish in appearance and character. His submarine had been lost in the Indian Ocean and after picking up him and his crew, the Japanese took them into Penang and tortured Fitz for information. They suspended him upside down and poured water into his nostrils, then laid him out and jumped on his stomach. During interrogation, they placed pencils between all his fingers and squeezed. But Fitz told them nothing and they eventually sent him to Ofuna and then Omori. He arrived in Tokyo after Watanabe had left, so he had no experience of the psychopath. We tried to advise him, but we knew he would have to learn the hard way. His passage with Watanabe was a bumpy one and finally the sergeant ignored him and used Captain Samson as senior POW officer.

Since the war, friends have often asked me how such things happened. 'After all', they say, 'the other man was senior', or on the subject of the treatment we received, 'But how could they do that? It's against international law! Couldn't you protest to a higher authority?' The answers are that the Japanese were not playing according to any rules we respected; they made up rules as they went along or they followed their Imperial Army regulations; further, there was no contact between us and any higher authority. That is why the International Red Cross should have devoted hours to listening to prisoners' complaints. But they did not. It was futile for us to pretend that we had any rights; the only sensible action was to try to persuade the Japanese to see things our way occasionally and so modify their orders. Also Japanese 'face' was at stake; having given an order, no Japanese was eager to retract it, for that would result in loss of face, an expendable commodity, and Japanese have been known to commit *seppuku* (*hara kiri*) through severe loss of face.

'Wasn't there anybody senior to Watanabe in that camp?' my kindly friends ask. Yes, there was—a lieutenant who had served in Omori for a few months, but he knew his place. He left everything to Watanabe, including all decisions on discipline, punishment and administration; he would never make rulings if cornered alone by our senior officer; he was a nonentity and a puppet and kept his mouth shut. I suppose this could only happen in the Japanese Army, but happen it certainly did.

With twelve extra officers in camp, we took over the fetching of supplies from the Aussies. It was good to walk out of camp, through streets of houses where people lived normal lives, to see children, to see female faces. We even got boyish pleasure out of swinging our loaded sledges round sharp bends, riding them down slopes and braking urgently as we rushed towards the river. From the *miso* factory, we brought back the camp's supply of this crushed soya bean paste and sometimes managed to obtain a small tinful each for our own use as a sort of peanut butter.

The snow lay deep over Naoetsu till April, then we watched it sink fast in fields and streets. The gutters ran like rapids. The ice on the river cracked into huge chunks and slices which sailed downstream, piling up against the bridge, then bursting through towards the sea. Whenever it piled high against the bridge, dynamite was used to break up the blockage.

As the snow melted away, we made new discoveries. That flat square of snow in front of a Japanese temple was not a simple courtyard but a cemetery with five-foot stone memorials we could never have guessed were there. Elsewhere, coal dumps, pillboxes, air-raid shelters, sheds and wood piles came to light. The bridge had four-foot parapets on each side which we had never suspected when it was over five feet deep in ice and snow. We saw the pig for the first time; none the worse for its entombment since the previous December. Hungry and emasculated as we were, we could not fail to catch some of the infectious excitement of spring as fresh green shoots of leaves and grass appeared on trees and in the dark earth left muddy by the snows. Now for news of a mighty offensive to end the war!

The Japanese newspapers had not lately devoted much space to the war in Europe, so in mid-April we thought the Allies were on the line of the Rhine. Then one day a Digger handed me a half front page with a small map of Germany on it. I fell to translating the report there and then under the light in the centre of the squadroom with a dictionary and the paper in my hands and my back to the doorway.

'Wow!' I shouted. 'Listen! The Americans have almost reached Leipzig and Dresden! They've cut right across Germany. They're almost at Berlin.'

A crowd gathered round me. 'Where exactly are Leipzig and Dresden?'

'Look at the map!' I almost shouted with happiness. 'They're near Czechoslovakia.'

'I don't believe it. You've got it wrong,' many doubted.

'I haven't got it wrong; this is what it says: "General Patton's Third Army continuing advance reported reached Chemnitz, near Dresden, and approaching Leipzig... something something.. another spearhead towards Regensburg".'

'It's impossible, you must have the names wrong.'

'It's *not* impossible. They broke through and there was nothing to stop them. Anyway I absolutely guarantee the names. Absolutely.'

We argued for several minutes and the majority refused to trust my translation— they had been disappointed so many times that they did not want to be caught again. At that moment a Japanese sentry in overcoat, belt, cap and nose-pad and carrying his rifle with bayonet fixed, walked into the squadroom. I stuffed the dictionary and newspaper inside my jacket and turned towards the sentry with an expressionless face. Thus, only moments after hearing the most sensational piece of news of the whole war there was an anticlimax of doubt and disbelief. It shows the power of propaganda when men refuse to credit news unfavourable to the enemy even when names and maps are clearly printed in an enemy newspaper. You would think we liked our monotony.

Early in May we heard and I translated reports that Germany had surrendered. We sighed almost with disbelief, and hoped now that Japan, with her face saved by her ally's capitulation, would sue for peace in a couple of months.

Meanwhile we had started farming once again. Japan, like China, is so highly cultivated that to find any flat land larger than a tennis court is virtually impossible. So the two-thirds of an acre that was found was over *six* miles from the camp! And was poor sandy soil spurned by neighbouring farmers. But six miles was much more than we had bargained for. It was an interminable march to make twice a day with a day's work in the fields in between, but once we got used to it, we were happy to be out of camp and in comparative freedom for twelve hours a day.

A wounded Japanese ex-serviceman, dressed in olive green semi-military uniform, *kokuminfu*, was our *hancho* or boss. He was a farmer by upbringing and a most obedient and loyal soldier by training. With him, alone and unarmed, we pulled a cart out to the farm each day, loaded with our messkits, farm tools and two barrels of camp manure. Human manure is so precious in Japan that you can't find it anywhere, you have to bring your own to your farmland.

We passed through pleasant countryside along the way; flat ricefields, vegetable plots, several villages, some groves of huge old trees, with three men pulling the cart and one or two of the other half dozen flitting out of the ranks now and then to snatch a carrot, some onions or leeks from the nearest plots. In some of the villages we passed through, the small boys were so behind with their war news that they jeered us and shouted '*Furyo!*' ('Prisoner of War!') and held up their hands in token of surrender, just as small boys had done in Taiwan and Korea long ago. The adults were careful to mind their own business. Japanese civilians kept away from the army; they feared it.

Every two or three weeks we would see two large flags draped across some front door as another son went off to the war, and now and then we would see a small flag hanging less brazenly outside a house and a pinewood tablet with sprigs of evergreen by the front door after a cubed white box had arrived and brought the ashes of a Japanese son to his ancestral home.

One day while farming, a single B-29 flew overhead reconnoitring the coast for defences. Weeks later a Superfortress dropped a few bombs on the Nippon Steel mill, missing the important buildings. We began to think that invasion was approaching. Most of Okinawa, if not all, was in American hands and there was talk of peace being negotiated through the Japanese Ambassador in Moscow or through Prince Konoye, an ex-premier. It sounded convincing to me. As for the townspeople of Naoetsu, they were so poorly fed that there was almost as much beri-beri amongst them as amongst us. Many also suffered from tuberculosis.

I was duty officer when Watanabe announced that a large party of American prisoners would arrive in two days time. Workmen came in and knocked windows and doors into the storerooms on the ground floor to convert them to squadrooms. The latrines were extended too, but when 400 men arrived the camp became woefully overcrowded.

The newcomers were mostly Americans from work camps in Kobe and Osaka, which had been burnt out in recent raids, but also a party of British from Thailand and, originally, Singapore. The whole group arrived with almost no baggage, torn and dirty clothing or ill-fitting Japanese uniforms and extremely low morale. The Aussies did not care for them and tended to keep their friendships among themselves. Too many of these men were demoralised and shifty. Stealing became commonplace. Four of the new arrivals were appointed cooks, but within ten days they were thrown out for sneaking extra rations to their friends and smuggling stolen food out of the galley to trade for tobacco or clothing.

There is, admittedly, not much tone about a prison camp, but the standard in this camp now fell sharply.

Gangs of these men scuffed about the camp seeking to trade their paltry belongings for food or tobacco. Overnight they transformed the whole appearance of the camp. They thronged corridors and blocked doorways offering their trades. They even woke men sleeping after a night shift. The place looked like a thieves' market or shoddy bazaar. There was a medieval look about these thin-nosed, grey-faced men in over-large greasy overcoats and oily caps, sneaking goods out of their sleeves. 'The only prop missing is the Hunchback of Notre Dame,' I said. In the end the Aussies began to hurl clogs at them and we forbade them in our room.

What these men were trying to sell was pathetic—old fountain pens, string lanyards, puttees, face towels—they might as well have offered lipstick. There are only six things a POW must have (and some had little more): a good pair of boots, one uniform, an overcoat, a spoon and a tin to carry his lunch—and a determination to survive. I gave away my last reserve cardigan and undershirt.

The British members of this contingent had all spent nearly two years in Thailand, working on the 'Death Railway'. They were still yellow and scrawny from tropical disease and overwork. Many had suffered from dysentery, malaria and huge tropical ulcers. One rarely heard a loud voice from any of them. They conserved strength, energy, voice, everything for the next harsh blow of fate. Twice, though, I heard a cry of pain and saw a man babbling and searching to discover who had stolen his bowl of rice. In both cases the thief, noticing the absence of a comrade after rations had been distributed, had hurriedly swallowed the other man's *gaoliang* then disappeared from the room with his own meal, remaining hidden until he had finished it. When he returned there was nothing his victim could do but curse him or fight him, usually the former. The thief would merely smile, knowing he had eaten a double ration and put one over on a fate that seemed intent on killing him.

Unprincipled as some of these men had become, there was some excuse for their behaviour. They had suffered hell, clearing jungle, cutting through rock, bridging rivers and laying over 400 kilometres of track so that the Japanese could supply their armies in Burma overland from Thailand. They had toiled through drenching monsoon rains, blazing heat and a miasma of disease to build this impossible railway. Civilian engineers in peacetime had refused the task because of the inevitable human cost. But the Japanese had *slave labour*. Some 60 000 British, Australian, Dutch and American prisoners of war had worked from both ends to construct this line, reinforced by over 150 000 Asian labourers from Malaya, Burma, Thailand and China. The latter had no discipline, organisation or sanitation and so they died plentifully. At the end, 13 000 British, Australian, Dutch and American prisoners had died in its construction. It was probably the worst experience suffered by any prisoners of the Japanese anywhere.[2]

Hearing of their tropical ulcers, dysentery, beri-beri and typhoid, of bonfires of cholera victims, of the lack of medication and surgical instruments, and no mail from home and only one Red Cross parcel, I realised that we were far better off in Japan. We probably received more beatings and equal or worse mental torture, we were repeatedly persecuted, but thank heaven we had not suffered nearly so many deaths and if the Japanese did not massacre us when the invasion began, then most of us would probably come through.

As so often, my impression of these survivors of the 'Death Railway' had come mainly from the behaviour of the worst third. The majority had not fallen so low, but as with us, scrupulously fair food distribution was a matter of the gravest importance.

These demoralised and stooping figures provided Watanabe with perfect subjects for his paranoid punching and screaming. We would hear them in room after room shouting '*Keirei!*' 60, 80, 100 times as Watanabe put them through their Japanese drill and subjugation to his will. And now he was assisted by a young Japanese interpreter with large black-rimmed spectacles, Private Kono. For months he had struck no one, but then, understudying Watanabe, he had become a roaring, strutting monster. He made no attempt to control his temper or his most brutal impulses. Carrying a bamboo *kendo* stick, he would patrol our barracks four or five times a day, smacking liberally at heads here and there with his *kendo* sword, shouting and threatening. He delighted in seeing fear in men's eyes. In Private Kono we witnessed the whole process of moral deterioration from a quiet human being to a roaring, Hitlerian animal, lusting to inflict pain and create terror. He moved rapidly up my hate list until he was second only to Watanabe—a feat of some distinction, showing his whole-hearted application to the

2. North Borneo was worse; only six Aussies survived out of 2500 POWs.

task. He had his moments of mad originality too; once he had two lines of men twisting each other's noses and pulling each other's tongues. 'Twisto! Hurto!' he shouted.

His, Watanabe's and Lieutenant Kato's were the only three names I would report for cruelty after our release. I had in POW camp long separated our captors into different types: the majority in Japan and Korea were indifferent to us and somewhat callous; some were harsh and contemptuous, but it was a minority, a comparatively small minority who were actively cruel or sadistic. And there were a few, like Professor Ukai, Colonel Noguchi, Lieutenant Morigishi, a Private Kano in Omori and perhaps 'Rochester', who were decent, humane individuals, harbouring no hatred, malice or inhumanity. Pity there weren't more.

After bombers passed regularly overhead at night towards Niigata, Watanabe wanted an air-raid shelter. Planks and posts were provided and much earth would have to be moved. The Japanese gave us wicker baskets attached to A-frame yokes, which we would strap to our backs to transport earth. We hesitated. *'Kurrah! Nanda?* Why you not working? Starto! Begin! Work! Work!'

And so we hoisted the panniers on our backs, had them filled with earth, carried them to the shelter and leant over to pour the earth into prepared cavities. No other work I did in prison camp made me feel such a slave as this. This was how the Great Wall of China and the pyramids had been built. Like oxen, we merely stood and waited while other men shovelled earth into our pannier, then walked to the site to pour it out. It was sub-human, deadening work.

Days later, our farmer-*hancho* jokingly remarked to Watanabe that we were rather lazy. In two minutes all the gardeners were on parade and a spluttering, exploding Watanabe ordered us all to work with the men's working parties.

We did not protest strenuously; we were too weary to care anymore; no work we did now could possibly assist the tottering Japanese Empire and we would just like to see the swivel-chair soldier in London or Washington who would try to tell us otherwise. Watanabe ordered us to the 'Barges'.

Next morning after *Tenko* at five o'clock and a seaweed breakfast, we were on parade with the barge party. We were clad like most of them in patched shirt and shorts with some kind of haversack containing a messkit, spoon and mug over one shoulder. Sixty of the men were British and 40 American, but impossible to differentiate as all had reached the grey, monotonous level of three-and-a-half-year prisoners.

The barges, after being filled with coal from one of the colliers standing out in the bay, were tugged up a canal to the steel mill and then unloaded into large coal pens on the bank. Our job was simply to unload the barges, using the same wicker back-panniers. Six men filled the baskets and the rest of us carried our baskets back and forth to the coal pen. We made about 30 journeys an hour, carrying 40 to 50 pounds of coal each time. Each man shifted about five and a half tons of coal a day.

It was dreadfully monotonous work. I took to repeating to myself every poem I knew. I had done this in Changi and while digging in Korea and learnt extra poems to lengthen my repertoire. So I would mouth through the iambic pentameters of Shakespeare soliloquies and a medley of poems, usually not more than two each, by Shelley, Yeats, Matthew Arnold, Stevenson, Housman, Poe, Browning and Masefield, ending with Abe Lincoln's Gettysburg Address and two perorations from Churchill's fighting speeches of 1940.

One day, returning to camp, tired, dirty, scabby, my hair full of coal dust, I had it all shaved off. It was an act of expiation. I was reminded of the story T. E. Lawrence tells of himself just after the liberation of Damascus by the Arabs in 1918—his crowning triumph. Entering the city among the first, he came upon a dysentery hospital full of patients, deserted by doctors and orderlies, its floors covered in excrement. He began to try to ease the sufferings of the patients, when a British officer strode in, took one look at the disgusting scene, decided that the figure in Arab dress was to blame and struck Lawrence several times across the face. The great guerrilla leader did not offer any protest; he felt so disgusted with war and politics and unclean himself that he regarded it as something of an expiation.

Author's sketch of Naoetsu camp, western Japan, where 700 POWs were held. The Nippon Steel mills visible in the distance and ricefields at right.

# 30

# Coalships

Once the barges had been emptied, our work transferred naturally to the coalships themselves. There was no harbour at Naoetsu; the coast was almost straight, consequently all colliers and freighters stood out at sea about three-quarters of a mile offshore. Behind a chugging tug, we glided over the grey-green water at the mouth of the river towards the coalships. Outside the moles of the river, the sea turned choppy. The empty lighters pitched and tossed, spray soaked us and a few men were seasick. But being in a boat moving straight out to sea and smelling salt spray gave us the illusion of freedom.

It ended too soon as the lighters were tugged into position alongside the coalship. Japanese longshoremen and foremen already aboard grinned and made obscene jokes as we climbed aboard up rope ladders. We were organised into four gangs, one for each hold while the winches began to work up steam and the hatches were uncovered. There was endless shouting by the No. 1 *hancho* in his olive uniform and brandishing his wooden sword.

Work started at a terrific pace to clear the hatch and get several feet below deck level so that the full squad could find room to dig. Once this bottleneck was cleared, we could spread out under the deck and keep the hatch clear for the raising and lowering of the nets. This was new work to us officers and we hadn't realised quite how fast our men had to work on these jobs.

There were four men to a net and five nets to each hold. When a net was carried towards your squad by the Japanese foremen below decks, you had just enough time to shovel like a demon and fill it before he was shouting for it to be rehooked, raised to the deck and carried out over the side to a lighter. The nets were filled and lifted in rotation and the empty nets descended rapidly and were cast towards each gang in rotation.

The first day, we found the work backbreaking and at the end of the day ached in twenty or 30 new places. I found it best not to straighten my back but to remain bent over and swoop with the shovel into the soft coal rather than to dig with it. My respect for manual labourers, already high after three years in prison camps, rose even higher.

The pace of the work was really set by the speed with which the winchman could raise and lower the hook five times in the hold and five times in the lighters alongside. If ever the hook hung idle for two seconds all the Japanese would shout furiously and beat any prisoner within reach with their wooden swords or even shovels.

It seemed probable to me that Watanabe would take the officers off this work after a few weeks, so I decided to do more than my share of work to give the men the maximum assistance as they would have to continue there indefinitely. I shovelled with several gangs and finally settled in with two tall, rangy American truck farmers from Boise, Idaho, and a small gingery American in a dirty white topee who did not look a good risk but was as fast and conscientious as anyone. All three had been captured as civilian construction workers on Wake Island in 1941. We were a good crew and knew that if anyone leant on his spade for a minute it was because he felt ill or really needed a momentary rest.

Unloading coalships! After the first one we did five more. How quickly one learnt the technique: to sweep with the shovel rather than to dig, to let rolling or sliding coal fill one's shovel whenever possible, not to struggle with an obstinate piece of coal and not to straighten one's back. How steadily too the coal surface moved downwards inside the huge hollow hull! Soon you would see the ribs of the hull curving round under you towards the propeller shaft. Finally we were standing on the damp bottom of the hull with the great ribbed sides curving above us like the belly of a whale and only corners holding the last remnants of coal.

When we climbed out on deck, we were wet, sweating and chilly, but the sun would warm us back to health. We would be ravenous for our meal of seaweed, *daikon* and *gaoliang* and some men might prospect for any food lying about in the ship.

One morning several men were caught stealing boiled rice and were dismissed with a clout across the ear by the *hancho*. Instead of curtailing their activities, the pilferers continued to take risks and be caught. Finally when some specially treated vegetable was dipped into, the Japanese demanded that the thieves confess. No one moved. We were sent back to work for the afternoon with the threat that if all the pilferers did not confess, the theft would be reported to Watanabe.

During the afternoon public opinion exerted its influence; 90 per cent of the prisoners had not even seen this special vegetable and we wanted the guilty to confess. Before leaving the ship, three men admitted their guilt.

We marched back into camp full of foreboding. It was late; the sun was low and other working parties were eating their supper. The *hancho* reported the thefts to Watanabe who immediately stamped out of the office, his lips tight with anger.

'*So!*' he shouted. 'Japanese *hancho* tell me that many men steal special begetable; only three men admit.' He paused, eyeing us all. 'Now, *ima*, ALL men who steal begetable come here. If not, I will punish *whole* party bery severely.'

We stood at attention and watched pessimistically. Four, six, seven, that was better; altogether eight men stepped forward and formed a line in front of Watanabe.

'*More!*' shouted Watanabe. 'More!'

But no one else stepped forward. This might have been the true total, but the sergeant kept shouting for more men. Slow minutes passed. Walking round the ranks of workers, Watanabe's eyes rested on me.

'Wado,' he said quietly. 'Go there.'

'Tinker,' he said. 'Go there.'

I wondered what was on his mind. Frank Tinker, a young, fair lieutenant in the American Army Air Corps, joined me. We were apart from the pilferers, but Watanabe now told us to join them. We did so, incredulously.

'These men,' he shouted indicating us all, 'are guilty of stealing begetable from Japanese. They must be punished. *You* will punish them. Ebery man must slap all ten men on the face, once this side, once that side. Understand?'

'*Hai*,' came the deep-throated roar from the party.

'But you must hit bery hard. *Bery hard*. If you do not, I will hit you and you must join with them also. Understand?'

'*Hai!*'

'*Oosh!* Begin.'

My face was red hot with rage. I felt sick at the injustice of it. Even after three and a half years as a prisoner in Japanese hands I was astonished at this most flagrant injustice of all. I wanted to kill that evil, sadistic brute, to smash his face—and all the time I was standing perfectly motionless at attention with Tinker on my left and the eight men beyond him. Watanabe ordered us to spread out so that the men would have plenty of room to swing their fists; then the parade began.

Slowly, painfully, endlessly the long column of barge workers came up one by one and, under the closest supervision of Watanabe and most other Japanese in camp who now gathered to watch the sport, swung their fully extended arms as ordered and struck each motionless punchbag once on each cheek. My cheeks were stinging and I cursed the well-meaning fellows who were hitting softly and therefore were ordered to hit again, lengthening the whole process. Many men tried to swing fast and connect more slowly; they did not brake fast enough; others thought a blow could be noisy, but gentle; untrue. There was no way anyone could reduce the number of slaps received; they could only increase it. Many men hated doing it I could see. A dozen British troops whispered 'Sorry, sir' just before they swung and next day apologised, telling me how badly they felt about it. There were 96 men in the squad and I suppose we were each struck about 220 times. It was almost dark when the cruel entertainment ended. Our supper had been waiting over two hours when we finally entered the barrack that night and Japanese food never tasted more bitter.

It was July and Japan had not yet sued for peace. Germany had been out of the war since May, so Japanese face was saved on the score of the failure of her allies. Admiral Suzuki was the second Prime Minister since Tojo resigned in July '44 and I could not believe that the present Japanese government was the most aggressive the country could produce. The Japanese press was praising the construction of wooden ships for coastal trading. Where then was the Japanese merchant navy but at the bottom of the sea? And most of her navy too. Our men in Tokyo and here knew that machines, vehicles, plant of all types was being patched and repatched to continue service. Yet the war continued. What was holding up the peace negotiations? When would the invasion of Japan come? The press reported a huge pile-up of men and ships in Okinawa. Would it be in August? I felt sure that Japan would prefer to surrender to the United States, Britain and China alone rather than to Soviet Russia as well—a closer and more fearful enemy from her point of view and one who would encroach and remain longer on Japan's doorstep. Yet if Japan hung on much longer Russia would certainly declare war. Was it only momentum that kept it going or did the Japanese want to fight to the death in their cities and mountains and die in their millions?

It would be in the mountains too, because there were no beach defences at all as far as we could see and we had heard nothing about the construction of any.

In moments of depression I began to wonder if the war might drag on through another winter, not through Japan's ability to fight, but through her ability to *wait*. And we all dreaded with horror the idea of a *fourth* winter in our physical state. The Japanese themselves warned us that food during the coming winter would be shorter than ever before, that prisoners of war would not be fed while Japanese starved and that fuel would be even more meanly rationed than during previous winters. Our doctors secretly voiced their fears to some of us that about one-third of all prisoners in Japan would not survive another winter, so even in warm, sunny July the thought of the cold, black deathly winter clouded our minds. Every day in July and August 1945 I found myself thinking of the coming winter. I therefore never missed the opportunity to eat anything that might be nutritious. Starting in Korea, I had eaten the kernel of every seed in every apple we had ever had, I had eaten the skin of every tangerine we'd ever been sold, I had eaten garlic raw and unwashed out of the fields, onions, leeks and carrots too. In Korea on warm summer days we had caught dozens of small frogs and eaten their legs, duly cooked; at the six-mile farm we had skinned and eaten snakes and several kinds of fungus guaranteed safe to us by a Guamanian who accompanied us twice. And this very month the cookhouse had been supplied with five dogs of varying sizes and colours and we had all eaten dog. I was determined to survive.

People in smug freedom and plenty say that they would never steal, never fight for food, never eat food that others leave on their plates, never pick food off the ground and eat it, but they don't know; they have never had the temptation. If they did they would know that blind, impelling self-preservation drives them on. I wonder if the reader can understand the strength of our determination to survive? With me, the *will* itself was absolutely ruthless though none of my actions had yet been. If only one prisoner were going to get out of Japan alive I was determined that it would be me.

Unexpectedly once more, things turned in our favour. One day in mid-July, Watanabe suddenly received orders to take over disciplinary command of a new camp in the mountains and a few days later was gone. The new camp was to be for officers, deep in the mountains, we heard, safe from liberation by invading forces, where all the officers that could be spared from work camps all over Japan would soon be assembled. I looked around; no doubt all except four or five would leave this camp. The rest of us, especially people like me whose name came so readily to Watanabe's lips, would certainly go to the mountain camp. I began to ask various Japanese what they knew about this new camp. 'Very good camp. All officers,' they said and nothing more.

Before he left, Watanabe punished Lieutenant Louis Zamperini, he said, for laziness as we did some building work in camp. He made him pick up a beam of wood, six feet long by four inches square, and hold it at arms' length above his head. He then sat on a nearby low roof in the sun chatting to passers-by. Louis Zamperini was a world championship class miler between 1938 and 1941, a long-legged, deep-chested athlete. Shot down in the Pacific, he and three other crew members climbed into a little life raft and began to drift across the Pacific. They had a pistol, emergency chocolate, a portion of emergency rations and no water. The first night the youngest crewman ate all the chocolate. They thought of killing him. The boy cried and they let him stay aboard. For days and very soon weeks they ate nothing but a few fish and birds and rainwater caught in a sailcloth. The chocolate-eater died; he had given himself an additional burden of guilt to bear and it was too much. On the 49th day they were picked up by a Japanese cruiser. None of them could stand or straighten their legs. Zamperini weighed only 79 pounds. The Japanese nursed them carefully on board and they began to recover strength and weight. Then they delivered them to Ofuna hell camp, from which Zamperini came to Omori and thence to Naoetsu. Now he was being crucified holding up this heavy beam of wood.

We went on working, glancing regularly at Zamperini and the clock. Finally Watanabe allowed the American to put down the beam. Louis could hardly move, hardly unlock his fingers. I looked at the clock. It had been 37 minutes. *Thirty-seven minutes.* I defy anyone to do it as long.

July went; it was now August. Nothing had improved for Japan; it was clear to us that she was defeated, but the war would not end. I spoke to a member of the camp staff one day.

'Have you heard from Sergeant Watanabe?' I asked.
'No. He in camp in mountains. Camp for officers.'
'Yes, I know. Plenty officers go there, maybe?'
He nodded.
'Why do you think they will put so many officers in one camp?'
He drew in his breath with a hiss. 'If American come Japan, fight, officers safe in mountains. If fighting bad—no good—they kill all officers.' And here he imitated

holding a rifle and pulling the trigger once, twice, three times, then drawing his finger across his throat for good measure.[3]

3. Precise and unequivocal orders for the massacre of all POWs in camps in Taiwan were later found and produced at the War Crimes Trials. They stated the '*aim not to allow the escape of a single one (POW), to annihilate them all and not to leave a trace*'.
Several camp authorities in Japan had short tunnels dug in hillsides in August 1945. It was learnt after the war that these were in preparation for the massacre and burial of all POWs.

# 31

# Liberation

I was having my head shaved by one of the Aussies when a POW came in straight from the steel mill and shouted that there was good news, the Japanese were all excited and worried. He thought that Russia had entered the war.

We had been waiting for this. We *knew* that the end of the war was near; we knew that Japan would surrender; we were only sceptical about exactly how powerful the last blow would have to be that would lead to the final capitulation.

The next day we learnt that the news was not Russia's entry into the war, but the dropping of what the Japanese press called 'an electron bomb'—a new and terrible weapon—on Hiroshima. Why Hiroshima, we wondered. It had not seemed an important town when we passed through by train on the way to Tokyo.

A day or two later a scrap of a Japanese newspaper was brought in to me to translate, but there was little need; a map of Manchuria showed three sharp arrows slicing from Siberia into Japanese-held Manchuria. We were elated, yet our excitement was not as great as during the B-29 raids on Tokyo or even at the fall of Italy. We were completely certain of Allied victory and our only anxiety was how to survive any massacre of POWs that might follow an American invasion of Japan.

Work continued at the steel mill, the carbide factory and the coalships. We wondered whether we would be safer at the end in this port on the west coast of Japan rather than No. 1 Camp, Tokyo, where we had been for sixteen months only to be removed after the huge fire-bomb raids of February.

One day at the worksites, the Japanese assembled for an announcement. Radio loudspeakers stood centre stage. It was 15 August. The Imperial Throne was to broadcast—the first time in history that the voice of the semi-divine Emperor would be heard on radio. The Japanese listened in silence, every head bowed. Some came out of the assembly with tears in their eyes. Hours later one foreman whispered that the Emperor had announced that there was to be no more fighting. Other *hanchos* confirmed this. The men returned from work jubilant. The night shift formed up. There was a delay, then the Japanese in the camp office told the POW labour officer that there would be no working until further notice. 'Dismiss the night shift.'

'Its over, its over!' yelled Theo Lee, the youthful Aussie labour officer, careering through our warehouse. 'The war must be over.'

We all howled and cheered; our ramshackle warehouse boomed with cheering. Next day only the cooks were working. We speculated endlessly; even the mountains and fields beyond our windows looked different. Two days later the Japanese camp commandant, with sword and gloves, stood on a box on the parade ground and announced that 'to avoid further bloodshed, the Emperor had made peace'.

We stood to attention, impassive, but inwardly we exulted. We've made it! we thought. My God, after three and a half years, we've made it! We've survived all their brutality, all their callousness, starvation and disease. We've survived everything. We're going to *live*!

We demanded more food, especially meat. We ceased saluting the Japanese. We informed them that we would hold our own *Tenkos*—roll calls, rather—and it was odd to number off in English again. We told the Japanese to keep out of our warehouse. Some of the officers sconced each other for using Japanese words any longer.

The Japanese interpreter, Corporal Kono, who had strutted through our barrack rooms morning and evening for months past, carrying a *kendo* stick and regularly roaring at some imagined misdemeanour and thrashing his bamboo sword two-handed at some unfortunate prisoner—this man never left his quarters for *eleven* days. When a prisoner looked in the room one day, Kono backed into the far corner with a gasp of terror. All the bullies hid; we heard that Watanabe had deserted his own army and fled. But the ordinary *heitais*, privates second and third class, were cool and detached. They hadn't hurt anyone. The bullies had always been a minority.

And we just laughed. We took no revenge. We were so glad after three years to be able to ignore them, to forget them, that we gave them not a glance, not a word, not a blow. We heard later that in a few camps, the worst bullies and sadists had been shot, but in most camps as in ours, the POWs took no revenge. We would give our evidence to those collecting data for War Crimes Trials and leave it to them.

The Japanese took defeat very quietly. There were no demonstrations, no speeches, no riots. They were stunned. As bad as things were, with shortages, huge cities destroyed and armies lost overseas, the thought of defeat and surrender had never crossed the minds of the vast majority. They could only obey and work, and start to rebuild.

The pig was brought out of his sty, destined for the cookhouse. It was weighed. 'Flamin' 'ell,' said an Aussie. 'He weighs less than when we put him in there two years ago.'

Days later an American Navy Hellcat painted ultramarine blue swooped over the camp so low we could see the pilot's features. He threw out a chocolate bar and a note: 'Back tomorrow with smokes—D. Wagner, Rochester N.Y.' For three days navy Hellcats and Corsairs roared and swooped overhead dropping occasional cartons of cigarettes and giving us a show. They recognised the 'PW 730' sign we had been instructed to erect on our roof and flew off to sea amid POW cheers.

Next morning a silver B-29 appeared overhead. Not any B-29, loveliest of aeroplanes though they were; on one wing, painted for all to read, were the words *'Food for POWs'*. We could hardly believe it; tears almost came to our eyes. The B-29 flew low over the ricefields alongside our camp and suddenly out tumbled bundles and drums. They splashed in the rice paddies. We grabbed the camp carts, many willing hands grasping the ropes and ran out of the gate past the startled sentry to the fields.

Some 44-gallon drums landed intact, others burst and khaki cans of food, chocolate, meat stew and half peaches lay splattered on the rice plants. We scooped the stew and peaches into our mouths straight out of the muddy water, loaded the drums onto the carts and tugged them back to camp. It took many journeys and left us limp and panting.

One bomber aimed for our tiny parade ground. A 44-gallon drum filled with boots crashed through the roof of the washroom outhouse and broke the leg of perhaps the youngest Aussie in camp, Frank Hole. 'Hard luck, chum,' we called as we trotted into the building with a stream of boxes, crates and bundles. Later we heard of four or five POWs killed by falling or bouncing crates.

Next day more B-29s came over; blue, red, yellow and white parachutes blossomed under them and drifted against the backdrop of hills on to the green ricefields. Plane after plane scattered its drifting flowers. Below, over 500 prisoners waved, cheered and skipped with pleasure among the fallen and bouncing boxes. It made a glorious, theatrical spectacle. Everyone except the sick and cooks was out in the fields. Teams were now set up in camp to count each item and divide by the 730 men in camp. Boots, overalls, zip jackets, underwear, cigarettes, field rations and chocolate were allocated, bulk bully beef and C rations going straight to the cookhouse. Seaweed and *daikon* disappeared forever, meaty stews were served and we needed less and less of our staple *gaoliang* or even white rice.

Some *sake* was purchased and was soon washed down. Honourable stomachs were at last satisfied and most men put on 25 pounds weight in two weeks. Our credit balances were paid to us. Theo Lee and I hired a taxi one day and drove twenty miles to Takata and bought a sword and two kimonos. Another day I bathed in the public bath-house—many women and men squatting and standing scrubbing out of small buckets before entering the common pool—and so renewed my acquaintance with the sight of the female nude. It was good to know that ivory, smooth female flesh still existed. Four men found a brothel and reported, beaming, to their comrades that their neglected equipment had actually functioned. Then the telephone rang. They called our senior officer, Lieutenant Commander Fitzgerald. 'Me? I don't know anybody in Japan.' But it was a commander on MacArthur's staff giving the time of our train to Yokohama.

Late into the night we packed. No one wanted to leave spare boots, overalls, etc. to the Japanese. Next morning we marched out of camp for the last time in sunshine, some laughing and joking, some thoughtful. With us last night's packing, also white boxes containing the ashes of the Australians who had died in Naoetsu camp. Japanese citizens in the streets watched us expressionless. Four or five waved goodbye and smiled. We smiled back. 'No more *daikon*,' the men cheered. 'No more punch-ups.' 'Plenty *yasume*.'

The train took us back over the mountains, then slowly through Tokyo, its centre intact, but mile after mile of it flattened to knee level. You could see the road network like a map with nothing but low black ruins in each block for thousands of yards. The Omori end was a little better, but Kawasaki and Yokohama were equally flattened. The devastation awed and silenced us. And all of it had been done in about seven months! The train pulled into an empty station. The carriage door opened.

'Welcome back, boys,' said a voice at whose owner I was staring open-mouthed.

Before me in immaculate khaki uniform and cap stood an American girl with a magazine-cover smile, faultless make-up and peroxide blonde hair. After three and a half years in prison camp, I had been liberated by the great American blonde! We tumbled out of the carriage, disbelieving this apparition. When she spoke men's mouths fell open or they stuttered.

'Did you get much to eat?' she asked.

'Not much from the Nips,' one POW replied, 'but when the B *ni-ju-ku*s came we had *takusan*.'

The nurse frowned.

'You dope,' someone said, 'you called a B-29 a B...'

There was a burst of laughter followed by a clearer explanation. Trucks drove us through bombed Yokohama to the docks beside a great floodlit customs shed. We jumped out.

'I like those little cars,' I said to a driver, indicating some fast-moving two-seaters twisting in and out of the trucks.

'Those are jeeps,' he said.

'Oh, *those* are jeeps!'

We were led towards a coffee and doughnut stall outside the shed. Hardly able to believe our eyes we stood at the counter and were handed cups of wonderful coffee by brisk American girls in white uniforms and lipstick.

'Take as many doughnuts as you want.'

'Didn't any men invade Japan?' I asked.

'Oh sure, there are some,' said a nurse, 'but our ship pulled in second and did it make the boys mad!'

Ahead was a white hospital ship and this was the 42nd General Hospital Unit. Men now guided us towards a shower and medical check. As we took the shower and were squirted with delousing powder, the medical corpsmen wanted to rid us of our clothes. 'But they're new,' we protested, so they let us keep our field jackets but accept new underwear. Part dressed, we passed through the hands of six specialists, one after the other. I was amazed at the thoroughness of this organisation working smoothly on

Yokohama docks only three days after the surrender ceremony on the USS *Missouri* out in the bay. I didn't receive a more thorough examination in England before I found myself a civilian once more.

At the far end of the shed some officers at desks asked a few questions.

'Okay, lieutenant, you'll be in Okinawa by morning.' One handed me a slip of paper on which were written just two words: '*Atsugi—British.*' It was my ticket to liberation accompanied by boundless courtesy, by air and sea, from Tokyo to London.

Joining my comrades again, I learnt that dysentery and beri-beri cases requiring immediate medical attention had been moved straight aboard the hospital ship alongside. We looked at the great white ship and noticed a prisoner being carried up the gangplank on a stretcher.

'Look, it's Charlie!' someone exclaimed.

Charlie, seeing us, raised his head and waved cheerily. He looked rather shamefaced at not being allowed to walk on board himself.

'Why, there's nothing much wrong with Charlie—he's been out to work for months,' I burst out and then bit my tongue for thinking like a Nipponese medical corporal.

Trucks appeared and drove us through the dark to Atsugi airfield, where C 54 Skymasters were taking off every three minutes. There were about 80 Skymasters and Dakotas on the airfield, many with engines running, making a deep-throated wolfish roar. Jeeps with men sitting on them ran about the tarmac in and out of the planes like silent toys. We ate a K ration and a cooked meal, were issued cigarettes, chocolate and an Armed Services Edition pocket novel and asked to wait our take-off. When it came twenty Aussies, four Americans, three Dutch and six British POWs left the soil of Japan bound for Okinawa.

'*Sayonara,*' I murmured, looking out of the Skymaster at the darkness below and behind. I realised I had seen only two armed American soldiers all this time and had not heard one Japanese shout of anger or defiance.

# 32

# The Long Way Home

Dawn and sunshine, C rations for breakfast. It was warm and brilliant sunshine when Okinawa hove into sight. In the bay lay a breathtaking concentration of shipping; over 1000 vessels: troopships, tankers and blunt-nosed landing ships—the invasion fleet for Japan. The island was gaudily colourful with green foliage, orange laterite roads, white beaches and blue water in innumerable shell-holes. We landed on an airfield with over 100 B-29s parked in astonishing lines. The American Red Cross canteen served us Coca-Colas and doughnuts from the hands of, to us, breathtaking American girls in white overalls and jaunty forage caps. But these girls in the Pacific theatre knew their routine: no sentiment or overt sympathy, just smiles or wisecracks and doughnuts and Coke.

Our truck was waiting to take us to the huge camp for liberated prisoners down a road reeling with hundreds of military vehicles. We soon had blankets, toilet articles, messkits and cutlery and were installed in empty tents. We dumped our stuff and ran out looking for friends. We found many from Naoetsu and Omori. None of the US Navy men were there; they had all been taken care of by their own service. From the Omori boys I heard that they had taken over their camp within hours of the surrender and that their liberation had come from the sea, when a line of fast landingcraft had torn across the bay and beached just outside the wooden walls of the camp to the cheers and waving flags of the 600 prisoners.

'What happened to Watanabe?' many asked me.

'He *deserted*! That super patriot deserted his own army and fled into the hills. I hope they catch him. We've no news yet.'

'Someone should have shot him. Couple of Aussies shot their worst bully...'

Loudspeakers dotting the camp blared Bing Crosby and all the latest tunes. It was like a fairground. North of the camp, bulldozers worked day and night flattening the next three hills to extend the encampment. We talked to every American soldier we could find. They talked about 'VJ Day' and 'VE day', while we couldn't stop saying '*sukoshi*' for little and '*takusan*' for many or much.

When an ex-prisoner admired a soldier's Sten gun and he asked if we hadn't had them, our man replied, 'No, we just had the regulation bow and arrow'.

Across the busy main road beside the camp were low rocky hills where we heard occasional shots as American patrols flushed out remaining Japanese snipers. Thousands of vehicles, from trucks to landing craft 'ducks' tore up and down that road and one day I thumbed a lift into shell-torn Naha to get a glimpse of its damage and its bewildered inhabitants. Preparations for an invasion of Japan were continuing, just in case. The whole American Army in Okinawa was an army with its shirts off, many in shorts and bare-legged and their suntanned bodies and healthy appearance were a wonderful testimony to the fine physique of American manhood after a couple of years in the Pacific. All this time in Okinawa, as in Yokohama before and Manila after, I never heard one single shouted command or angry altercation between service personnel. It was the smoothest running, most efficient army I have ever seen; how or when orders were given I could rarely see and they were never shouted. Everyone was working hard and fast and the face of the island was changing day by day.

I spoke with hundreds of my fellow British ex-prisoners and all were deeply impressed with the kindness, generosity and efficiency with which we were treated and smoothly shepherded from stage to stage in our swift journey homewards. The planning was so perfect one might have been excused for thinking that the whole American Army had been doing nothing else for months past but evacuate prisoners through this channel; in fact, the scheme was quickly improvised in late August, and, as one POW fortunate enough to have been liberated through those friendly hands, I salute with grateful appreciation the forethought, the hospitality and the generosity with which we were met on all sides through our evacuation and repatriation.

We were allowed to go through the meal lines twice if we wished and most of us did. At some issues of cigarettes and chocolate, liberated prisoners scrambled and fought in such a way as to bring looks of surprise to the faces of our benefactors. The prison camp habit of fighting for nutrition was still strong. In prison camp even one chocolate bar or a dozen peanuts would have been worth half a dozen camp meals and we had not yet learnt to allow ourselves to miss one morsel within reach, or wait and perhaps risk the food running out.

Two generals called at the camp unofficially: General Doolittle, who led the earliest raid on Tokyo, to see Air Corps friends; and General Stilwell, commander of one of the armies in Okinawa, to meet any prisoners who wished to meet him. I shook hands with 'Vinegar Joe' Stilwell, whom I had last seen as a lieutenant colonel of the 15th US Infantry in Tientsin in the '30s. He was dressed in olive-drab coveralls without a single badge, ribbon or sign of rank on him. He looked like an old house-painter until he spoke and then a sharp mind and keen personality came through. It wasn't hard to reconcile the appearance with the rank and record of the man.

After three days in Okinawa, my name was called for the flight to Manila. I didn't particularly want to leave. We felt so liberated already and enjoyed our present company enough not to be in a hurry.

'I bet you can't wait to get home?' they would say.

'No. I feel completely free and happy here. To be among friendly people *is* freedom and you have all done so much for us....'

'Forget it,' they would say. 'You go home; you've been through enough.'

A Dakota carried us the 1000 miles to Manila. We asked to fly in over Lingayen Gulf where the Japanese invasion of 1941 and MacArthur's liberation of 1944 had both come. Then over Cabanatuan. Perhaps that name means nothing to the reader, but it was one of a handful of names like Omori, Ofuna, Zentsuji, Kanchanaburi and Bunka that we had lived with for years. A pretty Spanish name, but the synonym for a horror camp where a thousand died through starvation and lack of medicine; Cabanatuan, where the Japanese grouped men into gangs of ten and when one of the ten escaped they shot the other nine. Yes, it really happened!

We flew in low over the stockade, the palm-leaf huts, a guardhouse and gate. But it did not look terrible, it didn't look anything! It was the cruel men, the circumstances and the suffering that made that camp a hell. Now that it was empty and the bullies and prisoners gone it held no horror, no evidence of its noisome past. That's how Omori would look to a stranger—and any prison or concentration camp. There was no measure of the pain and anguish that had once saturated the close lines of huts; that measure can only be learnt from the scattered ex-inmates whose minds and bodies still bear the scars of years of torture and neglect. And why should anyone bother to find out? Certainly the guilty will not want review of the case. No, since there is no public measure of his shame, man will always cause suffering to man.

The countryside below was green and beautiful; ricefields, tobacco and sugarcane; Filipino farmers in their wide palm-leaf hats looked up beside their carabao buffaloes in flooded fields. We saw the peninsula of Bataan, jungle-covered, with few roads, where the Americans and Filipinos had held back the Japanese Army for nearly five months. Corregidor passed beneath us and we saw about 1000 supply ships and transports in Manila Bay—an amazing sight. What caught the eye too was scores of sunken ships in the bay with funnels and masts leaning drunkenly. As we came in to land, we saw that the airport was surrounded by shelled and destroyed buildings and by heaps of crashed and crumpled Japanese planes, their red wingspots a last memorial to Japan's departed might.

We stayed in Manila six days at the 3rd Australian Reception Camp, a few miles out of town. The Australians and Americans did their utmost for us; however, as we were on twelve hours notice, we were not allowed to leave camp, which was rather confining to our expansive mood of freedom. I was brimming over with the excitement of being alive and so intoxicated with freedom that I had the same genial love of the world and of my fellow men as a merry drunkard. I wanted to talk and laugh with people, to admire and listen to women, to *do* things, never to waste a moment, to taste every morsel in freedom's feast of experience and to exercise all the emotions and actions that had been shackled so long. After all the self-control I had taught myself in prison camp, I was preparing to throw those hard-learnt lessons to the winds and become a pure hedonist.

Besides segregation by nationalities, officers were for the first time separated from men and it was strange how few of these British officers I knew. There was no one from Seoul or Omori and only one from Naoetsu. I had nothing in common with these undemonstrative strangers. They were intensely quiet; there was no laughter, no joking and no enjoyment of the moment; they sat in their tents or read or talked very quietly. They were still shut up inside themselves. Possibly they were thinking about the forthcoming reunion with their wife and family and worrying whether things would be different and how much they themselves had changed. Once they were home they would probably be brighter and happier, but at the moment they did not seem alive. Accordingly, I hitchhiked out to the American camp twice and saw all my Omori and Naoetsu friends. They had all been promoted one rank and were all discussing the opportunities open to them under the GI Bill of Rights. They were far brighter and more voluble—officers and men lived in the same lines and ate in the same dining hall.

Restless and curious still, I twice begged a lift into Manila to see more of a city I had known in peacetime. It was horribly ruined, the fine homes and hotels along Dewey Boulevard circling the bay were hammered and broken. The great granite government ministries were cracked and crumbling, their tall pillars bent like sagging knees. Far more of Tokyo was flat, but the sight of so many stone buildings crumpled and split by high explosive was perhaps more horrible and spectacular. We drove round the old Walled City, the original Spanish settlement in Manila. Here, the Japanese made their last stand and the American artillery had been obliged to pulverise many of the fine old Spanish houses with their iron grille balconies overhanging narrow streets. Yet in spite of so much evidence of the power of modern high explosive the ancient ramparts of the Walled City remained.

While we were in Manila, the first evidence of torture, brutality and criminal neglect was collected from us to be framed into charges to be brought by the War Crimes Commission against our former captors. As soon as I wrote the name Matsuhiro Watanabe, the interviewing officer said, 'Not the same Watanabe! We've got enough to hang him six times already.'

'Sit back and take it easy,' I advised. 'There's lots more to come; we're the experts.'

I gave details of only the worst dozen cruelties, all of which I had either witnessed from beginning to end or had myself been the subject. I did not revel in the task; I just did it as a duty and forgot some really ugly scenes, including the one where he ordered a whole working party to strike us on his behalf.

'We have a warrant out for his arrest,' the officer said, 'but we haven't traced him yet.' And in the many years that have passed since then, Watanabe has never been found. There is one story that, pursued by American and Japanese police, he was cornered in the mountains in northern Honshu and there committed suicide. But it may not be true and the Bully of Omori and the Terror of Naoetsu has never had to face charges in a court.

In 1989 I learnt that Prince Tomoshito Tokugawa, son of the wartime head of the Japanese Red Cross, had recently admitted to Dr Lloyd Goad, American doctor at Omori, that Watanabe was alive and well and living in Tokyo. So 'the wily Bird', as we sometimes called him, had successfully evaded all War Crimes trials and escaped all responsibility for his crimes and was living free and unfettered in the capital of his country

# 33

# Sentimental Journey

We were on a large American troopship, the USS *General W.C. Langfitt*, capable of carrying a vast number of men as we realised when 3000 filled the decks each day, talking, reading and sunbathing. Our route took us to Leyte, the site of the first American landings in the recapture of the Philippines. The ship had steel decks, a fortified bridge and considerable armament; the bunks were seven feet long to handle the tallest Texans and Westerners. I wondered how long it would be before Europe made beds seven feet long. The sun shone brilliantly and the Pacific Ocean was the most wonderful ultramarine blue.

Starting in Okinawa we had been trying to catch up on news of how the war had been won. I had already read about the two atomic bombs, Iwo Jima and penicillin; now, in *LIFE* magazines and other periodicals, I read of Hitler's end in the bunker, Belsen and Buchenwald, the battles for Okinawa and Manila, Burma and the surrender on the USS *Missouri*. As ex-prisoners we wanted to know so much about how the war had been fought, how the troops felt, what weapons they used, about the guerillas and so much more. It wasn't easy to find all the answers, not even when we reached England. But I read and sunbathed on deck nearly all day trying to catch up. Besides British ex-POWs, there were many Canadians and American Army personnel going home on leave or at the end of their tour of duty.

It was because of this contingent of Canadians that the ship changed its destination from San Francisco to Victoria, BC. I was sorry not to see California, but I had known since Naoetsu that my mother and sister had left San Francisco in 1944 and gone to England to do war work. And I had a godfather in Vancouver; I'd try to see him.

As our grey troopship glided past the headland into the harbour of Esquimalt, the Canadian naval base adjoining Victoria, we slowly realised that there was a tremendous welcome in store for us. The sirens of over twenty destroyers and corvettes, tugs and a cruiser shrilled and whistled to welcome the first Canadian ex-prisoners of war to return home from the Far East. Crews tumbled out on deck to wave and cheer. As we approached the dock, we saw that there were a thousand girls there, waving and cheering, and a naval band led by a drum major playing martial music. In spite of

Yokohama and Okinawa, we were still strangers to kindness. After years of bullying and contempt we could not believe that these sirens were screaming and these crowds cheering to welcome and honour us. They were glad we were free and safe. We were quite overwhelmed. We landed to hugs and kisses from females of all ages.

At an army camp we were issued with British battledress and regimental badges and insignia. A shopkeeper gave me an officer's cap and I bashed it about until I had it the way I wanted it and then we were off into Victoria to enjoy six days of leave with a few medical checks and some debriefing fitted in. I had just seen my first WRENs and thought how pretty they looked in uniform. Canadians shook our hands warmly or hugged us in the streets, they thanked us and blessed us. We went to private homes to lunches and teas, attended afternoon and evening dances and flirted with all the pretty girls of Victoria. I obtained permission to go to Vancouver for 24 hours and saw my godfather and a few old friends from China.

Only a week this lasted, but what a glorious, festive, friendly week it was! Women in queues for nylon stockings invited us to the front to 'get a few pairs for our girlfriends'; older men recognised our badges and spoke of Flanders. There were warm smiles everywhere, and threading all the way through the week was a haunting, significant tune, our melody of freedom and homecoming: 'Sentimental Journey'.

When we left Victoria, we learnt that three of our men had become engaged. We were all so susceptible to feminine beauty and gentleness that when later contingents passed through at least three ex-POWs married Canadian girls. In Vancouver outside the dockyard was a tremendous crowd. As we moved slowly through in coaches, they wrung our hands and cried, 'Thank you, thank you'. Many wept. It was highly emotional and intensely moving. The lustre in our eyes and the cheers in our ears never ceased all the way across Canada. At every station, large or small, crowds welcomed us with heart-warming friendliness. They were eager to see the first Canadian and British troops to return from the Pacific war and we were rapt at this attention and sought out the young and pretty girls to kiss until the bells clanged and the train moved off. There were moments of hysteria when even the young girls, embracing us, had tears in their eyes.

After the beautiful Rockies in autumn colours and the wide prairie, we curved south down the Hudson valley to New York. Straight to the docks we went, up the gangplank into the almost empty *Queen Elizabeth*. There were only 1000 people in that mighty ship; the majority were liberated prisoners from Japan, still many Omori and Shinagawa NCOs and men, but few officers I had known from Manila. To the handful of service personnel returning from staff appointments in Washington this trip appeared dreadfully dull, but to the ex-prisoners, whom you could pick out by their beaming faces, it was all still a party. Life stretched before us, broad, limitless and full of sunshine, and we walked with arms outstretched to take and enjoy all the good things the world had to offer, with no thought of disappointment or failure. My reunion with my mother and sister was close, but my father was still in his internment camp and would have to remain in China for many months. As the ship manoeuvred towards the dock in Southampton—five, six and even more years since most of us had seen England—our euphoria was tinged at last with realism, our excitement mingled with apprehension. We were home.

In the army reception camp an hour after landing, they asked us *one question.* 'You have to decide *now* whether to leave the army now or sign on for another year. Which do you want?'

We had been in England an hour, maybe an hour and a half; we had had no information from any source in Britain for four years; we knew nothing.

'I've just come from prison camp in Japan; can I have a couple of weeks to decide?'

'No, you must decide now.'

'I don't think I want to sign on for another year,' I said. 'I'd like to go to university.'

'Then you'll have to sign on for a year.'

'No, I don't want to commit myself to another year.'

'All right, sign this sheet and you'll be released immediately—after your leave of course.'

I signed, and the army considered its duty to me done.

I never received one talk, one leaflet, one pamphlet, any guidance or advice on how to return to civilian life in much-altered Britain after three years and seven months of prison camp and over five years of army service.

But I cannot end my account on such a bleak note; this would be to repudiate all the determination, hope and endurance of my prisoner-of-war years and beliefs which had sustained me for so long. The last word I write must be about the men with whom I shared three and a half years in prisoner-of-war camp. They were so self-reliant, good-humoured and resilient, they looked as if they could survive anything, as they had every intention of doing. They took all the blows of an unkind fate without serious murmur; they were unconquerable.

And Omori, where I had spent the longest time? There were worse places than Tokyo Headquarter Camp; it was the best informed camp in Japan, where one met new prisoners regularly or passing through. Just to see a man who had been free only days earlier was refreshing and encouraging. It was visible proof that the outside world was working towards one's liberation and seemed to bring it a step nearer.

I was glad I had shared my POW experience with Americans, Australians and Canadians (there were very few of the other nationalities). Their presence and slightly different viewpoints, opinions and language added another dimension to my experience, which would have been poorer without them. So too did some knowledge of our captors' language. To speak directly to a man in his own language is better, more immediate communication than to rely on second-hand interpretation. It is worth attempting. Absorbing too was the opportunity to study the Japanese character and spirit. If one advanced only a few paces towards understanding how their minds worked and what motivated them, it was an expansion of one's horizons. If one learnt to recognise decent and humane, even neutral and impartial Japanese from out of the mass, one would have ceased to lump them all together as the monolithic brutal enemy.

There was no need for those long years in camp to have been a totally negative experience; we all learnt more about ourselves and our fellow men in the camps; many found their moral principles confirmed by our experience and some found spiritual faith. It was our sojourn 'in the desert', where we found time to study ourselves and decide what equipment we valued, what we would jettison and what we would carry on the next march ahead.

There was a time in POW camp when I thought that a stanza from Kipling's 'The Galley Slave' summed up our experience:

> *By the brand upon my shoulder, by the gall of clinging steel,*
> *By the welts the whips have left me, by the scars that never heal;*
> *By eyes grown old with staring through the sunwash on the brine,*
> *I am paid in full for service. Would that service still were mine!*

But now I prefer the last two lines:

> *But today I leave the galley. Shall I curse her service then?*
> *God be thanked! Whate'er comes after, I have live and toiled with Men!*

# Postscript

James Bertram returned to Japan in 1946 and was instrumental in the release from Sugamo gaol of Private Kano, the helpful last interpreter at Omori; and later Louis Zamperini also visited Sugamo, forgave four guards from Ofuna for maltreatment and had Seaman Sasaki's eighteen-year sentence quashed.

Major Frankcom received the OBE for creating the POW post office.

# Index